CONTEMPLATIVE PRACTICES AND ANTI-OPPRESSIVE PEDAGOGIES FOR HIGHER EDUCATION

This volume explores mindfulness and other contemplative approaches as strategic tools for cultivating anti-oppressive pedagogies in higher education.

Research confirms that simply providing students with evidence and narratives of economic, social, and environmental injustices proves insufficient in developing awareness and eliciting responses of empathy, solidarity, and a desire to act for change. From the environmental humanities to the environmental sciences, legal studies, psychology, and counseling, educators from a range of geographical and disciplinary standpoints describe their research-based mindfulness pedagogies. Chapters explore how to interrupt and interrogate oppression through contemplative teaching tools, assignments, and strategies that create greater awareness and facilitate deeper engagement with learning contents, contexts, and communities.

Providing a framework that facilitates awareness of the links between historic and current oppression, self-identity, and trauma, and creating a transformative learning experience through mindfulness, this book is a must-read for faculty and educators interested in intersections of mindfulness, contemplative pedagogies, and anti-oppression.

Greta Gaard is Professor of English and Women/Gender/Sexuality Studies at the University of Wisconsin-River Falls, USA.

Bengü Ergüner-Tekinalp is Professor of Counseling at Drake University, USA.

CONTEMPLATIVE PRACTICES AND ANTI-OPPRESSIVE PEDAGOGIES FOR HIGHER EDUCATION

Bridging the Disciplines

Edited by Greta Gaard and
Bengü Ergüner-Tekinalp

NEW YORK AND LONDON

Cover image: © Jan Estep, Molokai Painting ii (detail), 2017.
Tempura paint on paper, 52" x 20". Courtesy of the artist.

First published 2022
by Routledge
605 Third Avenue, New York, NY 10158

and by Routledge
4 Park Square, Milton Park, Abingdon, Oxon, OX14 4RN

Routledge is an imprint of the Taylor & Francis Group, an informa business

© 2022 selection and editorial matter, Greta Gaard and Bengü Ergüner-Tekinalp; individual chapters, the contributors

The right of Greta Gaard and Bengü Ergüner-Tekinalp to be identified as the authors of the editorial material, and of the authors for their individual chapters, has been asserted in accordance with sections 77 and 78 of the Copyright, Designs and Patents Act 1988.

All rights reserved. No part of this book may be reprinted or reproduced or utilised in any form or by any electronic, mechanical, or other means, now known or hereafter invented, including photocopying and recording, or in any information storage or retrieval system, without permission in writing from the publishers.

Trademark notice: Product or corporate names may be trademarks or registered trademarks, and are used only for identification and explanation without intent to infringe.

Library of Congress Cataloging-in-Publication Data

Names: Gaard, Greta Claire, editor. | Ergüner-Tekinalp, Bengü, 1977- editor.
Title: Contemplative practices and anti-oppressive pedagogies for higher education : bridging the disciplines / edited by Greta Gaard and Bengü Ergüner-Tekinalp.
Description: New York, NY : Routledge, 2022. | Includes bibliographical references and index.
Identifiers: LCCN 2021047720 (print) | LCCN 2021047721 (ebook) | ISBN 9781032063492 (hardback) | ISBN 9781032063478 (paperback) | ISBN 9781003201854 (ebook)
Subjects: LCSH: Education, Higher--Social aspects—United States. | Social justice and education—United States. | Critical pedagogy—United States. | Transformative learning—United States. | Mindfulness (Psychology)
Classification: LCC LC191.9 .C66 2022 (print) | LCC LC191.9 (ebook) | DDC 378.73—dc23/eng/20211109
LC record available at https://lccn.loc.gov/2021047720
LC ebook record available at https://lccn.loc.gov/2021047721

ISBN: 978-1-032-06349-2 (hbk)
ISBN: 978-1-032-06347-8 (pbk)
ISBN: 978-1-003-20185-4 (ebk)

DOI: 10.4324/9781003201854

Typeset in Bembo
by Apex CoVantage, LLC

CONTENTS

Foreword   *viii*
    David Forbes
Preface   *xi*
Acknowledgments   *xiii*

PART I
Contemplative Theoretical Frameworks   1

1. Introduction to Contemplative Practices and Anti-Oppressive Pedagogies for Higher Education   3
   Greta Gaard and Bengü Ergüner-Tekinalp

2. Pursuing Antiracist and Anticolonial Approaches to Contemplative Practices   17
   Janelle Adsit

PART II
Contemplative Pedagogies for Environmental Justice   33

3. Eco-Grief and Climate Anxiety in the Classroom   35
   Jennifer Atkinson

4. Contemplative Pedagogies, Environmental Literature, and the Art of "Interbeing"   52
   Darin Pradittatsanee

5 Literary Reading, Mindfulness, and Climate Justice: An Experiment in Contemplative Ecocritical Pedagogy 71
Anne Raine

6 Mindfulness, Writing, and Sustainable Happiness in the Anthropocene 90
Greta Gaard

PART III
Contemplative Pedagogies Across the Disciplines 115

7 Inner Tracking: A Reflective Practice for Transformative Learning 117
David J. Voelker

8 A Mindful Approach to Teaching Art and Yoga as a Means of Liberation 133
Jan Estep

9 Contemplative Practices for Teaching the Sciences 149
Franklin M. Chen

10 Enhancing Students' Mindfulness Practice Through Philosophy of Mind 168
Sam Cocks

11 Creating Mindful and Self-Aware Counseling Practitioners: Centering Privilege and Oppression 185
Teysha L. Bowser, Renae Swanson, and Amney J. Harper

PART IV
Contemplative Practices for Community and Institutional Change 197

12 Reflections on Developing a Campus-Wide Workshop Series on Contemplative Practice and Social Justice 199
Jennifer Daubenmier, Christopher J. Koenig, Maiya Evans, Lisa Moore, and Michele J. Eliason

13 Using Neuroscience and Mindfulness to Form New
   Habits of Mind Around Race   217
   Renee Owen and Danaé Jones Aicher

14 Contemplative Learning Communities: Transforming
   Universities by Embedding Contemplative Practices in
   the Academic Life   231
   Bengü Ergüner-Tekinalp

Editor Bios   *247*
Contributor Bios *248*
Index   *252*

FOREWORD

As a mindfulness practitioner and progressive educator, I see personal growth, critical analysis, and the imperative to fight for social justice as inseparable. To say I had grown frustrated with the field of mindfulness in education, which tends to stare blankly at this integral vision, is an understatement.

In my book, *Mindfulness and Its Discontents* (2019), I sought to interrogate and clear the field of *un*mindful, unexamined practices and beliefs that contribute to its myopia and obstruct its contributions to education in the highest sense. The primary tool I applied was to ask the question:

> Do mindfulness practices serve to *accommodate and adjust* students and educators to an individualistic and inequitable education system and society? Or do these practices help us *transform* unjust personal and societal relationships and institutions, thereby contributing to optimal development for all?

This is a moral and spiritual question as much as a psychological and social one. What's more, to be critically mindful of the social context of how and why we practice mindfulness should be as much a practice of contemplative pedagogy as attending to one's thoughts, feelings, and sensations.

Critically mindful of social contexts, we can uncover the hidden, unaddressed structures, norms, and beliefs that condition us in unhealthy and unjust ways, preventing us from further growth. These beliefs fuel some of the basic cultural myths that govern our everyday thoughts and actions, yet tend to lurk outside our awareness and beyond the scope of traditional mindfulness inquiry. Some unacknowledged delusional myths are as follows:

> You are by nature a private, self-contained entity, separate from others, whose mission above all is to promote yourself and market your brand.

It is natural and necessary for you as an individual to compete against others for your basic needs.

You must pursue money and status, the keys to your social success and sense of security, and your education is a necessary path toward obtaining them.

Whiteness is the default standard of health and normality for you and everyone.

Instead of placing mindfulness within its moral and social contexts and helping us de-condition and *de-colonize* ourselves from harmful and unhealthy thoughts, actions, and relationships, I saw that mindfulness educators tended to *de-contextualize* the practice. But severing personal consciousness from our troublesome social relationships and institutions converts mindfulness into a neutral individualistic technology, and puts the onus for change solely on the privatized self. In the end such a mindfulness—rather than leading students and educators to contemplate, question, study, resist, and change both themselves and the interpersonal and structural relationships in which they engage—only serves the status quo. It adjusts them to an inequitable and stress-inducing society. Paradoxically, that individualistic, competitive, racist society is the very source of much of the anxiety, anger, unhappiness, and alienation students and educators experience—and that mindfulness purports to alleviate.

I then set out some future directions for an emergent, integral, critical, social mindfulness that counters the unaddressed normative, individualistic beliefs and practices within the field. These directions build upon the work of recent scholars in critical psychology, developmental psychology, integral meta-theory, critical social theory, critical pedagogy, antiracism, ecology, feminism, and cultural studies. The emergent perspective takes an explicit moral stance for social justice, antiracism, interdependence, democracy, inclusivity, and optimal self-development. It combines contemplative practices with an anti-oppression pedagogy and, instead of individualism, is premised on the interdependent non-dualism of self and other.

I aimed for a broad, inclusive perspective that would encourage and allow for prospective educators who shared an integral vision to build on the foundations. I hoped that someday, some like-minded educators would consider these foundations as groundwork for advancing critical contemplative pedagogies in practical and useful ways.

I didn't think it was going to happen for a while, if at all, and could not imagine what shape it might take.

But it did.

My book was implicitly calling for the next step, and here it is, in the form of this timely, innovative, encompassing, collaborative work, *Contemplative Practices and Anti-Oppressive Pedagogies for Higher Education: Bridging the Disciplines*.

I was excited when the editors, Greta Gaard and Bengü Ergüner-Tekinalp, shared this book with me and told me they saw it as building on some of the cornerstones I had proposed. While I'm happy our books share an emergent vision, I am even more delighted in how this volume takes it further in practical, scholarly, and conceptual ways.

This book exceeds my hope for more educators to link contemplative pedagogies in higher education courses with progressive, liberating, anti-oppressive practices. All the authors combine the scholarship, wisdom, and art of both approaches in unique, creative ways within and across academic fields. They succeed at what the editors call "triangulating" mindfulness practices, critical pedagogical tools, and scholarly course content in their respective (inter)disciplines.

In the spirit of an emergent integral worldview and practice, the authors share and build on the vision of inseparability, of the interdependence of self and other. They are mindful of the need to embody and hold both secular and religious aspects of contemplative practices, a rejection of either-or thinking. Not only do they aim to transcend the secular-religious divide; they are conscious of the quantitative-qualitative tension in research and insist on sharing both objective and subjective perspectives. In their courses the authors invite students to bridge the inner and outer, to delve deep into their own personal experiences through contemplative awareness along with critical analysis of the social conditions of their own lives, and in some to apply their wisdom to help their own college campuses become more mindful and just. A number of authors cultivate mindful social action and contemplative practices as ways for their students to confront with wise compassion both personal biases and social oppression around racism, sexism, and climate justice.

Contemplative practices along with anti-oppressive pedagogies can and should help us de-colonize and de-condition ourselves from deluded and ill-serving societal beliefs about ourselves and the world, enabling personal growth and social change. This book is a timely, significant advancement in this regard. It tackles head-on today's crises of racism, climate change, and students' mental anguish within higher education. The beauty of these chapters is their usefulness to other educators. They provide solid examples of teaching and scholarship informed by the authors' own contemplative practices and embodied commitment to anti-oppressive pedagogy and social change at both personal and institutional levels.

I am proud to share the vision that infuses this book. It deserves a broad readership.

David Forbes, PhD, LMHC
Emeritus Associate Professor, Urban Education Doctoral Program
CUNY Graduate School
Author, Mindfulness and Its Discontents: Education, Self, and Social Transformation

PREFACE

This edited volume explores contemplative pedagogies as a strategy for uncovering and transforming the mental and embodied beliefs that support oppression. Such pedagogies can be used to bridge course content with students' embodied awareness through practices such as poetry-writing, qigong, yoga, art-making, walking meditation, mindful self-compassion practice, and mindfulness of breath, sounds, thoughts, sensations. Of these many contemplative practices, mindfulness practices are shown to be quite effective, enhancing concentration and memory, reducing anxiety and depression, and improving general health and well-being. Mindfulness is also used as an *anti-oppression pedagogy*, strategic in helping students expose and examine deeply held prejudices around race, gender, sexuality, species, and more. To date, the scholarship on integrating contemplative practices in higher education in general and specifically anti-oppressive pedagogy and racial healing is growing, but an interdisciplinary book that provides guidance, and the contemplative methods for creating inclusive and transformative learning spaces, has not appeared. This volume fills that gap.

We begin with an introduction to contemplative theoretical frameworks, and the uses for contemplative, anti-oppressive pedagogies in cultivating awareness of mental habits that reinforce beliefs normalizing social injustice. These pedagogies are immediately useful in addressing the linked crises of our time—environmental, economic, multispecies, and climate injustices. Our second cluster of chapters explores contemplative pedagogies for teaching specifically about these diverse injustices, addressing "eco-affects" such as climate anxiety and eco-grief, exploring the art and awareness of interbeing, and the uses of these pedagogies to raise awareness in courses addressing ecocritical and multispecies interactions. A third cluster of chapters develops contemplative pedagogies across the disciplines of history, the sciences, art, philosophy, and counseling. We conclude with a fourth cluster focusing on contemplative practices that investigate and cultivate awareness about oppressive social and institutional structures across communities and institutions of higher education—and offer strategies for transforming those structures.

College and university educators who are committed to addressing social and environmental injustices through their pedagogies will appreciate this volume for its specific applications and assessments of a diversity of contemplative pedagogies, each with an awareness of adapting to the specific cultural and regional demographics where educators are situated. Not all practices work effectively with every student population, and this volume emphasizes how the preparation of the instructor's own daily contemplative practice provides a foundation for selecting and utilizing these pedagogies.

Throughout the volume, tools and tables offering course readings, contemplative practices, and assessment strategies are introduced, utilized, and evaluated. Every chapter addresses the value of both qualitative and quantitative assessments, pre- and post-implementation, and the practice of authenticity, being transparent with students about our own intersectional identities as well as the research-tested outcomes possible through contemplative, anti-oppressive pedagogies. Readers will find a wealth of curriculum and resources to support their teaching.

ACKNOWLEDGMENTS

We are grateful to the Center for Contemplative Mind in Higher Education (CMind), both for allowing us to reprint "The Tree of Contemplative Practices" and for hosting the annual Summer Session on Contemplative Practices in Education where many of us met, and where this volume originated. CMind's *Journal of Contemplative Inquiry (JOCI)* allowed us to republish "Reflections on Developing a Campus-Wide Workshop Series on Contemplative Practice and Social Justice," originally appearing in *JOCI* 7:1 (2020), 49–73. We also acknowledge the Association for the Study of Literature and Environment (ASLE) for accepting a panel proposal to explore "Contemplative Pedagogies for the Environmental Humanities" for the biannual summer 2019 conference, where several more contributors to this volume presented papers. Parts of ASLE panelist Janelle Adsit's Chapter 2 in this volume appear in Adsit, J., *Epistemic Justice, Mindfulness, and the Environmental Humanities: Reflections on Teaching* (Routledge, 2021). The Mind and Life Research Institute awarded a 2018 Think Tank grant to Greta Gaard's proposal for "Mindfulness Practices as Anti-Oppressive Pedagogy: Strategies for Preparation, Implementation, and Assessment," hosted at the Aldo Leopold Center, with keynote addresses from Beth Berila and Zenzele Isoke, bringing together even more participants who became contributors to this volume. For our volume's cover, we are delighted to display the artwork of Jan Estep, whose experiences teaching art and yoga are detailed in Chapter 8. We are grateful to David Forbes for his foundational work and his pedagogical passion that permeates our Foreword. We thank our colleagues who participated in the learning communities exploring contemplative pedagogies, and our universities for supporting this work. Finally, we thank Heather Jarrow, Rebecca Collazzo, and the team at Routledge for their clear and timely communications, advice, and support for this volume, from acquisition through production.

PART I
Contemplative Theoretical Frameworks

1
INTRODUCTION TO CONTEMPLATIVE PRACTICES AND ANTI-OPPRESSIVE PEDAGOGIES FOR HIGHER EDUCATION

Greta Gaard and Bengü Ergüner-Tekinalp

How do we bring together the different parts of our lives, using their synergy to create a greater whole? Contemplative practitioners in higher education have wondered at various times whether or how to use the tools of their own mindfulness practice in their college courses: could these practices help students calm their own minds and bodies? Connect their cognitive and affective responses to course materials, and form more complete analyses? Could these practices support students in bringing different parts of their own lives together—their values and compassion, sense of justice, and inquiry into course materials? Motivated by these and other questions investigating the uses of mindfulness practices as a liberatory pedagogy, over 200 educators convened at the 2017 summer session on Contemplative Learning in Higher Education, sponsored by the Center for Contemplative Mind in Higher Education (CMind)—and that's where this volume began.

In large presentations and small group discussions, mindfulness leaders and educators such as Steven Murphy-Shigematsu, Katja Hahn D'Errico, Beth Berila, Kakali Bhattacharya, Arthur Zajonc, and many others provided inspiration, resources, and examples of contemplative pedagogies. While Berila's *Mindfulness as Anti-Oppressive Pedagogy* (2016) provided a foundation and inspiration for seeking ways to link course content, contemplative practice, and resources for investigating and unlearning oppression, D'Errico's workshop gave participants the strategies for integrating these three areas (see Table 1.1 at the end of this chapter).

Several contributors to this volume met at CMind 2017 and began a more serious study and approach to developing their own uses of contemplative pedagogies. Other contributors attended a Mind and Life-grant funded Think Tank on "Mindfulness Pedagogy," held at the Aldo Leopold Center in 2018. And still others responded to an open call for proposals shared through the Association for

DOI: 10.4324/9781003201854-2

the Study of Literature and Environment (ASLE) discussion board, the 2019 convention panel dedicated to exploring "Contemplative Pedagogies for the Environmental Humanities," or were contacted by one of the co-editors. Through each of these channels, faculty were excited to discover peers who were seeking ways to offer the benefits of mindfulness to students struggling with academic, personal, and social issues such as reading comprehension and anxiety, and noticing, experiencing, and responding to social injustices.

Higher Education's Student Profiles of Stress

Multiple studies over the last decade have explored college students' mental health (Bauer-Wolf, 2018; Eva, 2019; Oswalt et al., 2020). An international survey of nearly 14,000 first-year college students across eight countries found that "35 percent struggled with mental illness, particularly depression or anxiety"—in the United States, anxiety is students' primary reported concern (Eva, 2019). Depression and anxiety are associated with lower academic performance, increased alcohol and drug use, self-injurious behaviors, suicidal ideation and suicide—with one-third of undergraduates exhibiting symptoms of mental health problems (Oswalt et al., 2020). Where do these mental health challenges originate? Reportedly, about one-quarter of U.S. residents ages 18 and older live with a mental health disorder each year, and half of all serious adult mental health disorders—notably major depression, anxiety disorder, and substance use—start by age 14 and present by age 25 (Kessler et al., 2005). While there has been an increase in the number of students seeking mental health and counseling services, at least 50% of college students who have struggled with mental health issues did not seek help (Oswald et al., 2020). What visible or invisible barriers prevented those students from help-seeking behaviors?

Perhaps the data is in plain view. The National Alliance on Mental Illness (NAMI) Survey Report on Mental Health, "College Students Speak Out" (Gruttadaro & Crudo, 2012), describes a national survey of "college students living with mental health conditions" administered between August and November 2011, and obtaining 765 survey responses. The report describes survey methodology and participant demographics—"individuals diagnosed with a mental health condition, who are currently or were enrolled in college in the last five years"—but omits using the demographics in data analysis. A search of terms used for identifying racial demographics in this NAMI report shows that groupings such as "African American," "Asian American," "Hispanics/Latinos," "American Indians," and "Pacific Islander" appear only once in the entire study—on the page where demographic data is provided. In contrast, LGBT students were mentioned three times, most notably in disclosing their mental health concerns (62%, a surprisingly high number for disclosure, given the combined stigma of queer identities and mental health). What's not evident from the NAMI survey is how many of those queer students were students of color, or how many of the overall survey population—beyond the 82% Caucasian and 82% female—were struggling with other challenges, such as economic stress, violence, race-based discrimination, harassment, or sexual assault.

In another study, analysis of 165 research sources on college students' mental health published from 2010 to 2015 indicates both "increasing demand for student services provided by campus counseling centers (113/165, 68.5%) and the increased mental health risks faced by racial and ethnic minorities (30/165, 18.2%)" (Payton et al., 2018). The study found six significant factors in mental health experiences—"age, race, crime, student services, aftermath, victim"—and two themes: again, the increased demand for campus counseling center services, but also the "increased mental health risks faced by racial and ethnic minorities" (p. 1). Presently, various stressors and traumatizing experiences prompt students to seek counseling services, and these stressors are not what mainstream mental health, DSM-V-trained counselors are expecting "sexual assault, food scarcity, violence, and racism" (p. 8). These data suggest there is an opportunity for contemplative educators to link our practices of mindful awareness with our social justice values by using contemplative pedagogies to teach students tools for more immediate well-being and simultaneously raising discussions of racial, economic, environmental, and gender justice in our courses.

Contemplative Pedagogies in Higher Education

Faculty and administrators in higher education have become increasingly aware of student mental health needs, the persistence of oppressive ideologies across the disciplines, and the immanent environmental challenges we face as a planet. Although application in higher education is relatively new, contemplative practices, including mindfulness, have been demonstrated to have a positive impact on mental health and wellness (i.e., Brown & Ryan, 2003; Hick & Bien, 2008; Rodríguez-Carvajal et al., 2016; Trautwein et al., 2016), as well as promoting social justice awareness and exploring differences with curiosity and compassion (i.e., Berila, 2016; Burgess et al., 2016; King, 2018; Forbes, 2019). The integration of mindfulness in higher education has benefits across the institution, including creating positive learning environments, promoting administration and faculty functioning, enhancing student life, and connecting with the larger community (i.e., Barbezat & Bush, 2014; Bush, 2011; Davis, 2014). Specifically, contemplative teaching practices enable deep engaged learning and promote a campus climate that enhances deeper personal and social awareness, encouraging critical inquiry (Barbezat & Bush, 2014; Rechtschaffen, 2014). Contemplative practices encourage us to move away from the "banking model of education" (Freire, 1993), which is a mechanical narration from the teacher, to a more holistic and liberatory education, where teacher and learner bring their whole selves to the learning process and engage deeply with the material, co-creating knowledge with their bodies, minds, and emotions.

As "The Tree of Contemplative Practices" (Figure 1.1; CMind, 2021) suggests, contemplative pedagogies are used to bridge course content with students' embodied awareness through a variety of practices: poetry-writing, qigong, yoga, art-making, walking meditation, mindful self-compassion, and mindfulness of breath, sounds, thoughts, sensations. Mindfulness practices, in particular, are shown to enhance concentration and memory, reduce anxiety and depression, and improve general health and well-being. Mindfulness is also used as an anti-oppression pedagogy (Berila, 2016), strategic in helping students expose and examine deeply held prejudices around race, gender, sexuality, species, and more.

Although the scholarship on integrating contemplative practices in higher education in general and specifically anti-oppressive pedagogy and racial healing

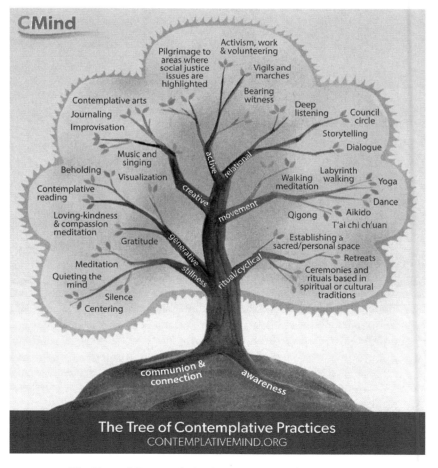

FIGURE 1.1 The Tree of Contemplative Practices (CMind)

is growing, a multidisciplinary book that provides guidance and the contemplative methods for creating inclusive and transformative learning spaces has not appeared. In short, there is no edited volume that builds upon the work launched by Barbezat and Bush (2014), advances Berila's (2016) work in anti-oppressive contemplative pedagogy, and applies Forbes's (2019) vision for a "counter-program" that transcends the secular-religious divide.

Our volume aims to fill this gap in the scholarship. In this book, we define oppression as beliefs that (1) construct a self that is separate from others, (2) value one's selfhood and group identity while ignoring or devaluing others, and (3) legitimate uses of power, privilege, and control over devalued others. Oppression is systemic and simultaneously sociocultural, institutional, interpersonal, and intrapersonal. It manifests through distinctions of race, ethnicity, gender, class, sexuality, age, ability, religion, nation, species, and more; it is variously articulated as hyper-achievement, perfectionism, overwork, and/or low self-worth, self-harm, and aggression (toward other humans and/or the community of life). Oppression produces trauma that may be stored in the body, repressed or "forgotten"; it is widely recognized that trauma often surfaces during mindfulness practices. Hence, our book also provides a framework and guidance on facilitating an awareness of the links between historical and current oppression, self-identity, and trauma, creating a transformative learning experience through mindfulness.

Another recent volume, *Contemplative Approaches to Sustainability in Higher Education* (Eaton et al., 2017), is both unique in this emerging field of mindfulness in higher education, for the ways it brings forward issues of environmental sustainability, and helpful in providing a model for the volume we have created. Each chapter in our volume examines the intersection between mindfulness and a specific scholarly discipline, exploring the ways that contemplative pedagogy can be integrated into course content, activities, and assignments to invite reflective awareness of structural injustices, cultivate empathy, bridge or release the boundary of separate selfhood, and provide tools and strategies for both dismantling oppression and supporting our students' resilience. Our contributors are responsive to student and regional demographics and the ways these contexts influence the approaches and goals for contemplative pedagogies: variously diverse in gender, race, and sexuality, our authors use their embodiment and that of their students to scaffold their uses of mindful anti-oppressive pedagogies strategically. Our fields range from the environmental humanities—literature, history, ecocriticism—to environmental sciences, ecocultural studies, philosophy, and social sciences—psychology and counseling. Although presented within their specific discipline, contemplative practices described in each chapter can be applied across the disciplines.

Secular or Spiritual?

Today's current debates regarding secularized versus contextualized contemplative practices in the United States are powered by the historic separation of church and state, enshrined in the U.S. Constitution and tested at the Supreme Court multiple times since World War II. Secular mindfulness practices were first popularized by molecular biologist Jon Kabat-Zinn in 1979 at the University of Massachusetts Medical School through his Stress Reduction and Relaxation Program (SR&RP), later renamed Mindfulness-Based Stress Reduction (MBSR), a practice aimed at using just one step from Buddhism's Eightfold Path as a strategy for "relaxation, paying attention, [cultivating] awareness and insight" (Wilson, 2014). Between the years 1980 and 2000, mindfulness practices and popularity proliferated, with developments in psychology—mindfulness-based cognitive therapy (Segal et al., 2001), mindful self-compassion (Germer, 2009; Neff, 2011), Dialectical Behavioral Therapy (Linehan, 2014), and Acceptance and Commitment Therapy (Hayes et al., 2016)—as well as in education, via the creation of the Mindfulness in Education Network in 2001, Goldie Hawn's MindUP program in 2003, Thich Nhat Hanh's contribution to mindfulness in education (Hanh & Weare, 2017), and the Mindful Schools in Oakland, California, in 2007, spreading nationally and incorporating as a nonprofit within three years.

Kabat-Zinn's definition of mindfulness has become the *sine qua non* for the secular mindfulness movement. The difference in contemporary debates, however, is that both secular mindfulness and dharma practice in the West have been "outed" for being either "McMindful" (Purser, 2019) and apolitical, emphasizing "momentary states rather than long-term transformation" (McMahon & Braun, 2017, pp. 210–211), or for involving primarily white practitioners, with practitioners of color joining white-dominant sanghas and forming people-of-color groups, and more recently expressing concern with the linked exclusions of people of color and the decontextualization of dharma practice, a "context-stripping" that obscures mindfulness practice's origins in Asian Buddhist cultures and people (Wilson, 2014; Batacharya & Wong, 2018; Forbes, 2019; Yetunde & Giles, 2020). Moreover, in the West, mindfulness and meditation practices are sometimes presented as the sum total of Buddhism, backgrounding or omitting integral practices of ethics and interbeing—generosity, effort, morality, gratitude, patience, and the wisdom of emptiness—that lead to spiritual, social, and ecopolitical awakening (Loy, 2018). This invisibility and exclusion of individuals of color through cultural appropriation in the West is similar to the invisibility of non-Buddhist practices of meditation. Integrating contemplative practices in higher education presents a challenge of secularizing practices that have religious, spiritual, and often mystic origins. At the same time, not all contemplative practices have religious/spiritual origins.

As contemplative faculty, we need to acknowledge the complexity and hold the contradiction of secularizing our practices and selves in the classroom. Contemplative practices are presented as invitations in the classroom, always with the option to participate or opt out; moreover, students are given a choice among multiple practices, and practice reflections are not graded. Anti-oppressive pedagogy asks us to notice, acknowledge, and be aware of the power we are given by the hierarchical educational institutions. No matter how egalitarian, contemplative, humanistic we are, we hold the power of grading in the student-professor relationship. We are all aware of how such power has been abused to exclude, discriminate, and oppress.

Where do these developments interface with contemplative pedagogies in higher education?

Contemplative Pedagogies and Anti-Oppressive Practices

This volume explores mindfulness and other contemplative pedagogies as a strategy for uncovering and transforming the mental conditioning and embodied beliefs that support oppression; as Forbes (2019) explains, an "emergent mindfulness" program does not "focus on individual mindfulness as a way to adjust to and cope with stress and injustice," but rather is a practice in which "community members further analyze, resist, and change those sources of stress and injustice" (p. 180). Our volume is responsive to cultural and demographic contexts, linking mindfulness and Buddhism when appropriate, as in courses taking place in Thailand (see Chapter 4), while in North America, not presenting contemplative pedagogies as requiring a specific spiritual practice. However, we do "practice what we teach": each contributor has an established mindfulness practice (as recommended in Hanh & Weare, 2017) and has observed in the habits of their own minds the ways that racism, sexism, heterosexism, and human centrism arise and can be interrupted, interrogated, and replaced with greater awareness of our interbeing with all life. Although not making direct links, one chapter is founded upon Sufi philosophy (Chapter 13) based on the author's culture and practice. Aware that leaving out parts of our whole selves enacts a colonial mindset, we are committed to bringing together the tools of our disciplines with the tools of contemplative pedagogies, and our whole human experience. What we each discovered was that a research model exists to provide the foundations for this nexus, but we would still have to build these discipline-specific anti-oppressive pedagogies ourselves.

Kumashiro (2000) summarizes and critiques the four main categories of anti-oppressive education: (a) education for the other (improving the experience of the Othered); (b) educating about the other (what students—privileged and marginalized—need to know about the Othered); (c) education that is critical of privileging and othering (examining how some are othered and some privileged, how this system is legitimized and maintained, and how educational institutions are contributing); and (d) education that changes the students and society (examining how certain discourses maintain oppression). Each of these approaches has strengths and weaknesses. Contemplative anti-oppressive pedagogy builds on these approaches, challenging the separation of self and other, and thus moving beyond educating for and about the other. Moreover, contemplative anti-oppressive practices invite faculty and students to take note of their own cultural conditioning and question its underlying assumptions, inspiring more authentic transformation and action.

Each chapter in this volume integrates and transcends the four main approaches to anti-oppressive education. Janelle Adsit (Chapter 2) uses the term "epistemic injustice"—a term taken up by both de Sousa Santos and Miranda Fricker, though with different orientations—that emphasizes the suppression of knowledges and, thereby, their knowers. Epistemic injustice is a manifestation and core logic of colonialism and white-supremacist-capitalist patriarchy (to use bell hooks's term). To identify the forms of epistemic injustice that Western contemplative pedagogies may risk, Adsit's chapter exposes, through close reading, the assumptions that are embedded in a selection of U.S. contemplative pedagogy texts.

Our second area of emphasis explores contemplative pedagogies as used in teaching about environmental and climate justice. Students who grapple honestly with the issues of climate change and climate justice do so both intellectually and emotionally, and responding to our embodied emotions for human, multispecies, and ecological suffering involves both eco-anxiety and eco-grief. Jennifer Atkinson's Chapter 3 examines the phenomenon of ecological grief among students, activists, and educators in the face of climate injustice and the ongoing assault on our biosphere. Atkinson resists conventional assumptions about grief as something to be resolved, and instead asks, how might grief serve as an ally and a contemplative pedagogy that promotes interspecies empathy and climate justice by cultivating awareness of our shared vulnerability, what Judith Butler calls "a point of identification with suffering itself"? This chapter offers concrete strategies for using contemplative inquiry to help students navigate grief and cultivate the resilience to stay engaged in climate solutions over the long run.

Using mindfulness pedagogy in Thailand, a traditionally Buddhist country, Darin Pradittatsanee teaches environmental literature that explores issues of place perception, inhabitation, toxicity, environmental justice, and postcolonialism. Her course utilizes contemplative practices to support students in cultivating awareness of "interbeing," starting from quieting the mind, being mindful of their existence and the interpenetration of all things, to imagining themselves in the position of others, extending compassion, and reflecting upon their responsibilities to the world. Presented from a nonsectarian stance, these practices are informed by Thich Nhat Hanh's notion of "interbeing," which articulates the Buddhist notion of dependent origination (*paticcasamppāda*) and non-self (*anattā*). Anne Raine's teaching takes place in Ottawa, Canada, many students feel removed from the immediate effects of climate change—even though the

Alberta Tar Sands are comparatively close by. Integrating mindfulness practice into an undergraduate course on the literature of climate change, Raine brings her contemplative pedagogy into dialogue with other fields such as affect theory, environmental justice studies, ecofeminism, and decolonization studies, all perspectives for anti-oppressive pedagogy in times that urgently call for this transformation. Section two concludes with Greta Gaard's explorations of contemplative pedagogy adapted to three rather different General Education courses: a Human-Animal Studies course, an Advanced Writing Course, and a second-year course in Composition, wherein she utilizes Ricard's (2003) Buddhist perspective on happiness with positive psychology's (Lyubomirsky, 2007) 12 happiness practices to support her students in exploring the intersections of climate change, the Sixth Extinction, and our global (rigged) economy. Students investigate and replace the three poisons identified by Buddhism—greed, hatred, and delusion—with generosity and gratitude, random acts of kindness, and nurturing relationships (interbeing) through the secular happiness practices (Lyubomirsky, 2007; Loy, 2018).

Supporting students' well-being and deeper engagement with the course content through mindfulness practices thematically ties together our third section, with courses on environmental history, environmental science, art and yoga, philosophy, and counselor education. Using a practice of "Inner Tracking," David J. Voelker's contemplative pedagogy draws on Macy and Brown (2014), giving students an opportunity to both think and feel the significance of their learning, working not only with the intellect but also with identity and their sense of how they fit into the world. Franklin M. Chen's pedagogy utilizes a variety of contemplative practices to promote student well-being, mental clarity, anxiety reduction, and concentration through mindful walking, contemplative listening to music or poetry, and reflective writing in his science courses. Jan Estep's course combines somatic, contemplative, and creative practices by linking art and yoga, promoting an increased awareness of embodiment and self-presence, greater connection to intuition and creativity, and a softening of self-judgment. Chosen for the cover of this volume to visualize how contemplative practice inspires a variety of pedagogies, as symbolized by the dragonflies taking flight from the hand, Estep's contemplative artwork is part of her teaching.

In his Philosophy of Mind course, Sam Cocks invites students to self-select a mindfulness practice and commit to a regular engagement with the practice throughout the semester, as part of a philosophical exploration of the *nature* of mind, consciousness, and subjectivity, exploring whether or how mindfulness increases students' awareness of habitual biases or ways of thinking. Teysha L. Bowser, Renae Swanson, and Amney J. Harper present ways to integrate mindfulness and reflection into counselor preparation courses in their program. Counselors are asked to be present ("here and now") and nonjudgmental, yet they are rarely taught *how* to do that. The practices these co-authors share are applicable to many disciplines.

Our final section addresses the ways that each of these contemplative classes would benefit from the supportive context of a contemplative campus and teaching communities of practice. Describing mindfulness "as an intrinsic aspect of interpersonal relationships" as well as "part of the call for social justice and a moral life," Forbes (2019) affirms that educational institutions also "need to create healthy, critically mindful cultures or we-spaces in order to develop relationships that foster trust, safety, respect, inclusiveness, caring, compassion, acceptance, healing, and connectedness" (p. 191). Jennifer Daubenmier and colleagues at San Francisco State University describe their work offering and assessing a campus-wide workshop series on contemplative practice and social justice, working to improve campus climate, enhance the well-being of campus members, and promote student success. Renee Owen and Danaé Jones Aicher describe their work teaching neuroscience and mindfulness in community workshops aimed at transforming racial bias and forming new mental habits around race. Bengü Ergüner-Tekinalp's chapter focuses on integrating mindfulness into higher education policy and practices through establishing learning communities. It describes the Contemplative Practices Learning Community at Drake University, and provides guidance on establishing and sustaining such initiatives, transforming institutions to become more mindful.

All of our chapters provide tools and tables offering course readings, contemplative practices, and assessment tools. Most contributors obtained Institutional Review Board (IRB) approval from their institutions to conduct their contemplative pedagogy research and utilized a variety of measurement tools. While the Five-Facet Mindfulness Questionnaire (FFMQ) was utilized in pre- and post-tests, as described in Chapters 4, 5, and 10, Chapter 6 utilizes a diversity of scales: the Perceived Stress Scale, the Toronto Empathy Questionnaire, and the Cantril Ladder. Other educators preferred surveys and varieties of qualitative self-reporting (see Chapters 3, 7, 8, 9, 11, and 13), and still others used both formal and informal reflective writing (Chapters 3, 4, 6, 7, 10, and 11). What we found overall was that any quantitative scale was incomplete without contextualizing the numbers with qualitative reflections (Forbes, 2019). In addition, our authors provided their positionality and intersectional identities as well as the context of their universities and student demographics, because all of these factors impact how faculty are presenting in the classroom, and the way students are engaging with contemplative practices.

Our Introduction concludes where each of us began, exploring the step-by-step strategies for infusing contemplative and anti-oppressive pedagogies into courses across the curriculum (see Table 1.1). We offer our readers these steps and the diversity of practices explored in this volume as strategies for infusing contemplative and anti-oppressive pedagogies into your own courses.

May you, your students, and all beings benefit from your contemplative practice and teaching.

TABLE 1.1 Strategies for Integrating Mindfulness and Anti-Oppression Pedagogy Into Your Existing Courses

1. **What mindfulness practices do you personally use?** There's an intimate connection between being a practitioner and being a teacher of mindfulness. If you want to add practices for your classroom, be sure to add these to your own practice. List these practices.
2. **What anti-oppression tools are in your own toolkit?** Ideas for this list include
    a. Classroom management—setting up safe space, inclusivity statement on the syllabus, etc.
    b. Specific short readings—i.e., Robin D'Angelo's "white fragility," Peggy McIntosh's, "Knapsack of white privilege," "Privilege in the Environmental Movement," etc.
    c. Specific activities or exercises
    d. What are the underlying anti-oppressive approaches of your course? (education for the other, education about the other, critical of privileging and othering, education that changes students and society?)
    e. What needs to be taken out or added to include contemplative anti-oppressive pedagogy?
3. **What are the key course activities?** Content? Readings? Films? Assignments? List them.
    a. Offer an overview of your course content and activities, asking
        i. Is self presented as separate from the other?
        ii. Are there implicit messages/tone if the separate other is less valuable?
        iii. What and who is privileged, normed and who holds the power?
    b. Reflect on the power you hold in the faculty/student dynamic. How can you make sure this power is acknowledged and balanced?
    c. Reflect on the politics of citation, who is cited, presented as the norm, as the expert; who is missing? What historical oppressive patterns might be repeated in course content?
4. **Create Learning Outcomes**, i.e., "After this class using mindfulness pedagogy, you will be able to. . .". Possibilities include
    a. Understand what mindfulness is and how it makes a difference
    b. Experience how mindfulness can improve your well-being and performance
    c. Be familiar with using a range of mindfulness techniques to enhance your learning
    d. Understand the causes, and be better able to manage stress, anxiety, and low mood
    e. Intentionally focus your attention
    f. Notice when your mind wanders
    g. Appreciate the difference between automatic thoughts that are useful, positive, and nurturing and those that are not useful, negative, and depleting.

STOP: LINK # 1-4.

5. **Provide resources on mindfulness within your syllabus or online course system**, i.e.,
    a. Mindfulness phone apps you use and enjoy, ones that students can download for free
    b. Short, guided mindfulness practices in transcript and audio links to university statements about mindfulness and higher education (i.e., Stanford, UCLA, UW-Madison, Brown University, Harvard, and more)
6. **Connect with your campus Counseling Services office:** explain your pedagogy and what might come up for students. Establish a ready support from Counseling Services as well as a list of area services if needed.

7. **Contact your campus Institutional Review Board (IRB), if you plan to assess your practice of this pedagogy, you may need IRB approval.**
   a. What assessment tools do you plan to use? What does research on mindfulness pedagogies in your subject area suggest?
   b. Consider using quantitative instruments (i.e., Five-Facet Mindfulness Questionnaire (FFMQ)) as well as qualitative self-reporting after various mindfulness practices throughout the term.
   c. Consider using pre- and post-tests with the same instruments, and a plan to follow-up query 6 weeks or more after the course has ended.
8. **Consent and nonparticipation.** When you introduce the mindfulness pedagogy at the start of the semester, obtain IRB consent forms, and provide the option of nonparticipation. Describe ways students can choose to not participate in a single event, to self-soothe in a practice they had entered but need to stop ("what ordinary activity could you bring to mind, to distract yourself if uncomfortable thoughts arise during the mindfulness practice? Doing laundry, grocery shopping, riding a bicycle?"), or not participate for the entire semester (i.e., remaining in class and sitting quietly, writing "I chose not to participate" if qualitative reports are invited after the mindfulness practice).
9. **Triangulate mindfulness practices, anti-oppression tools, and course content/activities (items 1, 2, and 3) to create your course schedule.** Make it clear on the syllabus what days you will introduce each new practice, or begin a class with a mindfulness practice, emphasizing punctuality for participation and explaining how to handle late arrivals.
10. **What would you add to this process?**

References

Barbezat, D. P., & Bush, M. (Eds.). (2014). *Contemplative Practices in Higher Education*. Jossey-Bass.

Batacharya, S., & Wong, Y.-L. R. (Eds.). (2018). *Sharing Breath: Embodied Learning and Decolonization*. Athabasca University Press.

Bauer-Wolf, J. (2018). Study Plumbs Sources of Students' Pain. *Inside Higher Ed,* October 25. https://www.insidehighered.com/news/2018/10/25/new-study-shows-causes-college-student-mental-health-problems.

Berila, B. (2016). *Integrating Mindfulness into Anti-Oppression Pedagogy: Social Justice in Higher Education*. Routledge.

Brown, K. W., & Ryan, R. M. (2003). The Benefits of Being Present: Mindfulness and Its Role in Psychological Well-Being. *Journal of Personality and Social Psychology*, 84(4), 822–848.

Burgess, D. J., Beach, M. C., & Saha, S. (2016). Mindfulness Practice: A Promising Approach to Reducing the Effects of Clinician Implicit Bias on Patients. *Patient Education and Counseling*, 100(2), 372–376. Doi: 10.1016/j.pec.2016.09.005.

Bush, M. (2011). Mindfulness in Higher Education. *Contemporary Buddhism*, 12(1), 183–197.

CMind. (2021). *The Tree of Contemplative Practices [Illustration]*. The Center for Contemplative Mind in Society. https://www.contemplativemind.org/practices/tree.

Davis, D. J. (2014). Mindfulness in Higher Education: Teaching, Learning, and Leadership. *The International Journal of Religion and Spirituality in Society*, 4(3), 1–6. Doi: 10.18848/2154-8633/CGP/v04i03/51091.

Eaton, M., Hughes, H. J., & MacGregor, J. (Eds.). (2017). *Contemplative Approaches to Sustainability in Higher Education: Theory and Practice*. Routledge.

Eva, A. L. (2019, January 11). How Colleges Today are Supporting Student Mental Health. *Greater Good Science Center/Education*. https://greatergood.berkeley.edu/article/%C3%ADtem/how_colleges_today_are_supporting_student_mental_health.

Forbes, D. (2019). *Mindfulness and Its Discontents: Education, Self, and Social Transformation*. Fernwood Publishing.

Freire, P. (1993). *Pedagogy of the Oppressed*. The Continuum Publishing Company.

Germer, C. (2009). *The Mindful Path to Self-Compassion: Freeing Yourself from Destructive Thoughts and Emotions*. Guilford Press.

Gruttadaro, D., & Crudo, D. (2012). *College Students Speak: A Survey Report on Mental Health*. National Alliance on Mental Illness (NAMI).

Hanh, T. N., & Weare, K. (2017). *Happy Teachers Change the World*. Parallax Press.

Hayes, S. C., Strosahl, K. D., & Wilson, K. G. (2016). *Acceptance and Commitment Therapy: The Process and Practice of Mindful Change* (2nd ed.). Guilford Press.

Hick, S. F., & Bien, T. (2008). *Mindfulness and the Therapeutic Relationship*. Guilford Press.

Kessler, R. C., Berglund, P., Demler, O., Jin, R., Merikangas, K. R., & Walters, E. E. (2005). Lifetime Prevalence and Age-of-Onset Distributions of DSM-IV Disorders in the National Comorbidity Survey Replication. *Archives of General Psychiatry*, 62, 593–602.

King, R. (2018). *Mindful of Race: Transforming Racism from the Inside Out*. Sounds True.

Kumashiro, K. K. (2000). Toward a Theory of Anti-Oppressive Education. *Review of Educational Research*, 70(1), 25–53.

Linehan, M. (2014). *DBT Skills Training Manual* (2nd ed.) Guilford Press.

Loy, D. R. (2018). *EcoDharma: Buddhist Teachings for the Ecological Crisis*. Wisdom Pubs.

Lyubomirsky, S. (2007). *The How of Happiness*. Platkus/LittleBrown.

Macy, J., & Brown, M. Y. (2014). *Coming Back to Life: The Updated Guide to the Work That Reconnects*. New Society Publishers.

McMahon, D. L., & Braun, E. (Eds.). (2017). *Meditation, Buddhism, and Science*. Oxford University Press.

Neff, K. (2011). *Self-Compassion: The Proven Power of Being Kind to Yourself*. HarperCollins.

Oswalt, S. B., Lederer, A. M. Chestnut-Steich, K., Day, C., Halbritter, A., & Ortiz, D. (2020). Trends in College Students' Mental Health Diagnoses and Utilization of Services, 2009–2015. *Journal of American College Health*, 68(1), 41–51.

Payton, F. C., Yarger, L. K., & Pinter, A. T. (2018, October–December). Text Mining Mental Health Reports for Issues Impacting Today's College Students: Qualitative Study. *JMIR Mental Health*, 5(4). https://mental.jmir.org/2018/4/e10032/.

Purser, R. E. (2019). *McMindfulness: How Mindfulness Became the New Capitalist Spirituality*. Repeater Books.

Rechtschaffen, D. (2014). *The Way of Mindful Education: Cultivating Well-Being in Teachers and Students*. W. W. Norton & Co.

Ricard, M. (2003). *Happiness: A Guide to Developing Life's Most Important Skill*. Nil Editions.

Rodríguez-Carvajal, R., García-Rubio, C., Paniagua, D., García-Diex, G., & de Rivas, S. (2016, October). Mindfulness Integrative Model (MIM): Cultivating Positive States of Mind Towards Oneself and the Others Through Mindfulness and Self—Compassion. *Anales de Psicología*, 32(3), 749–760.

Segal, Z., Williams, J. M. G., & Teasdale, J. D. (2001). *Mindfulness-Based Cognitive Therapy for Depression*. Guilford Press.

Trautwein, M., Naranjo, J. R., & Schmidt, S. (2016). Decentering the Self? Reduced Bias in Self-vs. Other-Related Processing in Long-Term Practitioners of Loving-Kindness Meditation. *Frontiers in Psychology*, 7, 582. Doi: 10.3389/fpsyg.2016.01785.

Wilson, J. (2014). *Mindful America: The Mutual Transformation of Buddhist Meditation and American Culture*. Oxford University Press.

Yetunde, P. A., & Giles, C. A. (Eds.). (2020). *Black & Buddhist: What Buddhism Can Teach Us About Race, Resilience, Transformation & Freedom*. Shambhala Publications.

2
PURSUING ANTIRACIST AND ANTICOLONIAL APPROACHES TO CONTEMPLATIVE PRACTICES

Janelle Adsit

We always write in the particularity of a moment. This moment is conditioned by the tenacity of antiracist protests and uprisings, born from deep roots of resistance. The breath is central to this resistance: the full-breath sounds of protests, interruptions of regular programming to call us back to the sound and presence of a human breath—accounting for how Black peoples' breath has been suppressed at the mercy of white knees, arms, and hands, suppressed by the fatal toxins poured into communities from continued environmental racism, suppressed by a health industry that fails to serve all communities and is needed in new ways during a global pandemic. When I think of the exigencies for scholarship at this time, I think of the utter and pronounced responsibility to seek radical transformation.

I write as a white woman who teaches in higher education, a system that perpetuates racism and maintains its legacy of white supremacy and its entrenched *noblesse oblige* orientation: the predominantly white university's assumption of "a model of 'uplift'—that is, the idea that the downtrodden must be lifted up to the social status of the privileged but ostensibly sympathetic activist-observer," as Justice (2005, p. 74) defines it. He continues, "In such a model, there's no reflection on whether or not the observer's *status quo* standards hold any appeal for anyone else and no thought that these standards and values might be considered dangerous or even corrosive to those being 'helped'" (Justice, 2005, p. 144, as cited in Leon & Nadeau, 2018, p. 74). Unless it has done transformative work, the predominantly white institution offers a racist education that reproduces inequities.

To write about the U.S. higher education system is to write within this context. I sit with the privilege of my breath moving in and out of my lungs and the stark questions that shape my embodiment in the world: What does it mean for me to teach? What does it mean for me to do the work of dismantling racism and interrupting the continued histories of interlocking oppressions? I write not

DOI: 10.4324/9781003201854-3

within a framework of answer-giving, but from the truth that there is no way of opting out of a response. We are always already in response. We respond in our living—in our choices and our actions, in the words we utter or don't. It is from this realization that I came to mindfulness and contemplative practice. In realizing that my life—my day-to-day, moment-by-moment—is a response, I also realize that my moments needed mindful attention.

In what follows, I offer a few notes of reflection about the relationship between contemplative practice and antiracist and anticolonial practice. In this, I am in close conversation with the many teachers and writers who also engage the relationship between anti-oppressive and contemplative practice (Batacharya & Wong, 2018; Berila, 2016; King, 2018; Magee, 2019; Manuel, 2015; Menakem, 2017; Orr, 2002; Polinska, 2018; Thompson, 2017; van der Kolk, 2014; Williams, 2002; Williams et al., 2016). In articulating an "equity-mindful approach," I consider questions of epistemic justice in the contemplative classroom, and I explore what it means to take an epistemic posture of cultural humility.

Equity-Mindedness as Equity-Mindfulness

Equity-mindedness, a term popularized by the Center for Urban Education (n.d.) and other Diversity, Equity, and Inclusion (DE&I) scholars, is a paradigm that that calls for attention to each individual's practice in an institutional and systemic context. Equity-mindedness, which we might think of as equity-*mindfulness*, means recognizing how, for instance, this comment on a paper, this choice in the classroom, this response to a colleague, all need an ongoing meditation on the ways that white supremacy and colonial logics are reproduced and reinforced. While mindfulness is not always explicitly named in theories of equity-mindedness, the words "consciousness," "awareness," "attention," and "self-reflection" regularly appear in DE&I literature. With the inclusion of such terms, we can read for the potential role that mindfulness can play in equity-minded work. Although the focus of "equity-mindedness" is also on institutional accountability, policy, and data-driven response, there is also the moment-by-moment awareness of the individual who occupies several roles—the individual as a potential agent for change as their awareness grows.

Multiple practitioners, including King (2018) and Magee (2019), have explicitly identified the role mindfulness can play within equity advocacy and antiracist transformation. As Magee writes of the role of mindfulness, "personal awareness practices are essential for racial justice work. For real change to occur, we must be able to examine our own experiences, discover the 'situated' nature of our perspectives, and understand how race and racism are mere cultural constructions" (7) that have a dire impact. Both King and Magee embody a mindfulness practice in the racial justice texts they've written—calling the reader to become more aware of their experience in the moment of reading. "What was it like for you to read those words?" Magee writes, "What thoughts are coming up for you? What do you feel in your body now? What emotions do you feel as you consider what you just read?" (16). These moments are written from the premise that "mindfulness is essential to developing the capacity to *respond*, rather than simply *react* as if on autopilot to what we experience" (Magee, 2019, p. 17). The distance that mindfulness creates between the fleeting thoughts of the mind and our experience of them is critical to moving from pre-programmed reaction to considered response. The pre-programmed reaction is prone to manifesting the dominant or status quo. Equity-mindedness calls us to do otherwise, and it is furthered by equity-mindfulness because, as Berila (2016) identifies,

> Oppressive ideologies insinuate themselves into our very selves, which means that they inevitably inform [our] mental chatter. . . . It takes the capacity to recognize the negative mental chatter and the skills to interrupt it if we are to truly unearth the seeds of oppression.
>
> (pp. 19–20)

This "mental chatter" (Berila, 2016) is "systemic chatter" (Prevatt-Hyles & Vinsky, 2009), a term used to describe how hegemonies are reinforced through our internal dialogues and decision-making patterns. One may be predisposed to read the world through scripts and understandings that are systemically provided to us. In turn, there is the potential to perpetuate or disrupt established scripts through our discourse and action. By mindfully slowing down the "automaticity" (Johnson, 2018; Lueke & Gibson, 2014) of our thoughts and our processing of the world, we come to notice internalized scripts and how they reproduce structures and forms of oppression in our society. Noticing requires breaking from the automaticity of our perceptions and interpretations: it requires "effortful processing" (Johnson, 2018) of scripts the mind draws upon to make its reading of the world, thus striving to break the white racial frame (DiAngelo, 2016; Feagin, 2013) and dominant narratives.

This is a starting place: "If the storylines we repeatedly narrate to ourselves are laced with oppressive ideologies . . . then the ability to pause those storylines and even rewrite them can go a long way toward creating a more just world" (Berila, 2016, p. 20). At times in my teaching, I will call attention to the language I use: for example, after unthinkingly using the words "firm-footed," I paused to notice with the students how this language could perpetuate ableism and is not inclusive of all bodies. What we said once is not what we cling to for all time; detachment and fluidity are necessary for embracing the possibility of revision, rethinking, reimagining—to prompt the changes that are most needed. This is mindful attention that we are called to as educators; it is also mindful attention that we invite our students to learn to be more present to each other. We can teach our students to pause, to notice the systemic chatter in their minds that might be ignited by a comment made by a peer or by something presented on the page or screen. The self-reflexivity enabled in mindful practices can help draw our awareness to how our presence, words, and action may be a form of resistance or merely a node in a matrix that maintains the status quo.

Contemplative Pedagogies and Colonialist Legacies

We see the value of mindfulness practices in equity work. Yet adopting mindfulness practices is not enough to dislodge and dismantle white supremacy. Some contemplative pedagogies may leave intact and perpetuate forms of white supremacist ideology, and the adoption of contemplative practices may be aligned with, rather than resistant to, colonialist logics. For example, an academic and colonial tendency to collect and appropriate from Indigenous cultures (Smith, 2012, p. 26) may be descriptive of contemplative practices in U.S. higher education. Removing belief systems, practices, and rituals from their contexts is an extension of the extractivist logics of continued colonial relations. This "cherry-picking" (Berila, 2016, p. 149) takes up certain ideas by snatching them from their rootedness in culture, history, and tradition. This is the orientation of a consumer: plundering an idea, like the cherry fruit, without understanding the tree, the broader epistemology, and cosmology that sustains it. We can see this tendency in how Traditional Ecological Knowledges have been taken up by some non-Native thinkers, or how Islam has been stripped from Rumi as the poet has been popularized in a U.S. context (Ali, 2017). We can also see this tendency in the engagement with mindfulness in the United States.

To shift the metaphor, mindfulness has at times been treated as a paper doll—popped out with perforated edges, dressed up in new clothes, and fitted within colonial logics, assumptions of universalism, neoliberal individualism, and Western capitalist consumerism. Mindfulness is taken up by white ideologies that are reinforced as "legitimate, objective, and socially acceptable" (Garcia, 2019, p. 18, as cited in Bonilla-Silva & Zuberi, 2008). In Western Anglosphere discourse, mindfulness is often pitched as a kind of "cure" or antidote—instrumentalized to give the assurance of any number of things: self-regulation, mental discipline, physical conditioning, stress reduction, pain management, and so on. In the United States, Wilson (2014) observes, mindfulness is employed "to gain control over mental illness, achieve self-fulfillment, and sell books" (p. 14). This need to "gain control" is a clear signifier of the detachment of mindfulness practices and pedagogies from their philosophical context of emergence.

Moreover, these culturally truncated mindfulness approaches seek to therapize the effects of oppressions without a critique of the systems that sustain them—an approach satirized as "McMindfulness" (Purser & Loy, 2013; Purser, 2019). Wong (2018) observes,

> Mindfulness has been commoditized as a cost-saving technique to be added to the Western toolbox to treat modern ailments such as stress and mental distress. This has been done without examining the socioeconomic and

sociopolitical conditions that contribute to the production of stress and mental health issues in this global, neoliberal capitalist era.

(p. 272)

In such circumstances, mindfulness approaches are tailored to fit into and perpetuate racialized capitalism and the inequities it perpetuates.

Interrogating the ways that Western approaches fall into the patterns of white supremacist thinking, Smith (2012) identifies a colonial orientation that

> assumes Western ideas about the most fundamental things are the only ideas possible to hold, certainly the only rational ideas, and the only ideas which can make sense of the world, of reality, of social life and of human beings. . . . Some indigenous and minority group researchers would call this approach simply racist. It is research which is imbued with an "attitude" and a "spirit" which assumes a certain ownership of the entire world, and which has established systems and forms of governance which embed that attitude in institutional practices.
>
> (p. 58)

This racist frame of superiority constitutes a form of *epistemic injustice*—a term popularized in Anglosphere research by Fricker (2007) and also core to de Sousa Santos's large body of scholarship on the topic focusing on the Global South. Epistemic injustice names the suppression of knowledges and, thereby, their knowers. Worldviews are discredited, marginalized, or eviscerated in a colonial regime. Given the continued global history of colonialism, we need to be continuously aware of how this white supremacist logic may condition our practice.

Multiple Cultural Roots of Mindfulness Practices

Mindfulness is not a dislocated object that we can pull from nowhere and take as needed; mindfulness is a practice and orientation that is rooted within varied cultural contexts. Mindfulness practices are embedded in a range of epistemologies, arising from multiple cultural traditions: from Kemetic yoga, Qigong, or Buddhism. These few examples are not meant to be representative of cultural groups, nor are these examples "stuck in time" as if they could be found, hermetically sealed and whole (Verran, 2018). Instead, these examples signal the need for honoring the radical and morphing epistemological diversity of the world—and to invite our students into sharing in humility toward this diversity. Contemplative practices are themselves pluralistic and cross-cultural. We come to them in recognition of different practices with different purposes and inflections, as the radical contingency of cultural embeddedness.

What does it mean to energetically respect the cultural specificity of mindfulness practices and, in so doing, make space for multiple ways of knowing while vigilantly attending to the workings of power? Diverse representation of authors and thought traditions on a syllabus is an important consideration; however, representation alone is not enough. Without active effort toward dismantling racism, representation sometimes can lead to tokenistic "multiculturalism." A diverse syllabus of texts will also represent different ways of knowing and ways of understanding the need for transformation. Making space for the epistemologies that manifest in the texts we study and in what our students make present in our classrooms entails reconsidering what content we infuse into the classroom and what we leave as empty space for students to fill in with their ways of knowing.

My environmental writing course begins each semester with Kimmerer's (2013) *Braiding Sweetgrass*, which invites students into epistemologies of animacy. Ways of knowing tied to Indigenous languages are part of Kimmerer's explicit discussion. With this opening text, students are able to see how their own ways of knowing may be shaped by the languages they know—just as Kimmerer is influenced by the languages of Western science, Indigenous languages, and more. The students write poems in which they adopt a word from a language they don't know; they research this word to understand its contours while also acknowledging all they don't know about the language, history, and culture that the word is rooted in. This is an occasion to discuss the radical contingency of our knowing. It is also an occasion to consider the relationship between endangered languages, endangered ways of knowing, endangered species on the planet, and colonial logics. What forces produce endangerment and pay no mind to, or even seek, eradication? Then, a discussion of Tuck and Yang's (2012) essay provides language for how settler-colonialism perpetuates these realities, while simultaneously disavowing them in "moves to innocence." We begin to investigate how colonial frames show up in speech patterns we might hear on campus. (Why, we ask, are phrases like "you rule" or "you're going to kill it" considered to be words of encouragement?) What epistemologies are we embedded in, and what do we reproduce?

When I introduce the Tree of Contemplative Practice (CMind, 2014), I contextualize it by stating that the trees of each cultural practice may look different, as an oak tree is different from the Ghaf tree—yet there is commonality too. In this conversation, I also seek to give a sense of my own history with contemplative practices and where my practice is rooted, as I invite students to find their own history to ground what is emergent.

This work requires acknowledgment of accompanying spiritual legacies, in the face of exclusionary tendencies of academic secularism that are described by Alexander (2006): "There is a tacit understanding that no self-respecting postmodernist would want to align herself (at least in public) with a category such as the spiritual, which appears so fixed, so unchanging, so redolent of tradition" (p. 15, quoted in Batacharya and Wong, 2018, p. 12). This aversion to the spiritual should give us pause, especially as we understand Western academia as an arm of colonialism, its classrooms used as a tool of assimilation, stratification, and domination (Boggs et al., 2019; Grande, 2015; Kuokkanen, 2007) and its version of research "inextricably linked to European imperialism and colonialism" (Smith, 2012). Kuokkanen (2007) puts it this way: "As long as it continues to ignore and shunt aside indigenous epistemes, individual academics and the academy as a whole will be continuing to support the imperialist project" (p. 5). Contemplative practice can counter academic suppression of epistemologies, cosmologies, and ways of life of many peoples around the globe, but this act is far more complicated than simply adding Indigenous cosmologies to existing secularized Western pedagogies. Indeed, an "addition" model that does not interrogate and dismantle white-supremacist-capitalist-ableist-colonialist heteropatriarchy—to adopt and modify bell hooks's (1984) hyphenated term—is insufficient at best, and may also be considered appropriative and white-washing by failing to account for cultural rootedness and one's positionality (i.e., what it means for me, in my identities and with my history, to engage here). Left unexamined, these practices serve to sustain histories of oppression and may continue "epistemicide" (de Sousa Santos, 2016), or the destruction of epistemologies and worldsenses.

Cultural Humility and Mindfulness

Resisting erasure and removal, contemplative practitioners can actively preserve coexisting languages and cosmologies, guarded against appropriation and extraction by hegemonic systems. This orientation lends itself to the pursuit of not only interdisciplinary but also multi*epistemic* approaches that broaden cultural understandings of interdependence in our difference. We respect multiple "tributaries of knowledge" (Maathai, 2007) as we work in community to address our central exigencies and concerns. We acknowledge that multiple cultural streams flow into the rivers that are the source of our knowledge. We carefully trace these waters and draw maps to better understand their complex cultural ecologies. These waters flow; they're not compartmentalized or frozen in time. At the same time, it is important to know the differences between one body of water and another, even as they may flow together as part of an interdependent earth system.

To honor the cultural waters and differing traditions of mindfulness is to take a culturally humble approach. Proposed as a counter to competence models that seek mastery of a finite body of cultural knowledge (Tervalon & Murray-García, 1998), a humility framework "incorporates a lifelong commitment to self-evaluation and critique, to redressing the power imbalances . . . and to developing mutually beneficial and non-paternalistic partnerships with communities on behalf of individuals and defined populations" (p. 123). Cultural humility dwells in the knowledge that one never fully knows another and that our worldviews and understandings may be radically different, based on our cultural inheritance, positionality, and more. Cultural humility is actively present to difference and is conscious of how continued histories come to bear upon our relationships as it seeks to redress continued disparities. The framework rejects simple conclusions or diagnoses made from the position of having "authority on" or "authority over."

Of course, humility and vulnerability mean differently for those who occupy different subject-positions in the world. As a generalized framework, we come to cultural humility with varied relations, given our different positionalities. Humility may feel different for those whose legitimacy has been questioned by the power regimes in place and the continued legacies of ongoing colonialism and racism. Being forced into a humble posture has had the most damaging, horrifically life-upending and life-ending effects on those already experiencing cultural marginalization.

Cultural humility is an act of resistance against hegemonic regimes of truth, a pronounced turn from "knowing best" and "knowing for" that is the stance of the missionary, the colonial figure, the master, the white savior. The authoritative stance of "knowing best" and "knowing for" is pervasive in a white supremacist, colonial culture, sometimes half-concealed in the language of "white allyship." As Regan (2010) writes, "the sympathetic humanitarian eye is no less a product of deeply held colonialist values, and no less authoritative in the mastery of its object than the surveying and policing eye" (p. 45). For example, a sympathetic white benevolence lurks behind some forms of "inclusivity" that serve "the colonizer whose benevolent imperialism assumes both herself or himself as the center of knowing and that everything can be known" (Jones & Jenkins, 2008, p. 24). We find this "benevolent" orientation in understandings of higher education that seek to "remediate" students' "deficiencies," "poor performance," or "achievement gaps" while keeping in place a fundamentally racist institutional system that, by definition, is responsible for those "gaps." The institution, and those who benefit from it, must account for the long legacy of reproducing racist stratification. Yet, rarely is this responsibility acknowledged; instead, "deficit model" thinking prevails whenever students' "lack" (of education, skills, ability, commitment, etc.) is what is blamed for the disparities that exist in education, in place of considering what the university education lacks in terms of representation, cultural relevance, equitable policies, humanizing and affirming practices, or otherwise.

Cultural humility stays with the possibilities of necessary transformation, without seeking "competence" in another's worldview. As such, cultural humility is radically pluralistic, recognizing that, in the words of the Zapatista movement, what is perhaps the most well-known line from the Fourth Declaration from the Lacandón Jungle (1996): "*Queremos un mundo donde quepan muchos mundos*" ("In the world we want, many worlds fit"; 2002, p. 250). Blaser and de la Cadena (2018) invoke the Zapatistas' words to describe the pluriverse, which they define as "heterogeneous worldings coming together as a political ecology of practices, negotiating their difficult being together in heterogeneity" (p. 4). Pluriversality is defined as "A kind of thinking that promotes decolonization, creolization, or mestizaje through intercultural translation" (Blaser & de la Cadena, 2018, p. 8).

Our classes can center this thinking. To do so, Keating (2013) suggests a practice "grounded in a framework of interconnectivity" (p. 11). Keating's approach to research and teaching is that of a "nepantlera, torn between theories, divided among worldviews, in love with authors and philosophers who rarely (if ever) speak to one another or even acknowledge one another's work" (p. 18). Keating finds connections between different thinkers, drawing "disparate worldviews into dialogue" and bringing together "areas of thought and perspectives that are too often kept far apart" (p. 18). This practice of reading for "complex commonality so spacious that it embraces difference—even apparently mutually exclusive differences" (Keating, 2013, p. 11) is done with full regard for risks of an "add and stir" (Mohanty, 2003, p. 242) melting-pot multiculturalism. The practice of reading determinedly preserves difference, as it also brings multiple texts together.

I read Keating's practice as a response to the bind that is usefully identified by Mohanty (2003):

> how do we undermine the notions of multiculturalism as melting pot, or multiculturalism as cultural relativism that so permeate U.S. consumer culture and that are mobilized by the corporate academic as a form of containment, and practice a multiculturalism that is about the decolonization of received knowledges, histories, and identities, a multiculturalism that foregrounds questions of social justice and material interests, which actively combats the hegemony of global capital?
>
> (p. 188)

Multi-epistemic reading practices resist normative pluralism and work instead from the Zapatistas' radical call from the Fourth Declaration: "In the world we want, everyone fits. . . . The nation which we are building is one where all communities and languages fit, where all steps may walk, where all may laugh, where all may live the dawn" (Ejército Zapatista, 2002, p. 250). This orientation does not collapse difference into the hegemonic, using difference for the role and purpose of the dominant. This orientation instead means decolonization and dismantling of the systems that are born of supremacist thinking.

In coming to consciousness of radical difference, there is no goal of "taking on." I can't simply step into a new epistemology, but I can adopt an active stance of "not knowing"—meaning that I let go of a desire to appropriate and fold into my existing schemas. By "not knowing," I pursue the art of seeking and staying with my awareness gaps, grappling with the complexities of what it means to stay present to an encounter, becoming more keenly aware without resting back in the status of "knowing."

This orientation is very different from—and, indeed, is actively opposed to—condoning ignorance. It counters the "sanctioned ignorance" that is perpetuated in predominantly white spaces, including the university (Kuokkanen, 2007, p. 1). The epistemic demeanor of cultural humility is aware, relational, and seeking, while an epistemology of ignorance (Mills, 1997) is unyielding, removed, and inert in its stance: "I have no need to know." This is a maintained ignorance.

As Polinska writes, "[R]acial ignorance is not a matter of simple neglect, self-deception, passivity, or accidental lack of knowledge. Rather, it is an ignorance that is actively created and managed" (Polinska, 2018, p. 328, following Spelman, 2007). The epistemology of ignorance accompanies "cognitive empire" (de Sousa Santos, 2018) that denies the radical plurality of lived knowledges as it rolls out its assurances and keeps divisions in place.

What we might call "pluriverse humility," as a form of cultural humility, fundamentally destabilizes the hegemonic "world of the powerful," or the "one-world world" that "has granted itself the right to assimilate all other worlds" (Blaser & de la Cadena, 2018, p. 3). Pluriversal cultural humility prompts criticality about the ways that "knowledge practices . . . are . . . conditioned to reinstate themselves" (Blaser & de la Cadena, 2018, p. 6) through ideologies and institutional practices. Even the momentary choice to use the word "we" may unintentionally universalize, cover over difference, and reproduce hegemony. If taken up uncritically within a one-world knowledge regime, mindfulness practices risk becoming part of the mechanism of reproduction and reinstatement. Without a recognition of radical difference, a trenchant mastery orientation may be fixed behind a contemplative practice, entrenched there beneath even gentle attention to breath.

As a way of fully countering sanctioned ignorance, we can, through contemplative practice, cultivate a posture that makes us real to one other—that fosters connection, trust, and "coming close" (Celidwen, 2020) in a respectful way without taking, in order to dialogue and understand. "This means never achieving and always becoming," Celidwen tells us: "This is a committed process." This is listening that undoes the regime of personal shame in not-knowing as it also undoes the systems that allow an epistemology of ignorance to continue. Okun (2019) has explained how white supremacy upholds a culture of shame and ignorance, producing defensiveness and rigidity from power-holders. Contemplative practice can be a resource for overturning this culture, as it allows us to find shared principles that can lead to a classroom culture that cultivates growth and community.

Early in the semester I ask the undergraduate students I teach to anonymously list on notecards (or an online bulletin board, such as Mentimeter) what they hope will characterize the community they're part of in our class. This is a space where students can make requests of each other. We read these anonymous thoughts aloud, sometimes passing notecards randomly around our circle and giving voice to each other's words as they are shared among us. As a way of linking the thoughts we hear from each other, we name five words that can help us to remember what was written (words like "honesty," "openness," "care" often appear on these lists). Then, for each reminder word, we imagine scenes from the weeks ahead: moments where honesty or openness might be especially important. What does honesty feel like in practice?

Later in the semester, I pose this question:

> Think of a time when you recognized the limitations of your lens or your perspective. Maybe you'll think of a time when you overlooked a harm or didn't understand what someone else was experiencing. How did you come to understand what you didn't at first see?

And, at the same time, I offer the alternative prompt: "Think of a time when you helped another person to see the limitations of their lens or worldview. How did you approach the communication with this person?"

Then I ask: "What needs to be present for one to be receptive to being 'called out' or 'called in' in these circumstances?" One group of students in my environmental writing class came up with the following list in response to this question:

> letting go of perfectionism, self-acceptance, self-forgiveness, knowing that we are understood for our blindspots (awareness gaps) and still valued/forgiven by the community, mindfulness about "what is showing up for me," humility and knowing I don't have all the answers, eagerness to learn from each other without demand, knowing that empathetic feedback is a gift shared, a learner's orientation/growth mindset, believing that it's valuable and necessary to be uncomfortable, understanding that cultural ideas are just around us—we receive problematic ideas from our world, but we can change how we think.

In the classroom, I try to craft a pedagogy that supports the culture and orientation toward one another that this list represents. I pose questions that are meant to prompt a self-forgiving—yet still accountable—way of recognizing thought patterns. A reading that explicitly exposes interlocking forms of oppression can be followed by questions such as: "What was your experience of our readings today? What did you feel? What thoughts went through your mind? What in your background, experience, or identity might condition your response to these readings?"

A slide or a pulled quote in an assignment sheet might have the header "pause and notice." I invite undergraduate students in my writing courses to "Notice your responses to the information presented in these articles that expose interlocking oppressions: Do you find yourself

> wanting to change things?
>> feeling daunted or frustrated?
>> feeling grief about the way things are?
>> feeling indignant and resentful that I've asked you to look at these materials?

wanting to shut down and ignore the writers you've been presented with today?
ready to take action?"

The worksheet continues with this language:

> There are many more words you might use to describe your emotions of course. Get curious about your reactions to what you read—and what those reactions mean for you. Take a moment to reflect on what showed up for you as you engaged these materials. Where do your reactions come from? Do you find yourself wanting to attach to your reactions? Are you able to simply observe your reactions with curiosity toward your ever-changing self?

I also include the note:

> A reaction to something just pops up within us; it is impermanent. A reaction does not define who we are. We can choose what we do next. What do you want to do with what you learned in the readings you engaged today?

My hope in posing these questions is to hold space for movement or change within each student (and within myself) while also actively cultivating community.

Conclusion

I write this chapter with awareness of how my teaching practices shift and change with every encounter I have with people who teach me so much, students and colleagues both. The approach and ideas I describe here may be practices I leave behind in the coming years, as I continue to learn new forms of responsiveness. I offer these momentary snapshots of what is said or written in my classroom with the hopes that they might open up ideas, awareness, and more conversation.

Writing this at a time when there is heightened awareness around the globe of the continued effects of colonialism and racism, I find myself using the word "hope" often—yet this is not hope in repose. Heightened awareness is not sufficient. As bell hooks (2002, p. 116) warns, "heightened awareness often gives the illusion that a problem is lessening. This is most often not the case. It may mean simply that a problem has become so widespread it can no longer remain hidden or be ignored." We must persist, sourcing the roots of resistance that long precede us. Mindfulness may be one resource for us, as we remain conscious of the fact that mindfulness's roots are long and varied. May we continue to acknowledge the diverse ancestries of mindfulness practices as we promote the diverse world-senses that sustain a pluriverse, that enable the hope of decolonization and the dismantling of racism and interlocking forms of oppression. May we do this in our classrooms (virtual or physical as they may be), in the streets, and in our moment-by-moment unfoldings.

Acknowledgement

Parts of this chapter appear in Adsit, J. (2021). *Epistemic Justice, Mindfulness, and the Environmental Humanities Reflections on Teaching*. Routledge.

References

Alexander, M. J. (2006). *Pedagogies of Crossing: Meditations on Feminism, Sexual Politics, Memory, and the Sacred*. Duke University Press.

Ali, R. (2017, January 5). The Erasure of Islam from the Poetry of Rumi. *The New Yorker*. https://www.newyorker.com/books/page-turner/the-erasure-of-islam-from-the-poetry-of-rumi.

Batacharya, S., & Wong, Y.-L. R. (Eds.). (2018). *Sharing Breath: Embodied Learning and Decolonization*. Athabasca University Press.

Berila, B. (2016). *Integrating Mindfulness into Anti-Oppression Pedagogy: Social Justice in Higher Education*. Routledge.

Blaser, M., & de la Cadena, M. (2018). Introduction: Pluriverse: Proposals for a World of Many Worlds. In M. de la Cadena & M. Blaser (Eds.), *A World of Many Worlds* (pp. 1–22). Duke University Press.

Boggs, A., Meyerhoff, E., Mitchell, N., & Schwartz-Weinstein, Z. (2019). *Abolitionist University Studies: An Invitation*. https://abolition.university/invitation/.

Bonilla-Silva, E., & Zuberi, T. (2008). *White Logic, White Methods: Racism and Methodology*. Rowman & Littlefield.

Celidwen, Y. (2020, May 29). *Indigenous Contemplative Science: An Ethics of Belonging and Reconnection*. The Center for Contemplative Mind and Society. https://www.youtube.com/watch?v=nJNNKLeB57g&feature=youtu.be.

Center for Urban Education. (n.d.). *"Equity-Mindedness." University of Southern California, Rossier School of Education*. https://cue.usc.edu/about/equity/equity-mindedness/.

CMind. (2014). *The Tree of Contemplative Practices* [Illustration]. The Center for Contemplative Mind in Society. http://www.contemplativemind.org/practices/tree.

de Sousa Santos, B. (2016). *Epistemologies of the South: Justice Against Epistemicide* (2nd ed.). Routledge.

de Sousa Santos, B. (2018). *The End of the Cognitive Empire: The Coming of Age of Epistemologies of the South*. Duke University Press.

DiAngelo, R. (2016). *What Does It Mean to Be White? Developing White Racial Literacy*. Counterpoints.

Ejército Zapatista de Liberación Nacional. (2002). Fourth Declaration of the Lacandón Jungle. (1996). In T. Hayden (Ed.), *The Zapatista Reader*. New York Thunder's Mouth/Nation Books.

Feagin, J. R. (2013). *The White Racial Frame: Centuries of Racial Framing and Counter-Framing* (2nd ed.). Routledge.

Fricker, M. (2007). *Epistemic Injustice: Power and the Ethics of Knowing*. Oxford University Press.

Garcia, G. A. (2019). *Becoming Hispanic-Serving Institutions: Opportunities for Colleges and Universities.* Johns Hopkins University Press.

Grande, S. (2015). *Red Pedagogy: Native American Social and Political Thought* (10th anniversary ed.). Rowman & Littlefield.

hooks, b. (1984). *Feminist Theory: From Margin to Center.* South End Press.

hooks, b. (2002). *Communion: The Female Search for Love.* William Morrow.

Johnson, J. (2018, May 4). *Automaticity to Authenticity: Efforts to Prevent Student Misgendering.* Presentation at Sacramento State University, Center for Teaching and Learning.

Jones, A., & Jenkins, K. (2008). Rethinking Collaboration: Working the Indigene-Colonizer Hyphen. In N. K. Denzin, Y. S. Lincoln, & L. T. Smith (Eds.), *Handbook of Critical and Indigenous Methodologies* (pp. 471–486.). Sage.

Justice, D. H. (2005). Review of *Real Indians: Identity and the Survival of Native America* by Eva Marie Garroutte. *Wicazo Sa Review*, 20(1), 201–203.

Keating, A. (2013). *Transformation Now! Toward a Post-Oppositional Politics of Change.* University of Illinois Press.

Kimmerer, R. W. (2013). *Braiding Sweetgrass.* Milkweed.

King, R. (2018). *Mindful of Race: Transforming Race from the Inside Out.* Sounds True.

Kuokkanen, R. (2007). *Reshaping the University: Responsibility, Indigenous Epistemes, and the Logic of the Gift.* University of British Columbia Press.

Leon, A. Y., & Nadeau, D. (2018). Embodying Indigenous Resurgence: 'All Our Relations' Pedagogy. In S. Batacharya & Y.-L. R. Wong (Eds.), *Sharing Breath: Embodied Learning and Decolonization* (pp. 55–83). Athabasca University Press.

Lueke, A., & Gibson, B. (2014). Mindfulness Meditation Reduces Implicit Age and Race Bias: The Role of Reduced Automaticity of Responding. *Social Psychological and Personality Science*, 6(3), 284–291. Doi: 10.1177/1948550614559651.

Maathai, W. (2007). *Unbowed: A Memoir* (Reprint ed.). Anchor.

Magee, R. (2019). *The Inner Work of Racial Justice: Healing Ourselves and Transforming Our Communities Through Mindfulness.* Penguin.

Manuel, Z. E. (2015). *The Way of Tenderness: Awakening through Race, Sexuality, and Gender.* Wisdom.

Menakem, R. (2017). *My Grandmother's Hands: Racialized Trauma and the Pathway to Mending Our Hearts and Bodies.* Central Recovery Press.

Mills, C. (1997). *The Racial Contract.* Cornell University Press.

Mohanty, C. T. (2003). *Feminism Without Borders: Decolonizing Theory, Practicing Solidarity.* Duke University Press.

Okun, T. (2019). *White Supremacy Culture.* DRWorksBook, 2019. Web. http://www.dismantlingracism.org/white-supremacy-culture.html.

Orr, D. (2002). The Uses of Mindfulness in Anti-Oppressive Pedagogies: Philosophy and Praxis. *Canadian Journal of Education*, 27(4), 477–490.

Polinska, W. (2018). Mindfulness Meditation as a Remedy to 'White Ignorance' and Its Consequences. *Buddhist-Christian Studies*, 38, 325–341.

Prevatt-Hyles, D., & Vinsky, J. (2009, July). *The LPI Reflective Practice Approach: Anti-Oppression (AOP) in Action.* Liberation Practice International (LPI). www.liberationeducation.com.

Purser, R. E. (2019). *McMindfulness: How Mindfulness Became the New Capitalist Spirituality.* Repeater.

Purser, R. E., & Loy, D. (2013, August 31). Beyond McMindfulness. *Huffington Post*. https://www.huffpost.com/entry/beyond-mcmindfulness_b_3519289.

Regan, P. (2010). *Unsettling the Settler Within: Indian Residential Schools, Truth Telling, and Reconciliation in Canada*. University of British Columbia Press.

Smith, L. T. (2012). *Decolonizing Methodologies* (2nd ed.). Zed Books.

Spelman, E. (2007). Managing Ignorance. In S. Sullivan & N. Tuana (Eds.), *Race and Epistemologies of Ignorance* (pp. 119–135). SUNY.

Tervalon, M., & Murray-García, J. (1998). Cultural Humility Versus Cultural Competence: A Critical Distinction in Defining Physician Training Outcomes in Multicultural Education. *Journal of Health Care for the Poor and Underserved*, 9(2), 117–125.

Thompson, B. (2017). *Teaching with Tenderness: Toward an Embodied Practice*. University of Illinois Press.

Tuck, E., & Yang, K. W. (2012). Decolonization is not a Metaphor. *Decolonization: Indigeneity, Education and Society*, 1(1), 1–40.

van der Kolk, B. (2014). *The Body Keeps the Score: Brain, Mind, and Body in the Healing of Trauma*. Penguin.

Verran, H. (2018). The Politics of Working Cosmologies Together While Keeping Them Separate. In M. de la Cadena & M. Blaser (Eds.), *A World of Many Worlds* (pp. 112–131). Duke University Press.

Williams, A. K. (2002). *Being Black: Zen and the Art of Living with Fearlessness and Grace*. Penguin.

Williams, A. K., Owens, L. R., & Syedullah, J. (2016). *Radical Dharma: Talking Race, Love, and Liberation*. North Atlantic.

Wilson, J. (2014). *Mindful America: The Mutual Transformation of Buddhist Meditation and American Culture*. Oxford University Press.

Wong, Y. R. (2018). 'Please Call Me by My True Names': A Decolonizing Pedagogy of Mindfulness and Interbeing in Critical Social Work Education. In S. Batacharya & Y.-L. R. Wong (Eds.), *Sharing Breath: Embodied Learning and Decolonization* (pp. 253–279). Athabasca University Press.

PART II
Contemplative Pedagogies for Environmental Justice

3
ECO-GRIEF AND CLIMATE ANXIETY IN THE CLASSROOM

Jennifer Atkinson

A student of mine once commented that if universities could monitor the collective pulse rate in environmental courses, they'd station medics in our classrooms. Given the way I taught during my first ten years, such a measure may have been prudent. Like many of my colleagues, I presented climate issues by feverishly pulling items from the bottomless grab-bag of ecological horrors and tossing them into students' laps like emotional grenades: mass extinction and dying oceans, community displacement and burning forests, melting icecaps, rising seas, suffering communities, and a diminished world for all who will come after us.

However, I rarely paused in those early years to ask students how this material made them *feel*. Doing so seemed to invite trouble: someone would end up in tears, or find herself trembling with anger or unable to speak clearly. I took it for granted that such moments detracted from student learning, and carefully steered around those "digressions" so we could quickly get back to the "real" content. And I'll admit that I was also seeking to protect myself. The daily poison drip of ecological outrage and injustice threatened to leave me emotionally depleted. How could I manage to keep teaching climate issues across the decades when I myself felt so overwhelmed by grief? Such efforts to bypass our feelings are, of course, bound to fail over time—especially when emotional attachment is itself the very thing that brings many of us to the field of environmental studies. Recognizing the inevitability of pain in the classroom ultimately led me to reverse course in my teaching and develop a seminar where students directly engage those challenging emotions.[1] In using grief as our starting point, rather than as an inconvenience to be sidestepped, the seminar seeks to bestow legitimacy on affective, intuitive, and ethical dimensions of environmental learning, acknowledging them as authentic sources of knowledge. We also center contemplative practices to help students reduce stress and anxiety, quiet the mind, enhance empathy and

DOI: 10.4324/9781003201854-5

creativity, and build the necessary resilience to avoid denial and despair in the face of climate injustice and eco-grief.

Within this chapter I use "grief" in the familiar sense of a deep sadness and psychological pain in response to the loss of someone or something for which we feel affection. What may be less familiar to readers is the use of grief in response to loss in the natural world—a realm that conventionally falls outside of what Western culture deems "grievable." As Cunsolo and Ellis (2018) argue, we tend to exclusively associate mourning with human loss. Yet, in an era marked by growing rates of environmental devastation, "ecological grief" is gaining currency as a way to describe the pain felt "in relation to experienced or anticipated ecological losses, including the loss of species, ecosystems and meaningful landscapes due to acute or chronic environmental change" (p. 275).

In confronting climate injustice and relentless violence to our biosphere, our impulse to look for ways to extinguish this grief is understandable. Yet the failure to process and mourn loss is but another form of collective denial, leaving us unable to respond effectively and creatively to growing environmental challenges (Davenport, 2017; Lertzman, 2015). As Nicholsen (2002) has observed, loss not fully faced "can lead one to fall under the spell of numbness and cruelty. It can lead to guilt and the wish to blot out the future" (p. 182). Yet suppressing grief is not only socially and psychologically harmful: it also misses an invaluable pedagogical opportunity to deepen student learning in environmental fields.

The aim of our seminar at the University of Washington, therefore, is to help students approach grief not just as something to be *resolved* by contemplative practice, but also as a valuable guide and contemplative practice in its own right. When paired with strategies for staying present with affective and embodied states, grief offers a powerful lens to examine and address root causes of social and ecological suffering. Grief can promote interspecies empathy by cultivating awareness of our shared vulnerability, and deepen curiosity and openness to intuitive knowing, helping us identify assumptions that perpetuate environmental racism and rationalist, patriarchal, capitalist ideologies (Cunsolo & Landman, 2017). Eco-grief is also a sign of deep attachment—a response that highlights our profound connection to others, including more-than-human lives and places. This makes grief a powerful but widely overlooked tool for cultivating hope and empowering ourselves to become agents of change. Finally, collective expressions of grief promote solidarity, helping those who may be emotionally moved but politically disengaged to overcome the sense of isolation that inhibits meaningful action.

The following discussion offers concrete strategies for using contemplative and reflective inquiry to help students, activists, and educators cultivate the resilience to promote collective solutions and stay engaged in climate work over the long run. After examining various ways that grief can be harnessed toward these ends, I outline a set of humanities methods for engaging in this work, including mourning rituals, movement-based activities, reflective writing, and creative play with sculpture.

TABLE 3.1 Eco-Grief Seminar in the Humanities: Course-at-a-Glance

Course Content	• Climate anxiety • Eco-grief • Environmental hope and despair (or more broadly, "ecological emotions") • Emotional resilience in support of climate justice
Contemplative Practices	• Reflective writing and journaling • Mourning rituals • Movement-based activities • Sculpture and art-making (creative play with clay)
Key Texts	• Butler, J. (2004). *Precarious Life* • Clayton, S., Manning, C. M., Krygsman, K., & Speiser, M. (2017). *Mental health and our changing climate: impacts, implications, and guidance.* • Cunsolo, A., & Landman, K. (2017). *Mourning nature: Hope at the heart of ecological loss and grief.* • Lanham, D. (2019). "Forever gone." • Macy, J., & Johnstone, C. (2012). *Active hope.* • Marshall, G. (2015). *Don't even think about it: why our brains are wired to ignore climate change.* • Nicholsen, S. W. (2002). *The love of nature and the end of the world.* • Orange, D. (2016). *Climate crisis, psychoanalysis, and radical ethics.* • Ray, S. J. (2020). *A field guide to climate anxiety.*
Assignments	• Reflective writing and journaling • Create a mourning ritual or memorial • "Spectrum Line of Ecological Emotions" (a movement-based activity) • Creative play with modeling clay to work through climate anxiety and grief

Student receptivity to exploring emotional content in this manner will clearly vary across cultural contexts. My own experience is based on work with students in the Pacific Northwest: many have had at least some experience with a mindfulness practice like yoga, meditation, controlled breathing, or prayer. Most also report high levels of concern for environmental justice issues. Nearly half of undergraduates at the University of Washington–Bothell campus are students of color, and many say that they or someone in their family suffers from health conditions exacerbated by pollution. Students from local tribal communities are also experiencing direct impacts of regional climate disruption. Finally, and perhaps most importantly, these students have self-selected into a seminar explicitly focused on eco-grief. For these reasons, I acknowledge that my students, on average, likely show greater openness to discussing climate emotions than students at other institutions. However, I have also worked with many students who resist approaches that center feelings in the classroom, whether they come from STEM fields or have simply internalized the mind-body divisions of Western education more generally (as discussed in this chapter). The strategies outlined here have indeed helped many of them make progress toward dismantling some of those barriers, but instructors should be explicit about their reasons for taking this unfamiliar approach. I have found it essential to offer this context at the outset, aided by several short readings that clarify our basic rationale.[2]

Eco-Grief and the Climate Generation

Living through an age defined by so much destruction of life has marked many of us by invisible traumas. In recent years terms like "climate depression" (Thomas, 2014), "ecological grief" (Cunsolo & Ellis, 2018), "climate anxiety" (Ray, 2020), and "pre-traumatic stress" (Kaplan, 2020) have become increasingly common. Meanwhile, a growing body of research is documenting the mental, emotional, and spiritual toll of climate disruption (Clayton et al., 2017; Albrecht, 2019; Pihkala, 2020a), including links to chronic anxiety and depression, post-traumatic stress, substance abuse, suicide or suicidal thoughts, and many other mental health impacts (Clayton, 2018; Hayes, 2018; Cunsolo et al., 2020). But one hardly needs to look at scholarly research to see that our students are struggling in the face of these intersecting crises. We can simply ask them. Here's a sample of typical responses from a first-day survey in my class, where students are asked to describe their feelings about climate change and the future more generally:

> "When I think about the future all I can imagine is apocalypse."
> "I feel . . . afraid, frustrated, but also hopeless and apathetic. I want to feel hopeful or even actively angry, but instead I feel resigned because as an individual I can only do so much."
> "I have nightmares about . . . water wars, mass extinction, infertile soil . . ."

The despair expressed in these responses is further compounded as students learn of the deep connections between ecological destruction and structural injustice: white supremacy and environmental racism, gender and economic inequities, xenophobic nationalism, speciesism, and all their toxic cousins. Intersectional approaches to environmental studies are vital to promoting climate justice, but they can be deeply unsettling to students immersed in those painful realities.

Unfortunately, students are rarely given the tools needed to cope with the emotional fallout of these wicked problems—let alone stay engaged with them over the long term. Like their instructors before them, they have internalized an approach to learning that elevates critical thinking and rational analysis as the ultimate outcome (Eaton et al., 2016). They come to our classrooms bringing their bodies, emotions, personal histories, and lived experiences but then are expected somehow to leave most of this at the door. Yet focusing exclusively on the intellectual dimension is simply not possible for most of us. Indeed, that compartmentalization runs contrary to how people actually learn. As scholars in affect theory have shown (i.e., Ahmed, 2010; Brennan, 2004), emotion is central to our ability to process information and think creatively as we connect material to our lived experiences, values, and internal states.

And it is not only students, but also educators and researchers who are harmed by the absence of opportunities to openly address painful emotions. Environmental scientists and justice scholars suffer high rates of eco-depression and despair (Clayton, 2018; Dahl, 2018). Climate scientists have described their experiences with their research as leading to "an acute mental health crisis" (Cobb, as cited in Corn, 2019) and "an eye-scratching, skin-tearing, dirt-in-hair-rubbing outpouring of grief" (Riley, 2016, p. 16). Lanham (2019) has characterized conservation as a profession where one is "marooned on an island of dwindling hopes" and burdened by ineffective policies that "can drive the conservationist into psychosis." And as a Black man working to stop violence against wildlife, Lanham's pain is amplified by the daily reminders that we live in a system where some lives do not matter, whether expressed through racism or species extinction. Indeed, Lanham's racial vulnerability has led him to identify with the plight of the birds he seeks to protect. As he writes,

> pushing a living being into the abyss of extinction is, in the end, a hate crime; a lack of compassion for another's implicit right to exist. I feel some kinship in that place, where my being is also seen by some as worthless.
> (Lanham, 2019)

And yet the simple act of discussing emotional responses like this can carry a deep stigma within a culture that prizes dispassionate discourse and objectivity (Fraser, 2013; Richardson, 2018). Some scientists worry that speaking openly about emotional pain may compromise their professional reputation—and this is especially true for women, who already struggle with institutional discrimination and stereotypes that impede professional advancement (Corn, 2019).

Yet it is students from marginalized and frontline communities who suffer the greatest harm from this failure to acknowledge the emotional toll of ecological loss, racism, and injustice in environmental education and advocacy (Burton, 2020; Higgins, 2020). My own seminar has included students from Indigenous communities where traditional fishing practices have been devastated by dams, pollution, and rising temperatures; children of undocumented farmworkers who suffer health effects from extreme temperatures and wildfire smoke; students displaced by extreme weather events; and many others whose cultural roots in the natural world put them at high risk of experiencing trauma from environmental loss. For these students, climate disruption is not an academic concept but an ongoing existential threat. To approach the issue from a purely analytical perspective, or impose reason/emotion dichotomies in the classroom without making space for students to process their pain, is simply another form of violence and erasure.

By using contemplative and reflective pedagogies to navigate anxiety and grief, educators can help students build the capacity to stay engaged with the realities of climate disruption without spiraling into despair. Moreover, integrating learning with lived experiences and affective responses helps students feel validated in their knowledge and see themselves as protagonists in a story of healing and change. One does not have to be a therapist to offer such support in the classroom. Students often gain tremendous benefit from simply having space and structure to participate in conversations about their emotional responses to the material, but in order to channel despair toward more empowering outcomes, we must first recognize the value and transformative potential of grief in relation to environmental learning. The following section outlines four insights that students and educators might consider as they get started.

What Good Is Grief?

First, in staying present with their affective and embodied states, students deepen understanding about grief as a fundamental sign of compassion and attachment. As one student put it in at the end of the term: "grief is the twin sister of love." From this perspective, the act of grieving—by its very nature—carries an element of hope. "Grief is praise, because it is the natural way love honors what it misses" (Prechtel, 2015, p. 31). Seeing grief as a function of love acts as a powerful affirmation of trans-species empathy, an acknowledgment that our identities and well-being are fundamentally entwined with earthothers. Keeping nature and humanity in separate categories prevents us from recognizing our living planet as a network of kinship to which all beings belong; grief, on the other hand, calls us back to an awareness of those bonds.

Second, grief for the natural world offers a resource for cultivating species humility and letting go of illusions of mastery and control. In grieving, we submit to something greater than ourselves: grief "undoes" us, decenters us, and reveals our powerlessness (Butler, 2004, p. 21). This vulnerability can deepen gratitude, which is itself an antidote to unsustainable first world consumption, entitlement, and arrogance (Macy & Johnstone, 2012). As one student wrote in their journal, "in a strange way, focusing on grief over ecological loss has deepened my sense of gratitude; more than ever, I want to minimize what I take and just protect what still remains." Another wrote, "I think what breaks my heart the most is to look around and see us turning living things into dead consumer things, especially when we already have more than enough and are drowning in our own waste. . . . [T]hat's the core logic of our capitalist way of life."

Third, contemplative practices rooted in eco-grief challenge oppressive boundaries imposed between humans and other species (and human "others'"). We live in a culture where some deaths receive elaborate mourning rituals and public tributes, while others are trivialized or ignored. Marginalized groups know how this absence of public grief dehumanizes them, which is why LGBTQ activists, people seeking justice for murdered Indigenous women, and the Movement for Black Lives all use protests, vigils, and other public acts to demand that those deaths aren't made invisible. When we grieve openly for animals, forests, oceans, or rivers, we assert that nonhuman lives are also worthy of mourning, and we challenge barriers that exclude those bodies from circles of compassion.

Finally, eco-grief can support anti-oppressive pedagogies by deepening understanding of the intersections among racism, sexism, speciesism, and climate colonialism. This clarity requires ongoing vigilance in acknowledging how the suffering and grief of certain bodies—Indigenous, queer, animal, women, and other marginalized groups—have historically been erased from public representation. Indigenous scholar Reed and sociologist Norgaard (2017) write about the disappearing salmon in their rivers: "[b]ecause the dominant non-Native society does not recognize the deep emotional ties we describe between humans and the natural world, Karuk grief and other emotions [related to] their loss is invisible" (p. 466). That invisibility or "disenfranchised grief" compounds the violence done to Indigenous people.

When we understand grief as central to the lived experience of climate colonialism and environmental injustice, we enter a powerful space for examining our own privilege/vulnerability in relation to eco-despair. Indigenous scholars like Simpson (2017) and Wildcat (2009) remind us that their communities have been experiencing "environmental crisis" since Europeans arrived in North America. As Leanne Betasamosake Simpson puts it: "Indigenous peoples have witnessed continual ecosystem and species collapse since the early days of colonial occupation. . . . We should be thinking of climate change as part of a much longer series of ecological catastrophes caused by colonialism and accumulation-based society" (as cited in Harris, 2019). Relatively well-off white folks, including college professors like myself and many of the grieving scientists I cited earlier, have historically been insulated from these impacts. Only when we join the ranks of the "threatened" do we begin to perceive climate change as a "problem" (Weiss, 2019). We need to address the myriad and uneven forms of "existential despair."

Environmental Humanities: Methods and Practices for Navigating Grief

Once students, activists, and educators recognize grief as a portal to wisdom and compassion (rather than a "dysfunction"), humanities tools and methods can more effectively be used to channel distress into healing. The four activities covered in this section were selected based on their adaptability for multiple contexts and accessibility among different participants—students or researchers in STEM fields, activists, social justice groups, and more.

1. Mourning Rituals

Coming to terms with any painful loss requires a process of personal transition. Mourning rituals create pathways for us to reorient our lives in the new reality of an absence, and they offer structure for interacting with community when we are bewildered and disoriented in our grief (Macy & Johnstone, 2012; Menning, 2017). Yet our most familiar mourning practices pertain almost exclusively to human death. Creating rituals that commemorate the loss of places or other creatures can therefore offer a corrective to social norms that trivialize the destruction of more-than-human life. These multispecies rituals also help us see beyond fallacies of human exceptionalism, the illusion of a separate human self, and Western society's aversion to death and grief more broadly—all root causes of our current ecological crisis.

Students in my seminars are invited to create rituals or memorials to acknowledge, process, and respond collectively to environmental loss. These have included vigils, art walks, mock-funeral services and eulogies, music, and public memorials that bring visibility to unacknowledged injustice. Some have staged funeral processions on our campus, taking inspiration from the "Remembrance Day for Lost Species"—a global series of events occurring annually to commemorate species driven to extinction.[3] Others have created video tributes to lost glaciers and coral reefs, held vigils for wildfire victims, given public readings that recognize wildlife impacted by construction around our campus, and created memorials that trace links between devasted rivers, Indigenous people, salmon, and Pacific Northwest orca populations. These practices promote not only visibility but also solidarity, since collectively grieving removes our isolation from others experiencing loss, providing an antidote to apathy or mass denial.

However, we remain vigilant about forms of catharsis that simply provide relief from discomfort so individuals feel absolved in returning to postures of inaction. With personal bereavement, we often play no part in causing the death of a loved one; yet when it comes to environmental loss, the grieving individual may be complicit, adding layers of guilt and denial to the underlying pain. "We must mourn not only what we have lost, but also what we have destroyed" (Menning, 2017, pp. 39–40). Yet even here, the guilty "we" is too often a construct offering political cover for privileged groups in the Global North who benefit from extractive practices that disproportionately harm marginalized groups (Guenther, 2018; Orange, 2016). Anti-oppressive strategies can be infused into mourning rituals to directly address these inequalities. For instance, while designing their ritual or memorial, students might consider a set of prompts, i.e.:

- How can your project make visible the role of privilege and the unequal distribution of benefits/burdens in an ecological reality shaped by white supremacy, patriarchy, climate colonialism, and consumer capitalism?
- Where have you benefited from or been harmed by conditions related to the loss addressed in your ritual?

- Who else profits from or is exploited within this dynamic, and how might those relations be rendered visible as you enact the ritual?

Importantly, the point here is not to amplify personal guilt—as doing so is *not* politically efficacious and often leads individuals to disengage (brown, 2017; Ray, 2020). Rather, the goal is *accountability*: a recognition of the direct or indirect role played in harm and loss; awareness of white supremacy, consumer capitalism, and other structural conditions that perpetuate this violence; reflection on the values and assumptions invoked to rationalize oppressive practices; and a commitment to specific action to prevent further violence and loss. Within my seminar, students are asked to address these four aspects as they develop their ritual. For example, a eulogy could explicitly name dimensions of one's complicity in a loss and then outline proposed reparations. Students can also submit written reflections discussing how those four elements of accountability inform the project.

2. Movement-Based Activity

While many of us have some familiarity with the language used to describe stages of mourning following the death of a loved one, we still lack a common vocabulary to describe the pain of lost ecosystems and species. This makes it hard to recognize—let alone articulate—connections between the natural world and our mental and emotional well-being. Using a simple movement-based activity can introduce concepts like eco-grief, climate anxiety, climate fear, and other ecological emotions while also helping participants visualize the complex ways we experience contradictory affects. Enacting these emotions also honors the embodied content that students bring to class, bestowing legitimacy on kinesthetic modes of communicating knowledge and experience in an education system that usually privileges verbal expression. Within my seminar I run a modified version of an activity called "The Spectrum Line of Ecological Emotions," by environmental theology professor Pihkala (2020b).

FIG. 3.1 Activity exploring the Spectrum Line of Ecological Emotions

> The activity begins with all participants in the middle of the room. Then a number of "ecological emotions" are mentioned, one at a time, with each word corresponding to an invisible line running across the room. One end of the line signifies that "I feel this emotion in relation to our ecological crisis (or climate crisis) strongly or very often." The other end expresses that "I feel this emotion seldom or not at all." As each word is shared, participants move to a point that matches the intensity of their response. A common sequence of ecological emotions that facilitators might use is "Concern," "Fear," "Anger," "Grief," and finally "Empowerment" or "Hope." After each round of positioning themselves along the spectrum, participants can share why they chose a particular point on the line.

This activity is especially powerful when run at an early moment in a course, since the line of bodies immediately reveals an invisible part of the climate story that many participants likely have not considered before. As one student put it in a written reflection:

> I didn't know how much this was affecting me until I started moving across the room, and seeing so many others headed in the same direction. I can also see eco-grief better now that I have a name for it, and am realizing that I've been in a state of mourning . . . for a long time without even realizing it.

Moreover, the exercise highlights that it's possible to experience (seemingly) conflicting responses simultaneously. When a person who's put themselves at the far end of the line to indicate "grief" goes to that same position in a subsequent round for "hope," they see that such affects are not mutually exclusive, and dark feelings need not preclude us from a sense of empowerment.

This activity includes all students as participants—even those who feel uncomfortable speaking in group settings—by using their bodies to articulate responses. In addition, movement activities can be powerful for participants whose disciplinary training has made them uneasy about voicing emotional responses to ecological loss (Head & Harada, 2017).

3. Reflective Writing/Journaling

Like many environmental humanities classes, our seminar on eco-grief uses writing to explore course issues, although these assignments are specifically structured to promote reflective and contemplative capacities. Our weekly journal prompt asks students to monitor their somatic, affective, and intuitive responses to reading and discussion material. Recorded observations have included notes like "my chest tightening," "shaking hands," "mental and emotional exhaustion," "rising anxiety," "awe and wonder at the beauty of life," and "gratitude for those working toward solutions." While monitoring both thought reactions and felt reactions to environmental issues, students also reflect upon what those responses might reveal about themselves as individuals, our culture, our educational system, assumptions or perspectives held by the author of a text, historical framings of the issue, and values or biases arising from a broader worldview.

This kind of reflective journaling can provide a "space of pause" when prompts are spread out over the term and scaffolded to slow down responses and impulses to leap to hasty conclusions (Killen, 2017). In encouraging students to monitor each step in their response, scaffolded writing can facilitate awareness of

> both how one was thinking about the event, which often surfaces assumptions, values, and basic positions regarding the reality that informs one's

thinking, and also, allows one to look again at the event or text, to notice what was missed or misconstrued.

(Killen, 2017, p. 45)

And beyond weekly responses, longer writing assignments can cultivate disciplined reflective practice when stretched across the entire term, further slowing down the process of interpretation and meaning-making. One overarching question for my seminar—"What good is grief?"—is addressed in a cumulative writing assignment developed from one week to the next as students regularly draw from and build on key insights from earlier journal entries.

In particular, written reflection can promote sustained attention to how our bodies and affective responses offer ways of knowing as we feel our way through the facts (Barbezat & Bush, 2014). One student surfaced this outcome in a powerful written reflection in my seminar:

> I have always accepted the facts of climate change so never considered myself as someone in "denial." But that was only a surface acceptance, because those facts didn't physically change anything I did in my life or influence how I acted in the world. It has only been through sitting with devastation, and letting those feelings sink into my core where they melt away at the numbness I've been living in. And once I can feel it gnawing at my stomach—actually causing me pain and mental anguish, that is what it takes to make me want to jump up and say *enough!* and throw myself in front of the death machines that are intent on burning every last drop of oil and the whole planet along with it.

In this compelling revelation, the writer overcomes an assumption that countless others carry in Western culture: the notion that allowing ourselves to experience pain will cause us to shut down or become paralyzed by despair. Yet in truth, it is the student's intellectual "numbness"—the habit of standing apart from his affective and intuitive responses—that had perpetuated inaction. That emotional denial is shaken only when he commits to staying present with difficult feelings—in this case, by recording them in weekly journal entries.

4. Sculpture

Creative play with sculpture can activate the imagination while helping individuals process and develop new understanding about ecological and climate justice issues in a non-linguistic format. Using modeling clay and one's hands, students explore subjective responses and experiment with communicating meaning visually through the use of shape, metaphors, and form. Especially among those with little to no art training, clay is one of the more versatile and accessible materials for engaging participants.

I was introduced to the concept of sculpture-based education by artist and restoration ecologist Amy Lambert, who explains that these activities "challeng[e] the privilege of language-based epistemologies" in humanities and social sciences pedagogy, while moving participants "further into the subjective and relational ways of knowing found in the arts." Art-making can be dismantling, she writes, because

> you don't always know where you're going, what you're creating (most of the time) and it's particularly powerful to discover something you didn't know about yourself and/or your relationships. What you create can be aggressive or even disturbing—something that makes others feel uncomfortable. That's the risk of art-making and the responsibility or art-making.
> (Personal communication, June 9, 2020)

Art-making also reminds us that language has limitations as a tool for developing contemplative and reflective capacities. The arts open up spaces for alternative forms of understanding and engagement. And in unsettling the ordinary, they can loosen our imaginations so we are better equipped to respond to emerging uncertainties with creative and meaningful action. It is especially helpful to emphasize ideas like "creativity" and "play" when facilitating these activities. This reassures participants that they don't have to be "good" at art. Here are the instructions I use in my seminar:

FIG. 3.2 Activity for creative play with sculpture

> Identify an emotion, experience, idea, memory, or question you have in relation to our climate crisis, and use the modeling clay to explore your response. It is not necessary to have a particular concept in mind before you start: just begin playing with the clay, observing how it feels in your hands and responds to pressure as you squeeze, flatten, stretch, or press it. Ideas or impressions may emerge or transform in the process of handling the clay. Do not feel bound to stick with your original plan if ideas shift along the way. For this activity, the *process* of creation and play is more important than any final product.

It is also helpful to offer prompts that participants might contemplate as they experiment with clay. Examples include:

- Working in an educational system where linguistic or numeric modes are dominant ways of representing meaning, how might the arts elicit different ways of knowing, feeling, perceiving?
- What does it mean for abstract concepts or feelings to take form through physical materials?

- How might the very division between the material/conceptual be complicated through this activity?

You can invite students to warm up before they respond creatively to the bigger issue of climate and environmental injustice. After getting comfortable with the properties of their clay and what it can "do," ask them to create something based on one or two words. For example: "you have one minute to create *commitment* or *brilliant*." The time limit will push participants to bypass their "thinking" and respond with basic shapes, sizes, weight, textures of clay that represent a feeling rather than a symbol that represents subject matter (e.g., the shape of a heart). If there is time, start with basic words that represent feelings and emotions (e.g., sad, happy, excited) and end with more complex concepts (uprising, trace).

In one recent workshop, participants explored their responses to the 2019 United Nations report on collapsing wildlife populations (Intergovernmental Science–Policy Platform on Biodiversity and Ecosystem Services, 2019)—a reading that presented particular challenges as we tried to process the incomprehensible figure of a million species at risk of extinction. Some clay sculptures were literal (a tombstone, a human figure doubled over with despair) while others were more abstract (a flattened disk with a sinking feature in the middle; a wad of material with a massive chunk violently ripped out). Some focused on the process rather than a final product, including a student who pulled out tiny pieces of clay from the main block and meticulously shaped them into various forms, then smashed them over and over to visualize the wantonness of extinction. As the participant explained in a subsequent reflective writing response, she had assigned herself the task of "doing this a million times"—knowing, of course, that that was impossible—but in so doing, the activity forced her to confront both the unthinkable scale of extinction as well as the tragedy and senselessness of destroying life after its wondrous evolutionary journey into its present form. During the process of sharing our objects with each other as a group, many other participants developed rich insights from discussing this particular clay project, including one who noted how it surfaced the limitations of statistical representation of death and suffering. While acknowledging the usefulness of numerical depictions in certain cases, the reliance on data-driven analysis in his own education had "deadened" his response over time. Others chimed in to contemplate ways that art could help overcome that numbness and help us feel the raw dimensions of loss anew, spurring a sense of responsibility and commitment to action.

Conclusion: Eco-Grief as a Portal to Solidarity and Connection

While there are considerable differences among the strategies discussed in the previous section, all of them begin with a commitment to acknowledge and stay present with our grief—an act that can seem radical in a culture that author

Stephen Jenkinson has called "death phobic and grief illiterate" (as cited in Hance, 2016). Directly engaging dark emotions that arise from environmental loss open a space to generate imaginative solutions while challenging dominant pedagogies that often fail to acknowledge affective, embodied, and intuitive elements as authentic sources of wisdom. One of the through lines of all such efforts to address grief via these contemplative, reflective, and humanities practices is that they build solidarity and, thus, help individuals overcome the very sense of isolation preventing us from taking collective political action. A significant part of our despair and anxiety in facing the growing climate emergency comes from feeling isolated; when people feel alone, they aren't empowered to act. This is why cognitive psychologists emphasize the importance of thinking of ourselves as part of a team; indeed, Stoknes (2015) has written that "participating in a community or group that works for a common cause is a good remedy (the only one, actually) for [our] toxic helplessness and passivity" (p. 101). Post-quarter surveys in my class have confirmed this, indicating that the single most helpful element for students was being in the room with others talking about their distress, and feeling heard and validated when they shared their own struggles. As one respondent wrote, "I thought it was relatively uncommon that people felt the same emotional response to the science that I did. One of the most valuable things I will take away from this class is not feeling quite so alone anymore." Another echoed this sentiment of previously feeling "alone in my grief," but after finding her community, she left the seminar "empowered to get involved in activist and community groups to keep that sense of camaraderie alive."

It is important to note that these post-quarter responses rarely, if ever, indicate that pain has been extinguished. Rather, students feel better equipped to draw on that grief to affirm a network of connection, responsibility, and reciprocity in the fight for climate justice. They come to understand that grief is not just a private, individual response to loss, but a phenomenon that comes to expression within a broader cultural, political, and ecological context. As one put it, "[t]here is obviously still deep despair here, there is no fighting that, but . . . I can wade in that with the communities around me. . . . It really does attach me to them so much more. We are in this together."

The hope of many environmental educators is, of course, that such a sense of connection will expand beyond interpersonal relations to also generate solidarity with impacted communities and more-than-human-species and systems. Grief is a powerful agent in broadening that web of moral consideration, particularly when we cultivate its capacities to disrupt barriers between self and others. Butler (2004) identifies this very potential in her remark that, through the transformative experience of grief, "something about who we are [is] revealed, something that delineates the ties we have to others, that shows us that these ties constitute what we are." As she concludes:

> It is not as if an "I" exists independently over here and then simply loses a "you" over there, especially if the attachment to "you" is part of what

composes who "I" am. . . . Who "am" I, without you? . . . On one level, I think I have lost "you" only to discover that "I" have gone missing as well. At another level, perhaps what I have lost "in" you, that for which I have no ready vocabulary, is a relationality that is neither merely myself nor you, but the tie by which those terms are differentiated and related.

(p. 22)

Love for our world is an easy thing to claim, but following that love into places of grief and pain is the next essential step to honoring the real meaning of this elemental connection, to acknowledging that our own distress is not the only suffering that matters, and to reckoning with the responsibilities and consequences of the world we are ushering in. It is precisely this political and ethical work of mourning that will enable us to fully know ourselves as beings entangled with nonhuman communities, and reinvent our role as healers and protectors within their midst.

Notes

1 The seminar discussed throughout this chapter, "Climate Grief and Eco Anxiety," has been offered annually at the University of Washington–Bothell since 2018. All student quotes in this chapter are taken from course surveys and learning assessments conducted from 2018 to 2020.
2 To provide this rationale I recommend Marshall's chapter "The Two Brains" from *Don't Even Think About It* (2015); Huntley's "Stop Making Sense: Why It's Time to Get Emotional About Climate Change" (2020); Norgaard's "Climate Change in the Age of Numbing" (2020); and Ray's chapter "Get Schooled on the Role of Emotions in Climate Justice Work" from *A Field Guide to Climate Anxiety* (2020).
3 For philosophical context, these activities might be paired with readings like Hance's "Why Don't We Grieve for Extinct Species?" (2016) and van Dooren and Rose's "Keeping Faith With the Dead" (2017).

References

Ahmed, S. (2010). Happy Objects. In M. Gregg & G. Seigworth (Eds.), *The Affect Theory Reader* (pp. 29–51). Duke University Press.
Albrecht, G. (2019). *Earth Emotions: New Words for a New World*. Cornell University Press.
Barbezat, D. P., & Bush, M. (2014). *Contemplative Practices in Higher Education: Powerful Methods to Transform Teaching and Learning*. Jossey-Bass.
Brennan, T. (2004). *The Transmission of Affect*. Cornell University Press.
brown, a. m. (2017). *Emergent Strategy*. AK Press.
Burton, N. (2020, May 14). People of Color Experience Climate Grief More Deeply Than White People. *Vice*. https://www.vice.com/en/article/v7ggqx/people-of-color-experience-climate-grief-more-deeply-than-white-people.
Butler, J. (2004). *Precarious Life: The Powers of Mourning and Violence*. Verso.
Clayton, S. (2018). Mental Health Risk and Resilience Among Climate Scientists. *Nature Climate Change*, 8(4), 260. https://doi.org/10.1038/s41558-018-0123-z.
Clayton, S., Manning, C. M., Krygsman, K., & Speiser, M. (2017). *Mental Health and Our Changing Climate: Impacts, Implications, and Guidance*. American Psychological Association, and ecoAmerica.

Corn, D. (2019, July 8). It's the End of the World as They Know it: The Distinct Burden of Being a Climate Scientist. *Mother Jones.* https://www.motherjones.com/environment/2019/07/weight-of-the-world-climate-change-scientist-grief/.

Cunsolo, A., & Ellis, N. (2018). Ecological Grief as a Mental Health Response to Climate Change-Related Loss. *Nature Climate Change,* 8, 275–281. https://doi.org/10.1038/s41558-018-0092-2.

Cunsolo, A., Harper, S. L., Minor, K., Hayes, K., Williams, K. G., & Howard, C. (2020). Ecological Grief and Anxiety: The Start of a Healthy Response to Climate Change? *Lancet Planet Health,* 4, e261–e263.

Cunsolo, A., & Landman, K. (2017). *Mourning Nature: Hope at the Heart of Ecological Loss and Grief.* McGill-Queen's University Press.

Dahl, K. (2018, December 31). *Feeling Blue about Climate Change? You're Not Alone.* Union of Concerned Scientists & EcoWatch. https://www.ecowatch.com/climate-change-grief-2624799890.html.

Davenport, L. (2017). *Emotional Resiliency in the Era of Climate Change.* Jessica Kingsley Publishers.

Eaton, M., Hughes, H., & MacGregor, J. (2016). *Contemplative Approaches to Sustainability.* Routledge.

Fraser, J., Pantesco, V., Plemons, K., Gupta, R., & Rank, S. J. (2013). Sustaining the Conservationist. *Ecopsychology,* 5(2), 70–79. https://doi.org/10.1089/eco.2012.0076.

Guenther, G. (2018, October 10). Who is the We in 'We Are Causing Climate Change'? *Slate.* https://slate.com/technology/2018/10/who-is-we-causing-climate-change.html.

Hance, J. (2016, November 19). Why Don't We Grieve for Extinct Species? *The Guardian.* https://www.theguardian.com/environment/radical-conservation/2016/nov/19/extinction-remembrance-day-theatre-ritual-thylacine-grief.

Harris, M. (2019, March 4). Indigenous Knowledge Has Been Warning Us About Climate Change for Centuries. *Pacific Standard.* https://psmag.com/ideas/indigenous-knowledge-has-been-warning-us-about-climate-change-for-centuries.

Hayes, K., Blashki, G., Wiseman, J., Burke, S., & Reifels, L. (2018). Climate Change and Mental Health: Risks, Impacts and Priority Actions. *International Journal of Mental Health Systems,* 12(28). https://doi.org/10.1186/s13033-018-0210-6.

Head, L., & Harada, T. (2017). Keeping the Heart a Long Way from the Brain: The Emotional Labour of Climate Scientists. *Emotion, Space and Society,* 24, 34–41. https://doi.org/10.1016/j.emospa.2017.07.005.

Higgins, A. (2020, May 11). Your Climate Anxiety is Another Person's Existential Crisis. *The New Republic.* https://newrepublic.com/article/157660/climate-anxiety-another-persons-existential-crisis.

Huntley, R. (2020, July 4). Stop Making Sense: Why it's Time to Get Emotional about Climate Change. *The Guardian.*

Intergovernmental Science–Policy Platform on Biodiversity and Ecosystem Services. (2019). *UN Report: Nature's Dangerous Decline "Unprecedented"; Species Extinction Rates "Accelerating".* https://www.un.org/sustainabledevelopment/blog/2019/05/nature-decline-unprecedented-report/.

Kaplan, A. E. (2020). Is Climate-Related Pre-Traumatic Stress Syndrome a Real Condition? *American Imago,* 77(1), 81–104. Doi: 10.1353/aim.2020.0004.

Killen, P. O. (2017). Using Reflective and Contemplative Practices with Integrity. In M. Eaton, H. Hughes, & J. MacGregor (Eds.), *Contemplative Approaches to Sustainability* (pp. 45–52). Routledge.

Lanham, D. (2019, March 11). Forever Gone. *Utne.* https://www.utne.com/environment/forever-gone-carolina-parakeet-zm0z19szhoe.

Lertzman, R. (2015). *Environmental Melancholia: Psychoanalytic Dimensions of Engagement.* Routledge.

Macy, J., & Johnstone, C. (2012). *Active Hope.* New World Library.

Marshall, G. (2015). *Don't Even Think about it: Why Our Brains Are Wired to Ignore Climate Change.* Bloomsbury Publishing.

Menning, N. (2017). Environmental Mourning and the Religious Imagination. In A. Cunsolo & K. Landman (Eds.), *Mourning Nature: Hope at the Heart of Ecological Loss and Grief* (pp. 39–63). McGill-Queen's University Press.

Nicholsen, S. W. (2002). *The Love of Nature and the End of the World.* MIT Press.

Norgaard, K. (2020, June 19). Climate Change in the Age of Numbing. The MIT Press Reader. https://thereader.mitpress.mit.edu/climate-change-in-the-age-of-numbing/.

Norgaard, K., & Reed, R. (2017). Emotional Impacts of Environmental Decline: What Can Native Cosmologies Teach Sociology about Emotions and Environmental Justice? *Theory and Society*, 46, 463–495. https://doi.org/10.1007/s11186-017-9302-6.

Orange, D. (2016). *Climate Crisis, Psychoanalysis, and Radical Ethics.* Routledge.

Pihkala, P. (2020a). Anxiety and the Ecological Crisis: An Analysis of Eco-Anxiety and Climate Anxiety. *Sustainability*, 12(19), 7836. http://dx.doi.org/10.3390/su12197836.

Pihkala, P. (2020b, April). *Spectrum Line of Ecological Emotions.* Eco-Anxiety & Hope. ecoanxietyandhope.blogspot.com/2020/03/spectrum-line-of-ecological-emotions.html.

Prechtel, M. (2015). *The Smell of Rain on Dust: Grief and Praise.* North Atlantic Books.

Ray, S. J. (2020). *A Field Guide to Climate Anxiety.* University of California Press.

Richardson, J. (2018, July 20). When the End of Human Civilization is Your Day Job. *Esquire.* https://www.esquire.com/news-politics/a36228/ballad-of-the-sad-climatologists-0815/.

Riley, H. (2016). Endlings. *Island*, 146(3), 15–19.

Simpson, L. B. (2017). *As We Have Always Done: Indigenous Freedom Through Radical Resistance.* University of Minnesota Press.

Stoknes, P. E. (2015). *What We Think about When We Try not to Think about Global Warming.* Chelsea Green Publishing.

Thomas, M. (2014, October 28). Climate Depression is for Real. Just Ask a Scientist. *Grist.* https://grist.org/climate-energy/climate-depression-is-for-real-just-ask-a-scientist/.

van Dooren, T., & Rose, D. (2017). Keeping Faith with the Dead: Mourning and De-extinction. *Australian Zoologist*, 38(3), 375–378. https://search.informit.org/doi/10.3316/ielapa.974707803247636.

Weiss, J. (2019, April 25). Who Gets to Have Ecoanxiety? *Edge Effects.* https://edgeeffects.net/who-gets-to-have-ecoanxiety/.

Wildcat, D. (2009). *Red Alert! Saving the Planet with Indigenous Knowledge.* Fulcrum Publishing.

4
CONTEMPLATIVE PEDAGOGIES, ENVIRONMENTAL LITERATURE, AND THE ART OF "INTERBEING"

Darin Pradittatsanee

The contemplative pedagogies presented in this chapter germinate from Thai Buddhist monk Buddhadāsa Bhikkhu (1906–1993), who deems education as a crucial means towards "the world's enduring peace and well-being" (1966, p. 22). Critiquing modern education for focusing solely on cultivating the intellect he advocates the significance of morality and spirituality in teaching (1990, pp. 3–8). He states that education's ideal goal is "the complete cessation of all suffering" while a teacher's aim is "to enable students to overcome their cravings and desires" (1966, pp. 14, 28).

The West has recently paid considerable attention to spirituality in education, especially mindfulness practices in contemplative pedagogies (e.g., Crawford, 2005; Zajonc, 2013). Mindfulness has been incorporated into college courses in science and humanities (Barbezat & Bush, 2014; Bush, 2013; Williams & Kabat-Zinn, 2013). Furthermore, the benefits of mindfulness practices have been substantiated empirically by neuroscientists and psychologists (Barbezat & Bush, 2014, pp. 21–38; Hanson & Mendius, 2009, pp. 85–86). Since Kabat-Zinn popularized Buddhist mindfulness through his Mindfulness-Based Stress Reduction program, the practice has also been used in psychotherapy (Tirch et al., 2016, pp. 88–89).

Drawing forward both the scientific findings affirming the usefulness of mindfulness, and my background as a Buddhist practitioner, I wanted to use Buddhist philosophy and meditation practices to design a contemplative course to educate students about environmental literature and sow the seeds of mindfulness. I started experimenting with mindful pedagogies in an undergraduate course, "Environmental Literature," for English majors and minors at the English Department, Faculty of Arts, Chulalongkorn University, in the academic year 2018. Presenting the contemplative strategies I have developed, this chapter particularly details those employed in 2019 when I conducted a research project to assess the

DOI: 10.4324/9781003201854-6

influence of mindfulness practices in supporting students' ability to achieve course learning outcomes. My research participants included 28 traditional Thai students ages 20 to 22 (23 female and 5 male), the majority of whom were Buddhists and Bangkokians. This chapter discusses first the course's conceptual frameworks, then the specific contemplative pedagogies practiced, and finally the empirical measures employed in my research and assessment of the learning outcomes.

Conceptual Frameworks

My contemplative pedagogies are founded upon Buddhist concepts and meditation practices. The Buddhist teachings are grounded in the Four Noble Truths about life's material conditions: the inevitability of suffering (*dukkha*), the origin of suffering (*samudaya*), the cessation of suffering (*nirodha*), and the path toward the cessation of suffering (*magga*) (Harvey, 2013, pp. 52–82). Suffering is caused by craving and egoism—all related to attachment to a sense of self (Harvey, 2013, pp. 62–65). The path toward the end of suffering centers on "moral virtue" (*sīla*), "meditative cultivation of the heart/mind" (*samādhi*), and "wisdom" (*paññā*) (Harvey, 2013, p. 82). The path of spiritual purification aims at enabling practitioners to attain an insight into the true nature of reality.

Buddhism postulates that all conditioned things are impermanent, unsatisfactory, and empty of an inherent essence. This view of reality is based upon the notion of dependent origination (*paṭicca-samuppāda*), which Thich Nhat Hanh refers to as "interbeing" (2012, pp. 411–412). To explain, all existence comes into being due to the concurrence of causes and conditions, thereby being subject to change and empty of an essential self (the notion of non-self or *anattā*) (Harvey, 2013, pp. 65–73). If causes and conditions dissolve, the existence also ceases to be as well. This notion dismantles the sense of a fixed, solid self and accentuates the intra-action of all things, aligning well with an environmental humanities vision.

To achieve insight into "interbeing," Buddhism suggests meditation practices accompanied by ethical behavior. It postulates that there are three kinds of wisdom (*paññā*)—(1) received knowledge learned from others, (2) intellectual wisdom, and (3) experiential wisdom—and that it is experiential wisdom gained through meditation practices that result in an insight into the true nature of reality (Harvey, 2013, p. 318). Fundamental to all types of Buddhist meditation practices is mindfulness (*sati*). Rooted in the Buddhist traditions, the mindfulness practices integrated into my course included breath mindfulness, mindfulness of physical sensations, mindful walking, loving-kindness meditation, and the practice of *tonglen*.[1]

Contemplative Pedagogies in Teaching Environmental Literature

My course aims to familiarize students with environmental literature through critical reading and analysis of selected texts, honing students' reading, writing, and critical thinking skills, and fostering ecological conscience. I communicated course objectives with students, interwove contemplative practices with selected texts, and designed concrete activities to flesh out students' experience of interbeing.

Setting up Goals and Communicating With Students

In line with the course's objectives, I chose the following texts: Daniel Quinn's *Ishmael: An Adventure of the Mind and Spirit* (1992); selected poems by Mary Oliver, Barbara Kingsolver's *Animal Dreams* (1991); Indra Sinha's *Animal's People* (2007); selections from John Joseph Adams's *Loosed Upon the World: The Saga Anthology of Climate Fiction* (2015) (Vandana Singh's "Entanglement," Chen Qiufan's "The Smog Society," and Paolo Bacigalupi's "The Tamarisk Hunter"); and Hayao Miyazaki's *Ponyo on the Cliff by the Sea* (2008a). Similarly pointing out the dangers of anthropocentrism, these texts question binary thinking and undermine readers' normative perception of their existence as humans as opposed to nonhumans.

As Killen suggests, educators need to set "a pedagogical purpose for using contemplative . . . practices" and "[a]rticulate how the practice contributes to the goals of a particular course" (2017, p. 63). I employ mindfulness practices to enhance students' understanding of the texts with their embodied experience; that is, to give them opportunities to "see" and "feel" the ideas presented in the texts in their own body. My intention to cultivate the art of "interbeing" for Environmental Literature students translates into five specific goals for the contemplative practices: (1) observing oneself and one's environment attentively; (2) acting in daily activities with awareness; (3) being aware of one's connectedness with the nonhuman world; (4) having sympathy and compassion towards those who are suffering; and (5) being responsible as a member of the planet.

As Barbezat and Bush (2014) point out, it is also crucial to consider students' backgrounds and make sure that students understand the goals of what they are instructed to do (pp. 68–69). Communicating with students on the role of contemplative practices in a classroom setting is thus indispensable. I think considering rhetoric that instructors use in communicating with students is also important. As Burke (1962) propounds, persuasion entails the process of "identification" or "consubstantiality" (p. 20). As he puts it, "a way of life is an *acting-together*; and in acting together, [people] have common sensations, concepts, images, ideas, attitudes that make them *consubstantial*" (p. 21, emphases in original). We need to seek some common ground with those whom we try to persuade.

One challenge that I had was how I could encourage my Thai students to engage in contemplative practices. Although Thailand is a Buddhist country and my students are familiar with meditation, quite a few of them are uninterested in Buddhism, while others may even have a negative attitude towards it. Viewed as tedious and outdated, meditation practices tend to be also regarded as suitable for troubled individuals or the elderly. Given this context, I wondered, what should I do to make mindfulness practices interesting to my students?

To begin, I used the first meeting to set the tone for the course and establish some common ground among class members. I informed students that course expectations included the exercise of rational, spiritual, and imaginative faculties and participation in diverse activities. Making it clear that contemplative practices were part of the course's activities, I tried to tap into students' curiosity, encouraging them to take the practices as experiments. I presented myself as a facilitator who journeyed along and learned with them. Furthermore, I chose not to discuss the Buddhist underpinning of my pedagogies since Thai students might find the explanation boring. I also reminded myself that my contemplative pedagogy should be conducted, as Barzebat and Bush put it, "in a spirit of inquiry rather than faith, even if [my] own practice is part of a spiritual path" (2014, p. 69). Therefore, I presented the practices in a nonsectarian manner, making sure that my pedagogy focused on the cultivation of universal qualities, such as lovingkindness and lessening of an ego, as well as the practical benefits of mindfulness for our daily existence and environmental concerns.

To highlight this significance of mindfulness, I engaged students in a discussion in which I drew upon our shared experience of living in a city like Bangkok. Students and I similarly felt an atmosphere of indifference, as most people were in such a hurry and so preoccupied with social media that they paid no attention to others. We agreed that we did not notice the sky or trees when commuting to campus. I then urged my students to reflect on how we could give our mind to nonhumans if we were not even aware of our existence or fellow humans. I further suggested that any changes we wanted to see in the environment might have to start within ourselves. This was where mindfulness practice might come into play. To foster ecological awareness, we should begin with the cultivation of mindfulness. I then invited students to start weaving mindfulness practice into their daily activities for seven minutes a day every day throughout the semester.

Interweaving Contemplative Practices With the Course Content

To design the course, I linked three interrelated worlds: the world created in literary texts, students' world, and their inner world. In teaching English literature to Thai students for whom English is a second language, encouraging them to consider the connection between their world and the worlds depicted in literary texts can be quite effective. Contemplative activities can further enhance students' understanding of literary issues by providing them with visceral and somatic experiences of their own inner lives.

In a semester system, our class met for 90 minutes twice a week. I usually allocated 10–15 minutes in each session for contemplative activities, except for the sessions when students made group presentations on the assigned texts. The practices were either at the beginning or the end of the session. I divided the course into four modules and took a step-by-step approach to achieve the five contemplative goals that I set. In each module, I interwove contemplative activities with the discussion of the selected texts. Activities requiring out-of-class experiential research—i.e., Speaking for Animals and a mindful campus walk—were scheduled both within and outside the regular class time (see Table 4.1).

A Warm-Up

In the first week, I used excerpts from the 2004 documentary film *Genesis* by Claude Nuridsany and Marie Pérennou to get students thinking about the origin of the planet Earth and its inhabitants. Since the film highlights how "we are members of the same tribe, the great tribe in the Living," we discussed the scientific notion of evolution which underpins the interpenetration of all organisms. I then left students with the questions of what it means to be "human" and how we are different from other beings.

Module I: Anthropocentrism and Human-Animal Relationships

Module I began with breath mindfulness practices in which we learned to be attentive to in-breaths and out-breaths to calm the mind and create awareness of our physical existence in the present moment. After the first meditation session, we discussed *Ishmael*, which captures dialogues between a gorilla, Ishmael, and a human narrator. This text challenges such binary concepts as humanity and animality. Ishmael's narrative about how he has been cruelly treated by humans galvanizes us to reflect on humans' brutality. Ishmael functions as a wise teacher who deploys his pedagogy to encourage critical thinking and awaken his student to realize that the environmental crisis is rooted in anthropocentrism. He elicits from his student an acknowledgment that the creation story constructed in human culture is based upon the idea that *homo sapiens* is the pinnacle of the evolutionary process and "[t]he world was made for [humans] to conquer and rule" (1992, p. 82). Replacing anthropocentrism with ecocentrism, he presents a new story founded upon the notion that humans "belong to the world" (1992, p. 239).

To deepen students' understanding, we proceeded to examine the debunking of "humanity" and "animality" from different perspectives through an analysis of selected poems by Mary Oliver. We focused on "Sleeping in the Forest," "The Fish," and "Bone Poem," which deconstruct our sense of self/other boundaries and the solidity of our illusory sense of an individual self. I also drew on Laird Christensen's ecological approach to Oliver's poems (2002, pp. 135–152). The notion of food chains and energy exchange helped students better understand the interrelatedness of all things. Through energy sharing, we cross the human-animal divide. Therefore, humanity and animality are no longer distinct; they are not qualities inherent in any creature, but mere concepts arbitrarily constructed by human culture.

During the discussion, I also evoked students' imaginative faculties. Since the three poems touch upon the idea of death, our discussion included imagining

TABLE 4.1 Course Contents and Contemplative Practices in Environmental Literature

Week	Class Topics	Readings	Assignments	Contemplative Practices
Week 1	Introduction to the Course; Warm-Up	Film Screening: *Genesis*	"7-minute a day: Mindfulness Practice in Daily Life" begins. Environmental Project begins.	Breath Mindfulness
Week 2	Module I: Anthropocentrism and Human-Animal Relationships	*Ishmael*		Breath Mindfulness
Week 3				Body Scan
Week 4		Poems by Oliver	Short Response 1 due	Body Scan (re-perceiving the self; deconstructing self-other dichotomy)
Week 5			Essay on "Speaking for Animals"	Speaking for Animals; Loving-Kindness Meditation
Week 6	Module II: Place Perception and Inhabitation	*Animal Dreams* (Presentations)	Quiz on nonhuman companions on campus	
Weeks 7–8			Short Response 2 due	Breath Mindfulness
Additional Session				"Mindful Walking on Campus" (1 hour)
Week 9		Midterm Exam		Breath Mindfulness before the exam
Week 10	Module III: Toxicity and Environmental Justice	*Animal's People* (Presentations)		

(*Continued*)

58 Darin Pradittatsanee

TABLE 4.1 (Continued)

Week	Class Topics	Readings	Assignments	Contemplative Practices
Week 11				Imagining Yourself as Animal, Loving-kindness Meditation
Week 12				Tonglen
Week 13	Module IV: Climate Change	"Tamarisk Hunter" (Presentations)		
Week 14		"The Smog Society" "Entanglement"		Imagining the times of climate change
Week 15	Epilogue	*Ponyo on the Cliff by the Sea*	Short Response 3 due	
Week 16		Reflection and Wrap-Up	Reflection Paper due	Breath mindfulness and meditation on joy
Week 17		Final Exam	Term Paper and Essay on Students' Environmental Project due	

our own death. Because such contemplative practice may be rather terrifying, I asked students to think of their teacher's death. I posed the question, "what would become of my body if they buried me in a yard?" One answer was that my body would dissolve into soil, nourishing trees and plants. If the trees blossomed, part of me would become flowers. Here, I adapted the Buddhist practice of meditation on death to fit the discussion of the texts. Aiming at shaking the ossified binary thinking in our perception, this imaginative exercise employed the notion of death as a means to illustrate the interrelatedness of all beings/things. This insight leads to the lessening of one's sense of self.

The discussion of these texts was followed by another contemplative session, which encouraged the re-perception of self in a non-dualistic manner. Its objective was to flesh out the notion of the interrelatedness of all beings in students' own bodies. We began with breath mindfulness to ground the mind in the present. Then, we proceeded to the body scan, slowly moving our attention from the head to different parts of the body down to the feet. With guided visualizations, we imagined ourselves as part of the intricate web of relations and extended ourselves in relation to other life forms. To discern that our existence depends on that of other beings, we imagined the human existence evolving from various animals, such as fish and mammals. As part of the evolutionary process discussed in *Ishmael*, we were aware of our kinship with the animals. Tracing humans back 750 million years to the first ancestors of all animals, we realized that the sponge was the bottom of the evolutionary tree. The sponge is thus our ancestor as well.

Next, we contemplated our body as being, in reality, composed of four basic elements: earth, water, wind, and fire. Looking deeply at our body, we could then see ourselves as being the earth, water, wind, and fire. We continued to think of the sun, imagining how the sun sustains our lives in innumerable ways. For example, plants use energy from the sun in photosynthesis to make food molecules. They become the food that we eat. In this sense, the sun becomes us, and we are imbued with the sun. This view can also be extended to the whole ecosystem, which gives support to human lives. Deriving our existence from it, we are entangled with the ecosystem. Then, we reflected upon how our existence is sustained by food that comes from other lives and how our existence is related to theirs.

Afterwards, we imagined a sense of sustenance that we both received and gave as part of this web of relations. We imagined it as a light illuminating in and out of our bodies. Wherever we looked, we discerned our ancestors and relations. We reflected upon how we were here to receive, give, and share with all life forms in the universe. Mindful of this magnificent gift, we felt blessed. Finally, we gratefully made a silent vow to cherish this special blessing and lead our lives in an attempt not to harm other beings. The session ended with a return to our breathing.

This session blended science with Buddhist meditation methods to debunk the human vs. nonhuman dualism. I employed evolutionary science to help students contemplate the genetic connectedness between humans and other creatures. Biology enabled them to see how human organisms cannot exist without the ecosystem. The contemplation of the four elements which constitute the human body was also integrated to enhance our reflection on the oneness of our body with what we regard as inanimate entities.

Module II: Place Perception and Inhabitation

Module II starts with students' reflection of their sense of place in Bangkok and their hometown, if they were not from the city. I specifically asked about their responses to this urban environment. Thinking about the fact that our university is situated in the hub of the metropolis and has surrounded itself with mega-shopping malls, we discussed the university's policy of renting its properties to developers and its attitudes towards the land. Some of the students shared their experience of place in their hometown in the country. I used this reflective discussion as a transition to the discussion of Kingsolver's *Animal Dreams*.

This novel explores how the ability to perceive one's hometown in physical, historical, cultural, and spiritual terms as well as environmental activism helps Codi, the protagonist, come to terms with her trauma, reconstruct her identity, and acquire a sense of belonging in her community. The novel also emphasizes the significance of the nonhuman in the lives of Codi, her sister, and Loyd, her boyfriend. Through Loyd, a Native American character, the novel highlights indigenous ecological and cultural practices which reflect non-anthropocentric relationships with the natural world.

Animal Dreams provides an opportunity for taking students outside and "[g]rounding our practice in place," an idea I learned from Hoelting's (2017) "The Practice of Inner Habitat Restoration" (p. 37). I conducted a one-hour activity of "Mindful Walking on Campus," which was scheduled one late afternoon outside of the class period. Bhikkhu Anālayo (2015) explains how the meditation of bodily postures anchors mindfulness practices in a tangibly "embodied form" (p. 73) and trains practitioners to blend the practice into daily activities. Furthermore, walking meditation on campus stimulated students to get in touch with their sense of place and nonhuman companions. Prior to the activity, I gave a list of questions regarding trees, plants, and animals on campus, assigning students to saunter around and find out the answers.

In this activity, we started with breath mindfulness and then took a meditative walk on campus together for 15 minutes. Inspired by Thich Nhat Hanh's *Present Moment, Wonderful Moment*, I told students to follow the monk's advice to "[w]alk as if you are kissing the Earth with your feet" (1990, p. 28). We gave full attention to our physical movement and the interaction of our feet with the Earth. After creating an awareness of our body's walking, we learned to be mindful of natural surroundings. Next, we proceeded to a 40-minute activity of "Meeting a Tree," which I adapted from Cornell's *Sharing Nature with Children* (1998, pp. 25–29). Telling students to pair up and having one person in each pair wear a blindfold, I instructed the leader to carefully guide their partner to a particular tree. On the way to the tree, the leader invited their partner to experience the place with audible and olfactory senses. When reaching the tree, the leader helped the blindfolded partner get acquainted with it by touching it, hugging it, and listening to its pulse. Then, the blindfold was removed so that the player could see the tree. Next, the pair changed their roles. Finally, we reconvened to share our experience of these three eco-contemplative practices.

Module III: Toxicity and Environmental Justice

This module focuses on exploring *Animal's People* while proceeding to cultivate sympathy and responsibilities for the world. Based upon the Bhopal gas tragedy of 1984 at the Union Carbide pesticide plant in India, the novel portrays the distressing effects of this incident upon the environment and indigent locals. Through the sarcastic voice of Animal, a 19-year-old boy whose spine was twisted at the age of 6 due to the gas explosion, the novel uses its story to exemplify the fact that polluting factories and waste disposal areas tend to be located in the communities of the marginalized. It critiques not only the American company and the corrupt Indian government, but also the injustice of international legal procedures. Moreover, the novel criticizes the quasi-humanitarian spirit that those in the First World extend to the underprivileged in postcolonial countries.

The issues raised by this text lent themselves very well to our contemplative activities. However, since an ability to feel for marginalized others required a certain level of understanding and engagement, I encouraged my students to connect the environmental problems presented in the text with their lives in Thailand, making a link between Animal's world and theirs. We explored the glaring contrast between our comfortable lives in Bangkok and the suffering of people living outside the city. While we enjoyed air-conditioned classrooms and shopping malls and used energy rather unthinkingly, locals from southern Thailand protested against the government's plan to construct a coal power plant in their village, and people in other provinces suffered from chronic illnesses caused by toxins from factories. In this light, we realized that we were, in fact, complicit with environmental injustices, even in our own country. We could also start questioning ourselves about our responsibility for these problems partly caused by our consumerist lifestyle.

The contemplative practices further stirred students to put themselves in the position of economically and environmentally marginalized others by imagining themselves as living Animal's life. We first did breath mindfulness, then reflected on the fact that we inevitably took others' lives in order to live and that our well-being hinged, to some extent, on the sufferings of others. Together we silently asked all beings for forgiveness and vowed to attempt to lead our lives deliberately. We ended this session by extending loving-kindness to ourselves and all beings.

Thai students were familiar with the loving-kindness meditation I used; that is, we extended our feeling of loving-kindness to ourselves first and then to other beings, wishing all to be happy, peaceful, and free from suffering. Another method that I employed in the following session was *tonglen*, as presented by Pema Chödrön. Taking in suffering with our inhalations, we visualize the suffering as a dark, hot, and heavy mass, and then we exhale something white, cool, and light (1994, p. 38). We "work with relieving a specific heartfelt instance of suffering," breathing in the pain of that being and breathing out loving-kindness (p. 43). Finally, we further "extend that wish to help everyone," "using specific instances of misery . . . as a stepping stone for understanding the universal suffering of people and animals everywhere" (pp. 38, 43). Following the discussion of *Animal's People* and the imagining of Animal's life, our practice of *tonglen* moved from Animal to all suffering beings. As it is a way to transform misery, this method may also help students overcome despair at such seemingly irreparable problems.

Module IV: Climate Change

This module focuses on another environmental problem that Thai students have experienced firsthand: climate change. Thailand is currently hard hit by the worst drought in 40 years. However, there is no sense of urgency to solve this problem. This may be because those heavily afflicted by the drought are farmers in rural areas, and the government's policies are more for the interests of the economically privileged. To illustrate this problem, I discussed the drought in combination with climate fiction to evoke students' awareness of "slow violence" (Nixon, 2011) and examine its various dimensions. "The Tamarisk Hunter" reveals the appalling consequences of severe drought upon the lives of the poor in a water-scarce environment. "The Smog Society" portrays the effects of the sky-darkening air pollution upon humans. "Entanglement" weaves the lives of characters from different parts of the world through their shared commitment to do whatever they can to protect the environment. I also employed this inspiring story to empower students to do what they can to help despite innumerable obstacles.

In our contemplative activity, students imagined their lives in times of climate change. I provided a specific scenario based on the situation presented in "The Tamarisk Hunter": drought, the limited amount of electricity, as well as scarcity of water and food. I asked students to work in groups to discuss the following questions and share their responses in class:

1. What does it feel like to live in such a world?
2. How will you cope with this crisis? What kinds of skills/attitudes will you need to survive?
3. How will you prepare yourself for such troubled times?

This activity aimed at stirring students' awareness of impending environmental crises while simultaneously equipping them with hope through their agency. In our discussion, students expressed their concern about the crisis. While they expected to see their government's responsibility in creating policies to counter global warming, they also reflected upon what each individual could do, such as weaning themselves from comfort addiction, adopting environmentally responsible lifestyles, and learning basic survival skills.

Epilogue

I ended the course with *Ponyo on the Cliff by the Sea*. Adapted from Hans Christian Andersen's "The Little Mermaid," the story focuses on the relationship between Sosuke, a five-year-old boy, and a goldfish princess from the sea who longs to be human in order to live with the boy she loves (Miyazaki, 2008b, p. 419). *Ponyo* accentuates the notion of boundary crossing as it dismantles the human/animal divide through the fluidity of Ponyo's physical form and the power of the boy's unconditional love for her. As Miyazaki points out, one needs both feminine (Ponyo) and masculine principles (Sosuke) for nature to restore balance (2008a, pp. 423–424).

Translating an Experience of Interbeing into Concrete Action

The course's contemplative activities not only provided students with an opportunity to experience "interbeing" but also fostered compassion for their fellow creatures—human and nonhuman—and spurred them to act in their own capacity to bring about change in the world. The course thus included two activities inviting students to express their ecological concerns and translate their embodied, empathetic insight into concrete action: "Speaking for Animals" and an environmental project.

"Speaking for Animals" was a simplified version of Joanna Macy's "The Council of All Beings" (1993, pp. 198–205) focusing on speaking on behalf of other life forms. To prepare for this activity, which took place after the discussion of *Ishmael*, I assigned students to research various animals to understand these species' lives, roles in the ecosystem, and ways in which their existence was adversely affected by humans. In students' solitary reflections, they imagined themselves to be chosen by one of these animals. With this empathetic identification, they crafted a speech in which they spoke on behalf of the animal to the human audience. In our class meeting, we started with breath meditation, then students delivered their speeches, and we ended with a loving-kindness meditation.

In the course's final session, students shared their reflections on their cumulative learning experience. After that, we practiced contemplation on joy to give a sense of closure to the course. We started with breath mindfulness and then meditated on the feelings of joy and fulfillment that arose from within. The practice of dwelling in joy generated by one's goodwill and deeds trains the mind to experience a different type of happiness, which derives not from external factors but from one's intent and attempt to act for the benefits of the planet. This activity also aimed at reinforcing students' appreciation of their admirable actions throughout the semester, and encouraging them to carry on their mission as stewards of the planet Earth.

Course Learning Outcomes

This section discusses the research methodology employed to assess the effectiveness of my pedagogies, the research results, and my students' responses to the learning experience.

Measures and Procedures

To determine to what extent my contemplative pedagogies enhanced students' intellectual learning and cultivated the art of interbeing, I employed the following methods:

1. *Pre- and post-tests.* I used select items from the "Five-Facet Mindfulness Questionnaire" (Baer et al., 2006), as well as "The Self-Compassion Scale" (Raes et al., 2011) and "The Compassionate Scale" (Pommier et al., 2019). The select 50 items formed five subscales which corresponded with the five goals of contemplative practices. They were given a pre-test at the beginning of the semester and the post-test at the end.
2. *Three short responses over the semester.* I provided two prompts for each assignment:

    a. I asked students how the texts discussed in class stimulated them to reflect on themselves in relation to the issues addressed;
    b. I inquired to what extent and how their engagement in contemplative activities helped them understand the course materials/topics.

While the prompts were used as measuring tools, these responses simultaneously served as contemplative practices, as students got to reflect on their experience in both academic and contemplative activities and on the specific ways their learning was relevant to their own lives. The first assignment was given after Module I, the second one after Module II, and the last one after Modules III and IV.

3. *End-of-semester questionnaire.* This questionnaire aimed at finding out the difference between students' understanding of the issues of the four modules before the course started, and after the 16-week course concluded. Participants were asked to answer 8 questions using a 5-point Likert-type scale, ranging from 1 (almost nothing) to 5 (a lot of ideas and viewpoints)—to assess how much they knew about the themes of the four modules before the course began in the first four, and how much they have learned about these themes by the course's end in the other four. Students were also asked to respond to my prompts on what they had known before the course began, what they had learned throughout the semester, and the usefulness of the contemplative practices.

I used line graphs to illustrate the extent to which my contemplative pedagogies achieved their objectives in (1) enhancing students' understanding of the course contents, and (2) cultivating their ecological awareness, which I interpreted as constituting the five points in the art of "interbeing."

Results

Since the purpose of the chapter is to share contemplative practices in teaching, and the statistical significance is not a concern, I will be providing nonparametric mean analysis of pre- and post-tests.

I. Students' Understanding of the Course Contents

Comparing the overall score of the first four questions in the end-of-semester questionnaire with that of the other four for each student, Figure 4.1 illustrates the self-perceived improvement in each student's understanding of the topics discussed in the four modules over the 16 weeks. The x-axis signifies students' scores showing the level of their understanding of the course contents (out of 20 points), while the y-axis refers to students.

II. Students' Ability in the Art of "Interbeing"

To measure ability in the art of "interbeing," I compared the overall score of the five subscales in the pre-test with that in the post-test for each student. Figure 4.2 illustrates that students' post-test scores were higher than their pre-test scores, indicating that the use of contemplative pedagogies enhanced the participants' ability in the art of "interbeing." The x-axis signifies students' scores on the overall scale (out of 250 points).

Results in Figures 4.3–4.7 show that for each of the five subscales, post-test scores are higher than in the pre-test. The x-axis signifies students' scores in each of the five subscales (out of 50 points). Out of 28 students, 25 had higher scores in the post-test for an ability to observe their sensations and happenings in the world, an awareness of one's connectedness with the nonhuman world, and sympathy for those that are suffering; 24 scored higher in the post-test for their

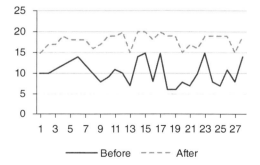

FIGURE 4.1   Students' understanding of course contents

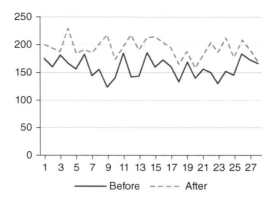

FIGURE 4.2 Ability in the art of interbeing

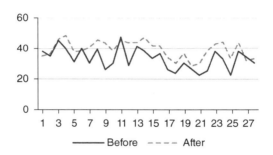

FIGURE 4.3 Ability to observe one's sensations and happenings in the world

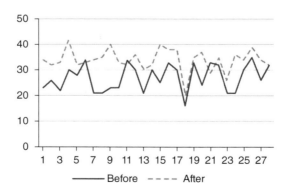

FIGURE 4.4 Ability to act with awareness

Contemplative Pedagogies **67**

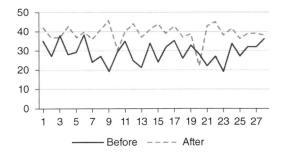

FIGURE 4.5 Awareness of one's connectedness with the nonhuman world

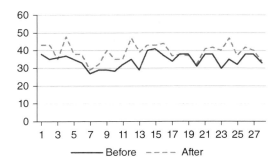

FIGURE 4.6 Sympathy for those who are suffering

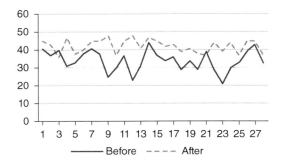

FIGURE 4.7 Sense of ecological responsibility

ability to act with awareness, and 26 improved in terms of their sense of ecological responsibility.

Students' voices (from short responses, reflection essays, and end-of-semester questionnaires) substantiated my argument that the contemplative pedagogies effectively enhanced students' learning ability and fostered their ecological awareness. Students found that mindfulness helped them feel calm and less distracted. They also realized that mindfulness was the cornerstone of their attempt at ecological protection. Moreover, contemplative activities played a crucial role in helping students feel connected with the natural world. For example, students found that "Speaking for Animals" generated empathy, which was based upon their awareness of all lives' vulnerability, stimulating them to reflect upon how they would treat other beings. As for mindful walking, students took delight in being connected with beings around them and started establishing bonds with nature. Imagining the life of Animal and *tonglen* helped facilitate students' connectedness with those who are suffering. Finally, students' cumulative experience showed that contemplative pedagogies provided experiential learning, which induced them to find peace and appreciate the world around them. Students' sense of ecological responsibility founded upon their own experience of interconnectedness was also imbued with hopeful enthusiasm to bring about changes to the world without being too critical of themselves or others. The following are some examples from students' writings:

> "By imagining myself to be the animal I was impersonating, I forged the sense of empathy in its strict sense of the capability to imagine ourselves with others' emotions. . . . As a result, this makes me more vocal in my protest against any animal cruelty and more conscious of my own course of action, for animals and I are all the same in our fragility."
>
> "My eyes are opened for the peculiar but funny Babao tree, and my nose can smell the gentle and sweet cork tree's flowers, all of which I have never noticed before. . . . My partner . . . took me to the giant raintree. With its curvy branches like the open arms, it hugged me and I gratefully wrapped my arm around [it] in return. At that moment, I could feel the warmth and love from the tree, as if we were friends."
>
> "Interestingly, to understand the issues and ideas more vividly, it can be done with my eyes closed. With visual distraction gone, it is easier to imagine myself as someone else, feel their pain, and ease them with relief during Tonglen practice. Together with mindfulness practice, it allows me to [be] compassionate [towards] other beings as well as myself."
>
> "The practices . . . help us bring the things in the book and class to actions. I think the most effective way of learning is experiencing. Before taking this course, I always knew of many ways I can help save the world, but I could hardly do it. . . . But with the practices, I appreciated every

minute of them for [they] made me focus on myself and the good things I can give to this world."

In blending contemplative practices with environmental humanities, my work creates education that advocates the interconnectedness of self and the other and the cooperation of body and mind. I believe that mindful education nurtures the interiority of learners' minds without ignoring external realities. It trains the learners to sharpen their awareness and learn to monitor their thoughts, speech, and deeds in interactions with all beings. Finally, I think mindful education has an ideal, yet not unrealizable goal of alleviating the world's problems through gradual changes that individuals generate from within themselves through a lifelong commitment to the practice. Just as the seeds sown in soil germinate and gradually become shady trees, so the learners trained in mindful education will grow in harmonious coexistence with all beings and help create, in Buddhadāsa's words, "the world's enduring peace and well-being."

Acknowledgement

I wish to express my gratitude to my *dhamma* teachers and friends from all religious traditions. I am indebted to Captain William Whorton, who commented on the drafts of this chapter. My special thanks goes to my students, especially the class of 2019. I am grateful to Professor Greta Gaard for her invaluable advice and support. I also thank the Faculty of Arts, Chulalongkorn University, for granting me travel funds to the 2019 ASLE Conference to present a paper that has blossomed into this chapter.

Note

1 The texts that I used include *Satipaṭṭhāna-sutta*, or the "Discourse on the Establishments of Mindfulness" (1995); *Anāpānasati-sutta,* or "Discourse on Mindfulness of Breathing" (1995); and *Visuddhimagga*, or "The Path of Purification" (Buddhaghosa, 2010).

References

Adams, J. J. (2015). *Loosed Upon the World: The Saga Anthology of Climate Fiction.* Saga Press.
Anālayo, B. (2015). Understanding and Practicing the *Satipaṭṭhāna-sutta.* In E. Shonin, W. V. Gordon, & N. N. Singh (Eds.), *Buddhist Foundations of Mindfulness* (pp. 71–88). Springer International Publishing.
Anāpānasati-sutta. (1995). In *The Collection of the Middle Length Sayings (Majjhima-nikāya)* (I. B. Horner, Trans.) (Vol. 3, pp. 121–129). Pali Text Society.
Baer, R. A., Smith, G. T., Hopkins, J., Krietemeyer, J., & Toney, L. (2006). Using Self-Report Assessment Methods to Explore Facets of Mindfulness. *Assessment, 13,* 27–45. Doi: 10.1177/1073191105283504.
Barbezat, D. P., & Bush, M. (2014). *Contemplative Practices in Higher Education.* Jossey-Bass.
Buddhadāsa, B. (1966). *Kansueksachanitthinamlokpaisukhamwinat* [*Education That Leads the World to Ruin*]. Karnphimphanakorn.
Buddhadāsa, B. (1990). *KansueksanaithatsanakhongThanBuddhadāsa* [*Education in Buddhadasa Bhikkhu's View*]. Atammayo.

Buddhaghosa. (2010). *The Path of Purification (Visuddhimagga)* (B. Nāṇamoli, Trans.). Buddhist Publication Society. (1956).
Burke, K. (1962). *A Rhetoric of Motives*. University of California Press.
Bush, M. (2013). Mindfulness in Higher Education. In J. G. Williams & J. Kabat-Zinn (Eds.), *Mindfulness: Diverse Perspectives on its Meaning, Origins and Applications* (pp. 183–197). Routledge.
Chödrön, P. (1994). *Start Where You Are: A Guide to Compassionate Living*. Shambala.
Christensen, L. (2002). The Pragmatic Mysticism of Mary Oliver. In J. S. Bryson (Ed.), *Ecopoetry: A Critical Introduction* (pp. 135–152). University of Utah Press.
Cornell, J. (1998). *Sharing Nature with Children*. Dawn Publications.
Crawford, J. (2005). *Spiritually-Engaged Knowledge: The Attentive Heart*. Ashgate.
Hanson, R., & Mendius, R. (2009). *Buddha's Brain: The Practical Neuroscience of Happiness, Love & Wisdom*. New Harbinger Publications.
Harvey, P. (2013). *An Introduction to Buddhism: Teachings, History, and Practices* (2nd ed.). Cambridge University Press.
Hoelting, K. (2017). The Practice of Inner Habitat Restoration: A Contemplative Approach to Sustainability Studies. In M. Eaton, H. J. Hughes, & J. MacGregor (Eds.), *Contemplative Approaches to Sustainability in Higher Education: Theory and Practice* (pp. 28–39). Routledge.
Killen, P. O. (2017). Using Reflective and Contemplative Practices with Integrity. In M. Eaton, H. J. Hughes, & J. MacGregor (Eds.), *Contemplative Approaches to Sustainability in Higher Education: Theory and Practice* (pp. 55–68). Routledge.
Kingsolver, B. (1991). *Animal Dreams*. Abacus.
Macy, J. (1993). *World as Lover, World as Self*. Rider.
Miyazaki, H. (2008a). *Turning Point: 1997–2008* (B. Cary & F. L. Schodtl, Trans.). Viz Media.
Miyazaki, H. (Director). (2008b). *Ponyo on the Cliff by the Sea* [Film]. Studio Gibli.
Nhat Hanh, T. (1990). *Present Moment, Wonderful Moment*. Parallax.
Nhat Hanh, T. (2012). *Awakening of the Heart: Essential Buddhist Sutras and Commentaries*. Parallax.
Nixon, R. (2011). *Slow Violence and the Environmentalism of the Poor*. Harvard University Press.
Nuridsany, C., & Pérennou, M. (Directors). (2004). *Genesis* [Film]. Les Films Alain Sarde.
Oliver, M. (1992). *New and Selected Poems*. Beacon Press.
Pommier, E., Neff, K. D., & Tóth-Király, I. (2019). The Development and Validation of the Compassion Scale. *Assessment*, 27, 21–39. Doi: 10.1177/1073191119874108.
Quinn, D. (1992). *Ishmael: An Adventure of the Mind and Spirit*. Bantam/Turner Book.
Raes, F., Pommier, E., Neff, K. D., & Van Gucht, D. (2011). Construction and Factorial Validation of a Short Form of the Self-Compassion Scale. *Clinical Psychology & Psychotherapy*, 18, 250–255.
Satipaṭṭhāna-sutta. (1995). In *The Collection of the Middle Length Sayings (Majjhima-Nikāya)* (I. B. Horner, Trans.) (Vol. 1, pp. 70–82). Pali Text Society.
Sinha, I. (2007). *Animal's People*. Pocket Books.
Tirch, D., Siberstein, L. R., & Kolts, R. L. (2016). *Buddhist Psychology and Cognitive-Behavioral Therapy: A Clinician's Guide*. Guilford Press.
Williams, J. M. G., & Kabat-Zinn, J. (Eds.). (2013). *Mindfulness: Diverse Perspectives on its Meaning, Origins, and Applications*. Routledge.
Zajonc, A. (2013). Contemplative Pedagogy: A Quiet Revolution in Higher Education. In L. A. Sanders (Ed.), *Contemplative Studies in Higher Education* (pp. 83–94). Wiley.

5
LITERARY READING, MINDFULNESS, AND CLIMATE JUSTICE

An Experiment in Contemplative Ecocritical Pedagogy

Anne Raine

Traditionally, the English honors seminar has been framed as a milestone in students' careers, an opportunity to demonstrate expertise in literary history, proficiency as critical readers and persuasive writers, and readiness for graduate studies or professional employment. But how can we prepare students for life in environmental and climate crisis? The climate emergency calls for deeper reflection on what humanities education is for, and what pedagogies can best help students develop the knowledge, skills, *and* affective resources they need to live well as engaged citizens and embodied beings in catastrophic times. My seminar, "Literature, Mindfulness, and the Climate Crisis," explores how mindfulness-integrated pedagogy can help students develop those affective resources.

Contemplative Pedagogy and the "Affective Turn"

Literary studies is itself a valuable form of contemplative pedagogy, and mindfulness practice deepens students' capacity to *embody* what they learn rather than understanding it only intellectually (Berila, 2016). Ecocritical analysis helps students critique cultural narratives that normalize climate change denial. But literary reading also has a contemplative dimension: it trains students to bring patience and curiosity to whatever arises in the reading experience, to stay open to more than one possible interpretation, and to attend not only to what's explicitly stated but also to the feel of things, or what we might call the "body language" of the text. Mindfulness practice extends this attention to the body of the reader as well, fostering experiential knowledge of the emotions and bodily sensations that shape how we interpret texts, inhabit the world, and interact with other beings. It helps develop a felt sense, as well as intellectual understanding, of how habits of attention and emotion management are shaped by internalized social norms and affect our capacity to respond to the climate crisis (Norgaard, 2011). And it fosters new

DOI: 10.4324/9781003201854-7

affective capacities—equanimity, resilience, courage, emotional intelligence, a felt sense of interconnection with more-than-human others—that can help students participate in the necessary shift from a culture of anxiety and denial to one of collective responsibility and climate justice.

My course combines affective ecocriticism, climate justice studies, and contemplative pedagogy to teach mindfulness not as individual self-care, but as an embodied, relational, ecopolitically oriented response to unsustainable and exploitative systems. Recently, scholars and activists have called for greater attention to the affective dimensions of public discourse and socioecological relations. Ecocritics use affect theory to explore the ecopolitical implications of neuroscience's recognition that "we process stories with a cognitive apparatus that is not wholly distinct from our bodies, our feelings, and—quite literally—our guts" (Bladow & Ladino, 2018, p. 2). Environmental educators recognize that teaching climate change involves helping students process difficult emotions and resist both naïve hope and debilitating despair (Fiskio, 2016). Ray (2020) argues that mindfulness and emotional intelligence are as important for climate justice work as scientific literacy. But, as Ray points out, humanities scholars are trained to approach our work intellectually, through textual analysis rather than embodied practice (p. 48). Given academia's valorization of intellectual over emotional and spiritual work, and the popularization of mindfulness as privatized self-care (Purser & Loy, 2013), we may feel uneasy incorporating mindfulness practice into our teaching. However, recent work on contemplative practices in social justice education and activism (Berila, 2016; Batacharya & Wong 2018; Rowe, 2016) helps restore the transformative potential that is too often lost when mindfulness is reduced to a technique for individual stress management or self-improvement. This chapter presents one example of what a mindfulness-integrated course on literature and climate justice might look like.[1]

"Staying With the Trouble"

Mindfulness pedagogy helps address two key challenges. One is the need to connect literary reading with more public and collaborative forms of engagement. As LeMenager (2017) argues, teaching cli-fi can help build public support for climate action: if literary genres produce "habitual feeling-states" or "affective expectations" that constitute "emotional and social infrastructure" for socioecological systems (Berlant, cited in LeMenager, 2017, p. 476), then the new genre of cli-fi invites us to experiment with new structures of feeling that unsettle normalized expectations of freedom, security, and prosperity made possible by colonialism, extractive capitalism, and cheap oil (LeMenager, 2014) and help us transition to more just and sustainable socioecological relations. By combining mindfulness pedagogy with climate justice studies, we reframe literary reading not as private catharsis for individual readers (LeMenager, 2017, p. 476), but as a shared project of building emotional and social infrastructure for climate action.

A second challenge is how to help students confront the climate emergency without exacerbating the mental health issues many already struggle with—which means finding ways to address both anxiety *and* denial. Environmental studies students may begin their studies "in anguish" about the climate crisis (Fiskio, 2016), but many of the English undergraduates I teach inhabit the same state of denial as most Canadians, who are increasingly worried about climate change but don't fully grasp the urgency and scale of the actions needed to address it (Hatch & Granados, 2021). Haraway (2016) asserts that in troubled times, our task is both "to make trouble, to stir up potent response to devastating events," *and* "to settle troubled waters and rebuild quiet places" (p. 157). Indigenous land protectors like Unist'ot'en spokesperson Freda Huson insist on the necessary connection between healing the people and healing the land (Rowe & Simpson, 2017). And Western health professionals now recognize climate-related anxiety, grief, and PTSD as a growing problem that requires both new therapeutic methods *and* collective action to address systemic causes of climate disruption (Cunsolo et al., 2020). In this context, Haraway's call to settle troubled waters and rebuild quiet places suggests the need to repair both outer and inner landscapes: to restore calm to mind and body, process difficult emotions, stay present in "the spaciousness of uncertainty" (Solnit, 2016, p. xiv), and cultivate the resilience, compassion, courage, and more-than-human solidarity that support both personal well-being and effective participation in climate action. Mindfulness pedagogy encourages students to make space for this inner work, and to recognize its value as part of an embodied learning process that connects literary reading with practical response.

Course Objectives

My seminar invites students to explore what happens when we combine literary reading with mindfulness practice as complementary strategies for engaging with the climate emergency. We discuss a variety of cli-fi texts—including ecopoetry, nonfiction, and graphic memoir as well as novels—and consider what each suggests about how to respond to the planetary crisis. And we use a regular practice of in-class and at-home meditation to deepen our engagement and reflect on what form our own responses might take. Our guiding questions are these:

FIG. 5.1 Guiding Questions for 'Literature, Mindfulness, & the Climate Crisis'

---

1. If most of us know we're in a climate crisis, why are we still acting like we're not? What are the emotional and social factors that get in the way of climate action?
2. How can meditation complement ecocritical analysis in attending to the feelings and sensations that shape our experience, behavior, and interactions with others? What happens when we recognize this emotional work as part of our learning process?
3. How can literary reading and mindfulness practice help us shift from a culture of anxiety and denial to one of collective responsibility and climate justice?

Students readily grasp how mindfulness practice might help them process climate anxiety. But they need to understand that the meditation component is not just a therapeutic add-on; rather, it's an integral part of the embodied learning process the course aims to foster. In addition to the many ways in which mindfulness can enhance students' learning and well-being (Cottrell, 2018), mindfulness-integrated pedagogy supports a number of learning objectives specific to our goal of developing affective resources for the climate emergency:

- *. To become more aware of how internalized norms of attention and emotion management affect experience and behavior—and how these norms participate in the capitalist, colonialist, human-exceptionalist systems that produced the climate crisis;
- To expand our attention from individual to systemic, more-than-human scales;
- To unlearn denial and process difficult emotions that get in the way of climate action;
- *. To cultivate compassion and collaboration with diverse human and nonhuman others;
- *. To become more comfortable with silence and uncertainty, and more patient in seeking solutions to complex problems;
- To experience ourselves not as isolated individuals but as co-emergent social-material actors with the capacity to contribute to systemic change.

Most of these objectives are already implicit in ecocritical studies; mindfulness pedagogy helps extend them into embodied practice.

Unit 1: Course Introduction

In the first few weeks of the course, we practice meditation in an open-ended way, guided by Cottrell's *Mindfulness for Students* (2018) and Chödrön's *How to Meditate* (2013). We build our conceptual framework with readings on ecocriticism, the emotions of climate change, and mind-body practices in activist movements. Later, we include meditations that "apply" mindfulness skills to particular ecopolitical challenges explored in the cli-fi texts. Each week we use concepts from Kaza's *Mindfully Green* (2008) to frame our meditation and our literary discussion, so that conceptual and experiential learning proceed together.

Because regular practice is needed to develop the capacity to settle the mind and observe whatever arises with equanimity, I ask students to meditate at home, at least four days a week, silently with a timer or with audio guidance,[2] and to keep a journal where they reflect on their experience as it changes over time. The journals are private, but I invite students to share observations and questions in meditation surveys every few weeks. This allows me to see how things are going and address any questions or difficulties they encounter.

FIG. 5.2 Contemplative Practice for Course Introduction

Introduction to Meditation

Appreciating stillness/noticing habits of attention: We begin our first class with a five-minute meditation, noticing what feelings arise as we suspend the usual class activities to observe the breath and sit silently in a room together. After meditation, students reflect privately in their journals, then share observations if they feel comfortable doing so. This encourages them to allow more space for listening to themselves and others, and to reflect on what assumptions they've internalized about what to spend time on, pay attention to, feel, or talk about (Norgaard, 2011, p. 132). In weeks two and three, we expand our practice to include mindfulness of sounds and body scanning.

> * *Important*: Students need to know that while mindfulness meditation has many benefits, it can intensify symptoms of traumatic stress. Students should opt out of any practice that feels unsafe, and know that I will support them in adapting the mindfulness component as needed (Berila, 2016; Treleaven, 2018).

Themes	*Readings*	*Practices*
• Climate anxiety and denial • Affect and embodiment	• Cunsolo et al., "Ecological Grief and Anxiety" • Norgaard, "The Emotions of Climate Apathy" • Ray, *Field Guide*, chapter 2 • Bladow and Ladino, Introduction	• Appreciating stillness/noticing habits of attention
• Starting a meditation practice	• Cottrell, from *Mindfulness for Students* • Chödrön, from *How to Meditate*	• Mindfulness of breath and/or sounds
• Mindfulness as ecopolitical praxis • Intersectional climate justice	• Kaza, *Mindfully Green*, "1: Reducing Harm"; "2: Being with the Suffering" • Rowe, "Zen and the Art of Social Movement Maintenance" • Hopkins, "Racism Is Killing the Planet" • Ghosh, "Stories"	• Body scanning

To help students understand how mindfulness practice relates to the ecocritical part of the course, we begin with articles on the emotions of climate change, and use Norgaard (2012) and Ghosh (2016) to articulate our central problem: that some of the affective habits we've internalized—including those embedded in academic practices and literary genres—help perpetuate denial, inaction, and injustice. I ask students to place themselves on a scale of 1 (living in denial) to 10 (overwhelmed by climate anxiety). Then, we consider how mindfulness can be part of the solution. Ray (2020) explains how mindfulness can help us question unsustainable cultural narratives and cultivate resilience and emotional intelligence for climate justice work. And Bladow and Ladino (2018) help us explore how mindful attention to affective experience might enrich literary reading and foster ecological awareness. While they don't consider how meditation provides experiential knowledge to complement theoretical understanding, they help introduce our mindfulness-based study of cli-fi by presenting reading and thinking as embodied activities. And by combining affect theory with new materialist attention to nonhuman agency, they prepare us think in less anthropocentric ways about how affective relations between bodies and environments are represented and mobilized in literary texts.

Similarly, Kaza's *Mindfully Green* (2008) supports our mindfulness-based engagement with the climate crisis by situating mindfulness within "an ontology and an ethic of interbeing" that foregrounds our interdependence with and responsibility to diverse human and nonhuman others (Wong, 2018, p. 267). This relational, ethical, more-than-human dimension too often goes missing when mindfulness is separated from its Buddhist roots and operationalized by medical science or popularized in self-help books and corporate wellness programs (Grossman & Van Dam, 2011; Purser & Loy, 2013; Wong, 2018). In contrast, Kaza presents mindfulness not as a tool for individual happiness or productivity, but as an ethical and ecopolitical response to human and nonhuman suffering. For Kaza, mindfulness begins not with attention to the present moment, but with three principles informed by ecological systems theory and North American engaged Buddhism: committing to reduce harm, witnessing suffering, and recognizing interdependence and mutual co-arising. These provide "an ethical foundation and a pragmatic direction" for our ecocritical study and meditation practice (Kaza, 2008, p. 3).

Some students may be wary of Kaza's Buddhist language or her reliance on a somewhat dated model of White-led environmentalism rooted in deep ecology and peace activism. We therefore complement Kaza's *Mindfully Green* with Ray's (2020) discussion of how Buddhist psychology intersects with affect theory and cognitive science, and with articles that connect contemplative practice with current critiques of white supremacy and economic injustice. Rowe (2015) shows how mind-body practices can contribute to social and environmental activism, but only if combined with structural analysis and respectful dialogue that centers Black and Indigenous perspectives. Hopkins (2020) explains why tackling climate change requires addressing capitalism, colonialism, and environmental racism, and his moving account of a drumming ritual at a Black Lives Matter protest corroborates Rowe's point that mind-body practices have always been integral to activist movements. By connecting Buddhist psychology with systems theory and environmental ethics, Kaza helps students connect the phenomenological with the systemic and understand mindfulness as ecopolitical praxis. And by situating *Mindfully Green* in an intersectional climate justice framework, Rowe and Hopkins help us explore how mindfulness can help build a climate movement that recognizes climate action as inseparable from decolonization and racial and economic justice.

Unit 2: Changing Habits of Attention

Themes	Readings	Practices
• Thinking beyond the human • Starting a process of self-education	• Kaza, "3: Embracing the Deep View"; "4: Entering the Stream" • Squarzoni, *Climate Changed*	• Meditation on interbeing • Mindful seeing

Kaza (2008) emphasizes that reducing environmental harm involves ongoing research into systemic causes and possible solutions; accordingly, we begin with *Climate Changed* (2014), which narrates a process of self-education about the science and politics of climate change. Like Kaza, Squarzoni encourages readers to expand our attention from personal to more-than-human scales and learn about how our habitual actions affect and are affected by ecological and socioeconomic systems. But where Squarzoni presents the narrator as separate from the systems he studies, Kaza connects systems theory with Thich Nhat Hanh's concept of interbeing to offer an ecological view of the self as "a flowing stream of information and communication" that "co-exists and co-arises with all other life" (Kaza, 2008, p. 46). This helps connect Squarzoni's account of the earth's climate systems with the experiential inquiry of meditation.

> *Meditation on interbeing*: We explore Kaza's "systems view of self" by noting that the breath enacts our participation in the systemic processes (the water cycle, the carbon cycle) that constitute all life, and by gradually expanding our attention from breath and body sensations to the space and sounds around us. We practice shifting from self-focused thoughts and emotions to a more expansive, dynamic sense of how we co-emerge with other beings and phenomena, from cultural narratives and social systems to the weather, the food we eat, and the matter and energy that circulate through the earth's systems. This practice helps generate positive affects that encourage closer attention to and care for our surroundings. And it can help soften our attachment to fixed social identities and build new emotional infrastructures grounded in embodied awareness of interdependence and change.

Climate Changed also echoes Ghosh's (2016) claim that dominant genres perpetuate climate change denial: through recurring allusions to classic films, Squarzoni shows how they distract from ecological problems and fail to help us imagine a satisfactory ending. And the graphic novel form invites reflection on the interplay between analytical and contemplative inquiry. While the text-heavy panels that convey information and argument, the wordless images may function as mindful pauses, or what Ghosh calls "moments of recognition" of nonhuman agency, if approached in a contemplative way.

> *Mindful seeing*: After discussing Squarzoni's argument, we choose a visual sequence, such as the images that register feelings of unease, or portray the death of his dog, or evoke landscapes we might normally dismiss as mere setting. We pause to contemplate the images with open-minded attention, then discuss how the experience changes our interpretation of the book. This helps us consider what nonhuman interlocutors we may be overlooking in real life when the mind is cluttered with thoughts and emotions shaped by familiar human-centered stories.

Unit 3: Doing the Emotional and Interpersonal Work

Themes	*Readings*	*Practices*
• Witnessing suffering • Processing difficult emotions	• Kaza, "5: Engaging Skillful Effort" • Kolbert, "The Sixth Extinction?" • Spahr, "Gentle Now, Don't Add to Heartache," "Unnamed Dragonfly Species"	• Ecological *tonglen* • Contemplative reading
• Practicing compassion • Learning from diverse others	• Kaza, "6: Seeking Wisdom Sources" • Kingsolver, *Flight Behavior*	• Metta practice

Kaza's fifth chapter pairs well with Spahr's (2011) ecopoetry, since both emphasize the need to work with difficult emotions and restore affective bonds with nonhuman others. After discussing Kolbert's (2009b) article to introduce the problem of anthropogenic mass extinction, we consider whether Spahr presents the expression of love and remorse in "Gentle Now" as a remedy for the anxiety and denial in "Unnamed Dragonfly Species," and whether the glacier scene in "Unnamed Dragonfly Species" represents a ritual of mourning, a "moment of recognition" (Ghosh, 2016), or an example of how desire can be mobilized in misguided ways (if desire for personal catharsis distracts us from collective action). And we discuss how the poems' inconclusive endings foreground the need to transform grief, remorse, anxiety, and desire into resources for action.

> *Ecological tonglen* (Kaza, 2008, p. 75): After grounding ourselves with mindfulness of breath and body scanning, I ask students to recall an instance of environmental harm that worries or saddens them—reminding them to choose one that's not too overwhelming and to opt out if it feels unsafe. Breathing in, we focus on this troubling situation and notice how anxiety or grief are felt as physical sensations in the body. Breathing out, we practice releasing those feelings into a sense of connection and solidarity with others who share our feelings and concern.
>
> *Contemplative reading*: We then read Spahr's "Gentle Now" together, taking turns reading each sentence aloud. As we practice meeting awkwardness with equanimity and relaxing into the time it takes to attend to each word, the reading becomes a shared ritual that enacts the speaker's co-emergence with and recognition of harm done to the more-than-human community. This may help us connect with the speaker's love and sorrow, or prompt reflection on our limited ability to care about life forms we know only as names.

Kingsolver (2013) also foregrounds the need to practice compassion for nonhuman beings, as well as to develop the emotional intelligence required to work with other humans across economic, political, and religious differences. Kaza's sixth chapter encourages students to learn from unlikely teachers, including trees, animals, and places as well as people; Kingsolver's portrayal of a community's response to an unexpected visitation of monarch butterflies helps us explore what it might mean to regard nonhumans as teachers. And her attention to the fraught relations and potential common ground between urban scientists, rural working-class White Americans, and displaced Mexicans helps us explore how building a strong climate movement requires attention to economic inequality and willingness to "be less right and more in relation" (Ray, 2020, p. 97).

> *Metta practice*: After grounding ourselves with mindfulness of breath and body scanning, I ask students to focus on an area where they feel pleasant sensations, then imagine those sensations filling the whole body and expanding outward as they offer kind wishes first to

> themselves, then to someone they love (human or nonhuman), then to a neutral person (someone they have no strong feelings about), then to someone they find difficult,* and finally to all beings, near and far, human and nonhuman.³ We then reflect on how we might view an animal or plant as a teacher, or a difficult relationship as an opportunity for learning.
>
> * For the "difficult person," students should choose a relationship that's challenging but not traumatic; it's important to acknowledge that some relationships are abusive and systemic oppression is real. We discuss how practicing compassion and learning from others does not mean agreeing with everyone, condoning abuse, or abandoning responsibility to prevent injustice and harm (Salzburg, 2020). Over time, students can begin to *feel* how metta practice can foster both the openness and compassion to collaborate across differences *and* the courage and clarity of purpose to stand our ground.

Unit 4: Energy, Desire, Action

Themes	*Readings*	*Practices*
• Dealing with climate disaster	• Kaza, "7: Understanding Energy" • Lustgarten, "How Climate Migration Will Reshape America" • Rich, *Odds Against Tomorrow*	• Meditation on energy
• Intersectional climate justice • Desire vs. need	• Kaza, "8: Working with Desire" • Butler, *Parable of the Sower*	• Practicing contentment

Rich's (2013) and Butler's (1993/2000) novels focus on how humans can survive and rebuild once climate disaster has struck. Like Lustgarten's (2020) article on climate migration, which we also read in this unit, both novels emphasize that the post-apocalyptic future is already here. And both foreground the emotional work of climate adaptation, exploring how anxiety, fear, empathy, and desire inhibit or enhance characters' capacity for action. Kaza's (2008) account of how energy and desire circulate in ecological, socioeconomic, and psychophysiological systems helps us consider what the novels suggest about how affects can be mobilized for collective rather than just individual survival.

Students often find *Odds Against Tomorrow* perplexing, but a mindfulness-informed reading helps us see that what Rich's novel offers is neither the cathartic pleasure of "disaster porn" nor simply an ironic critique of disaster capitalism, but an uneasy exploration of the reckoning with vulnerability the climate crisis demands. How can we live with the knowledge that suffering and risk are inevitable, while taking action to prevent what harm we can? Kaza argues that reducing the harm caused by overconsumption of fossil fuels is not just a technological problem but requires mindful use of personal energy *and* building social energy for systemic change. This helps us consider what Rich's characters do with the nervous energy generated by fear of disaster and death: do they try to profit (or escape) from existing systems, or build more just and sustainable alternatives? Kaza's discussion of impermanence and interdependence helps us see that while Mitchell's fear of disaster is well-founded, his obsession with doomsday scenarios impedes his ability to protect the most vulnerable, address systemic causes of harm, or recognize Elsa's decisions as efforts to turn existential dread into eco-political action.

> *Meditation on energy*: Kaza's seventh chapter shows how "energy" is not a mystical idea but a materialist one: we participate in energy systems by metabolizing food that plants produce with energy from the sun; we know what it feels like to be low on energy, or to be energized by the mood of a crowd, the rhythm of a song, or a compelling idea. In meditation, we practice experiencing the body not as a fixed object but a field of sensations and flows of energy, and we explore how both excitement and nervousness can be experienced simply as energy that can be channeled in various ways.

Vulnerability is painfully concrete in Butler's (1993/2000) novel, which insists that there is no going back to old emotional and social infrastructures based on expectations of unlimited prosperity on a stable, hospitable planet. By focusing on the poor and racially diverse people who appear only briefly in Rich's novel, *Parable of the Sower* emphasizes that climate-related drought, fire, hunger, homelessness, and violence are already a daily reality that disproportionately harms poor, Black, Indigenous, and people of color. Kaza's chapter on resisting consumerism seems far removed from these life-or-death struggles. Yet by identifying the root of consumerist desire in the natural drive for self-preservation, and discussing how mindfulness helps distinguish between desire and need, Kaza raises questions that are central to Butler's novel: What do we need to keep ourselves alive? How much can we take before consumption becomes theft? When is it justifiable to use weapons and walls to protect what we have from others? And, as Lauren's gratitude for "Good, clean, free water from the sky" helps us contemplate (p. 48), what can we do now to appreciate what's truly valuable, and ensure that there is enough for all?

Moreover, Butler's Earthseed verses show how mindfulness is not just a luxury for the privileged, but a survival and resistance strategy for marginalized communities. We explore why putting ideas into verse was necessary for Butler to write *Parable of the Sower* (Butler, 1999, p. 336) and Lauren to "pry [herself] loose from the rotting past" and start "building a future that makes sense" (Butler, 1993/2000, p. 79). Kaza argues that both practical action and mindful practices of "not doing" are needed to replace exploitative systems with new infrastructures that support collective well-being. By adding a contemplative dimension to Butler's action-oriented novel, the Earthseed verses similarly suggest that climate adaptation and climate justice require both practical skills and contemplative practices for working with uncertainty, impermanence, and interdependence.

> *Practicing contentment*: This week we explore Kaza's suggestion that meditation trains us to resist the marketing of dissatisfaction that fuels overconsumption (pp. 131–136). We practice being content with whatever is happening in the present moment—whether that's enjoyment, discomfort, or boredom. We explore how it feels to suspend the desire for things to be different. And we consider how to balance practicing contentment with taking action to ensure that we and others have what we need to be safe and well.

Unit 5: Inhabiting Uncertainty

Themes	Readings	Practices
• "[P]ositive groundlessness"	• Chödrön, *Practicing Peace* (excerpts) • VanderMeer, *Annihilation*	• Working with uncertainty
• Working with diverse others • Unlearning capitalism and colonialism • Thinking toward action	• Kaza, "9: Practicing Peace" Hern and Johal, *Global Warming and the Sweetness of Life* • Kolbert, "Green Like Me" • Klein, "Stop Trying to Save the World All by Yourself"	• Three-part meditation (breath, body scan, metta practice)

Our final unit pairs VanderMeer's (2014) unsettling cli-fi novel with Hern and Johal's (2018) collaborative experiment in ecopolitical nonfiction. Both provide opportunities to practice "don't-know mind," or what Solnit (2016) calls "the spaciousness of uncertainty," and prepare students for their final assignments: a literary-critical essay and a personal, creative, or activist project that investigates and reflects on some form of environmental praxis.

Rather than using realist narration to portray climate impacts, *Annihilation* immerses readers in an uncanny textual landscape that blurs distinctions between natural and sociotechnological, human and nonhuman, self and other. Ghosh (2016) helps us read the novel's indeterminacy as a critique of scientific modernity's anthropocentrism and privileging of intellectual over embodied and emotional intelligence. And Kaza (2008) and Chödrön (2006/2014) help connect this indeterminacy with the state of openness we cultivate in meditation. Chödrön suggests that the open, spacious quality of "positive groundlessness" can emerge not only during peaceful contemplation, but also when something unexpected happens that jolts us out of habitual patterns (Chödrön, 2006/2014, pp. 83–84). This helps us recognize how *Annihilation* offers valuable training in staying present with uncertainty: the novel's unsettling beauty helps readers *feel* how uncertainty can inspire curiosity and wonder as well as caution and care.

> *Meditation on uncertainty*: After grounding ourselves with mindfulness of breath and body scanning, I ask students to recall a situation when they felt unsettled or unsure what to do, when their usual habits or assumptions suddenly didn't work—reminding them to choose something challenging but not traumatic, and to opt out if this practice feels unsafe. We breathe through the remembered experience and practice *feeling* how an unsettling moment might become a space where new insights or ways of responding can emerge. As we do this, we maintain contact with our present surroundings and the earth under our feet, noting that we can support ourselves this way whenever we find ourselves in an unsettling situation.

Global Warming and the Sweetness of Life (2018) explores uncertainty of a different kind: how to feel about the uncannily ordinary city at the heart of Canada's oil industry (p. 115), and how to think beyond the seeming inevitability of colonialist and capitalist development. We focus on the authors' experimental, collaborative approach, and their effort to see what they can learn by traveling to the tar sands and listening to people whose lives and politics differ from their own: European philosophers, Indigenous scholars, diverse Canadians whose jobs depend on oil extraction, and Indigenous people whose communities are directly harmed by it. This project politicizes Kaza's (2008) practice of "finding teachers everywhere" and her argument that environmentalism involves peacemaking—where peace means not just absence of overt conflict but ongoing effort to end systemic violence. Similarly, Hern and Johal argue that the climate movement needs an affirmative vision of the future that addresses the needs of people currently dependent on the oil economy while respecting Indigenous sovereignty and rematriating Indigenous land. Like Hopkins, they insist that climate justice means dismantling capitalist and colonialist systems that reduce some humans and all nonhumans to exploitable resources. And like Kaza, they present politics as "corporeal," involving both new ideas and "renovated way[s] of being in the world" (Hern & Johal, 2018, p. 20).

In seeking a new set of affective expectations and "possible relationships to each other, to other species, to the land, to the future" (p. 29), Hern and Johal find inspiration in Agamben's notion of "the sweetness of life," in Latin American models of *buen vivir* and *sumak kawsay*, and in Simpson's model of Indigenous theorizing as rooted in "full body intelligence" and "relational way[s] of being" with neighboring animal, plant, and human nations (cited in Hern & Johal, 2018, p. 65; Simpson, 2017). Simpson's argument that extractive capitalism is rooted in settler anxiety—that we must keep "developing" because "we do not have sufficient resources, . . . we are vulnerable, . . . we always need more" (Hern & Johal, 2018, p. 17)—adds a decolonial politics to Kaza's account of the emotional roots of consumerism. And the formal indeterminacy of Hern and Johal's book—the interplay between narrative, interviews, reflection, and argument, and between the text and Sacco's cartoons—self-consciously resists the "desire for clarity, for finality, for relief from anxiety" that fuels self-righteous approaches to climate politics (p. 22). This affirms the value of "staying with the trouble" (Haraway, 2016) even when our efforts are awkward, imperfect, or incomplete. Echoing Kingsolver's emphasis on multidirectional learning, Hern and Johal call us to inhabit the uneasy, often contested space of working with diverse others to build "an ongoing set of relations where we can find what the sweetness of life might mean" (p. 175).

Three-part meditation: Our last two meditations integrate five minutes each of mindfulness of breath, body scanning, and metta practice. We reflect on how this embodied and relational practice can support engagement with the koan-like challenge of staying open to diverse perspectives yet strong in our commitment to confront injustice and prevent harm. And we consider Hern and Johal's experiment as one model for end-of-term projects involving field research, collaboration, or interviews with people whose perspectives differ from our own.

From Cli-Fi to Mindful Climate Justice

Mindfulness pedagogy is valuable in part because it challenges us to suspend "business as usual" judgments about what counts as scholarly, productive, and important; it makes space to reflect on how some of our institutional and disciplinary habits may contribute to a culture of anxiety, denial, and injustice. Because of this, it raises some practical challenges.

First, time management: the mindfulness component will not be effective unless we spend time in class practicing meditation and discussing how it relates to the course readings and goals—so we may need to reconsider how many novels we assign or what level of literary analysis we can expect. By making time for meditation, we enact the guiding premise that addressing the climate emergency requires both systemic analysis *and* experiential learning that "cannot be understood in the abstract" but "*must be practiced*" (Berila, 2016, p. 17, emphasis in original). Because academia tends to view embodied and emotional intelligence as private or therapeutic matters rather than vital components of knowledge production, some students may begrudge the time spent on meditation ("I attend class to learn, not to meditate"). Others have trouble sitting still or relaxing in a group setting; and some need trauma-informed modifications and support. But the majority look forward to our in-class meditation and find that it helps them focus, get more out of discussions, or feel more at ease and connected with their classmates. This sense of community enhances learning and supports the idea that mindfulness can help build the affective foundation for collective action.

A second challenge is how to support students' at-home practice without reinforcing the culture of performance anxiety that mindfulness aims to counteract. Students need structure to help them practice consistently enough to start feeling the benefits. But since the goal is to foster equanimity, flexibility, and self-compassion, they also need to be free to adapt their practice to their temperaments and circumstances, without worrying they're "doing it wrong" or striving for an A+ in meditation. To recognize the time and effort involved, the mindfulness component is worth 10% of the final grade. But everyone receives full credit if they submit all five surveys throughout the semester, indicating how often and how long they meditated, what they noticed about their experience, and any connections they see between their practice and our course readings. This scoring method provides incentive to take the practice seriously as part of the learning process, but minimizes the pressure to judge themselves or the assignment harshly if they find meditation difficult or regular practice hard to maintain. It also enables me to offer clarification, guidance, and support as needed.

While writing assignments can assess how well the course succeeds in teaching ecocritical skills and concepts, measuring how well it succeeds in developing affective resources for the climate crisis is a third challenge. Here, assessment tools like the Five-Facet Mindfulness Questionnaire (FFMQ) (Baer et al., 2006) can be helpful. As Grossman and Van Dam (2011) argue, identifying specific cognitive capacities as measurable indicators of mindfulness, while useful, necessarily isolates those capacities from the complex ethical and experiential processes inherent in Buddhist (and ecological) conceptions of mindfulness—processes that develop slowly over time and are difficult to quantify (pp. 223–224). Given the limited time most students can devote to meditation, it may not be realistic to expect dramatic change in a single semester.[4] Instead, we might think of the benefits of mindfulness pedagogy in terms of "changes in value system"—students "learning to *value* aspects integral to the cultivation of mindful awareness," such as "appreciation of stillness, attentiveness, and patience"—rather than "mastery" by the end of the course (p. 226). Nonetheless, the FFMQ can help assess the extent to which students leave the course with renovated habits of attention and affective capacities that can help them respond more effectively to the climate crisis. In the undergraduate version of my course, students' average FFMQ scores increased by 15.5%, with the most significant increases in "observing" (25%) and nonreactivity (17.9%). In the graduate version, average scores increased by 13.7%, with the most significant increases in nonreactivity (28.3%) and nonjudging of inner experience (22.9%).[5]

Empowerment and Action

The seminar aims to redefine mindfulness as a relational and ecopolitical practice rather than a private therapeutic one—and students' comments show that they recognize the need to move from building personal resilience to taking action to address systemic causes of harm. As one pointed out, meditation itself can be used to "distrac[t] [ourselves] from thinking about the problems that arise from global warming," thus contributing to denial and inaction. But students also grasp how mindfulness practice can do the opposite: "Noticing, understanding, and being okay with your feelings are the first steps to engagement with the climate crisis. Meditation has helped cares surface [that] I didn't even know I have." Students agreed that meditation practice can make climate anxiety less overwhelming, but also that "a little bit of anxiety is necessary if one wishes to actually enact change in the world." "In meditating," another observed, "we learn that it's okay to not be okay"; this helps us "come to terms with how we feel and channel that energy into doing something productive" rather than "immediately turning away" from the uneasy affects that emerge when we pay attention to the climate news.

But do these insights move students to action? The course supports that movement in two ways. First, there are the meditation practices that loosen our attachment to fixed and limiting conceptions of selfhood and foster a felt sense of ourselves as co-emergent social-material actors with the capacity to contribute to systemic change. This renovation of emotional infrastructure is essential, but it is incomplete unless it helps us connect with and expand the *social* infrastructure that can transform socioecological relations on a necessary scale. Kaza makes this point throughout *Mindfully Green*, and we end with two articles that encourage students to position themselves not as isolated individuals but as engaged members of local, national, and international climate change publics.

One is Kolbert's (2009a) critique of the film *No Impact Man*, which suggests practical ways to focus less on individual consumer choices and more on working with neighbors and lawmakers to effect systemic change. Similarly, Klein's (2015/2019) commencement address calls students to shift from green consumerism to political action, but emphasizes that "you personally do not have to do everything," because "you are part of a movement" that includes people taking all kinds of action all over the planet (pp. 135–136). To expand our sense of what might be possible, we brainstorm a range of options: from writing a poem, making a video, or discussing climate issues with family; to going vegan, attending a demonstration, or joining a letter-writing campaign; to launching an emissions reduction project in their community, changing their career plans, or running for political office. Like *Mindfully Green*, these articles reassure students that it's okay to start where you are and take inspiration and courage from others who are doing the same. In this respect, our final assignment is too open-ended for its success to be measured precisely. Building on the felt sense we've developed of our interdependence with others and the earth, I encourage students to view the end-of-term project as one step in an ongoing practice of multidirectional learning, "staying with the trouble," and staying open to possible futures they might not have imagined before.

Notes

1 I am grateful to Nicole Merola, whose syllabus on the emotions of climate change was an inspiring model for my seminar.
2 It's hard to find a meditation app that fits perfectly with the course's ecopolitical goals, but here are some to consider: Buddhify; Healthy Minds Program (from the University of Wisconsin–Madison); Liberate (a new app by and for BIPOC meditators); Mindful USC; UCLA Mindful; or Mindfulness Daily (not the smartphone app, but the free online course by Tara Brach and Jack Kornfield).
3 My approach to metta meditation is inspired by Cayoun (2015). Unfortunately, it's surprisingly unusual for meditation courses to extend metta practice to nonhumans.
4 Most mindfulness-based stress reduction and cognitive behavioral therapy programs recommend two 30-minute meditation sessions every day, which is not realistic for most students.
5 These figures are approximate, since not all students submitted both the entry and the exit survey.

References

Baer, R. A., Smith, G. T., Hopkins, J., Krietemeyer, J., & Toney, L. (2006). Using Self-Report Assessment Methods to Explore Facets of Mindfulness. *Assessment*, 13(1), 27–45. DOI: 10.1177/1073191105283504.

Batacharya, S., & Wong, Y.-L. R. (2018). *Sharing Breath: Embodied Learning and Decolonization*. Athabasca University Press.

Berila, B. (2016). *Integrating Mindfulness into Anti-Oppression Pedagogy*. Routledge.

Bladow, K., & Ladino, J. (2018). *Affective Ecocriticism: Emotion, Embodiment, Environment*. University of Nebraska Press.

Butler, O. (1993/2000). *Parable of the Sower*. Grand Central Publishing.

Butler, O. (1999). A Conversation with Octavia E. Butler. In *Parable of the Sower* (pp. 333–341). Grand Central Publishing.

Cayoun, B. A. (2015). *Mindfulness-Integrated CBT for Well-Being and Personal Growth*. Wiley-Blackwell.

Chödrön, P. (2006/2014). *Practicing Peace*. Shambhala.

Chödrön, P. (2013). *How to Meditate*. Sounds True.

Cottrell, S. (2018). *Mindfulness for Students*. Palgrave Macmillan.

Cunsolo, A., Harper, S. L., Minor, K., Hayes, K., Williams, Kimberly G., & Howard, C. (2020). Ecological Grief and Anxiety: The Start of a Healthy Response to Climate Change? *The Lancet Planetary Health*, 4(7), e261–e263. DOI: 10.1016/S2542-5196(20)30144-3.

Fiskio, J. (2016). Building Paradise in the Classroom. In S. Siperstein, S. Hall, & S. LeMenager (Eds.), *Teaching Climate Change in the Humanities* (pp. 101–109). Routledge.

Ghosh, A. (2016). *The Great Derangement: Climate Change and the Unthinkable*. University of Chicago Press.

Grossman, P., & Van Dam, N. T. (2011, May). Mindfulness, by Any Other Name... Trials and Tribulations of Sati in Western Psychology and Science. *Contemporary Buddhism*, 12(1), 219–239. DOI: 10.1080/14639947.2011.564841.

Haraway, D. J. (2016). *Staying with the Trouble: Making Kin in the Chthulucene*. Duke University Press.

Hatch, C., & Granados, M (2021, March). What Do Canadians Really Think About Climate Change? A Summary of Public Opinion Research for Climate Communicators. *Climate Access*. climateaccess.org/blog/what-do-canadians-really-think-about-climate-change.

Hern, M., & Johal, A. (2018). *Global Warming and the Sweetness of Life: A Tar Sands Tale*. MIT Press.

Hopkins, H. (2020, June) Racism Is Killing the Planet. *Sierra Magazine*. www.sierraclub.org/sierra/racism-killing-planet.

Kaza, S. (2008). *Mindfully Green*. Shambhala.

Kingsolver, B. (2013). *Flight Behavior*. Harper Perennial.

Klein, N. (2015/2019). "Stop Trying to Save the World All By Yourself." In *On Fire: The Burning Case for a Green New Deal* (pp. 129–136). Knopf Canada.

Kolbert, E. (2009a, August). Green Like Me. *The New Yorker*. www.newyorker.com/magazine/2009/08/31/green-like-me.

Kolbert, E. (2009b, May). The Sixth Extinction? *The New Yorker*. www.newyorker.com/magazine/2009/05/25/the-sixth-extinction.

LeMenager, S. (2014). *Living Oil: Petroleum Culture in the American Century*. Oxford University Press.

LeMenager, S. (2017). The Humanities After the Anthropocene. In U. K. Heise, J. Christensen, & M. Niemann (Eds.), *The Routledge Companion to the Environmental Humanities* (pp. 489–497). Routledge.

Lustgarten, A. (2020, September). How Climate Migration Will Reshape America. *New York Times Magazine*. www.nytimes.com/interactive/2020/09/15/magazine/climate-crisis-migration-america.html.

Norgaard, K. M. (2011). *Living in Denial: Climate Change, Emotions, and Everyday Life*. MIT Press.
Norgaard, K. M. (2012, December). The Emotions of Climate Apathy. *Mobilizing Ideas*. mobilizingideas.wordpress.com/2012/12/03/the-emotions.
Purser, R., & Loy, D. (2013, August). Beyond McMindfulness. *Huffington Post*. https://www.huffpost.com/entry/beyond-mcmindfulness_b_3519289.
Ray, S. J. (2020). *A Field Guide to Climate Anxiety*. University of California Press.
Rich, N. (2013). *Odds Against Tomorrow*. Picador.
Rowe, J. K. (2015, March). Zen and the Art of Social Movement Maintenance. *Waging Nonviolence*. wagingnonviolence.org/feature/mindfulness-and-the-art. DOI: 10.1080/07393148.2016.1153191.
Rowe, J. K. (2016). Micropolitics and Collective Liberation: Mind/Body Practice and Left Social Movements. *New Political Science*, 38(2), 206–225.
Rowe, J. K., & Simpson, M. (2017). Lessons from the Front Lines of Anti-Colonial Pipeline Resistance. *Waging Nonviolence*. wagingnonviolence.org/feature/lessons-front-lines.
Salzburg, S. (2020). *Real Change: Mindfulness to Heal Ourselves and the World*. Flatiron Books.
Simpson, L. B. (2017). *As We Have Always Done: Indigenous Freedom through Radical Resistance*. University of Minnesota Press.
Solnit, R. (2016). *Hope in the Dark*. Haymarket Books.
Spahr, J. (2011). *Well Then There Now*. Black Sparrow Press.
Squarzoni, P. (2014). *Climate Changed: A Personal Journey Through the Science*. Abrams.
Treleaven, D. (2018). *Trauma-Sensitive Mindfulness*. W. W. Norton & Co.
VanderMeer, J. (2014). *Annihilation*. HarperCollins.
Wong, Y.-L. R. (2018). 'Please Call Me by My True Names': A Decolonizing Pedagogy of Mindfulness and Interbeing in Critical Social Work Education. In S. Batacharya & Y.-L. R. Wong (Eds.), *Sharing Breath: Embodied Learning and Decolonization* (pp. 253–277). Athabasca University Press.

6
MINDFULNESS, WRITING, AND SUSTAINABLE HAPPINESS IN THE ANTHROPOCENE

Greta Gaard

After teaching courses on "Critical White Studies," "Feminist Science Studies," "Ecofeminism," and "Socially Engaged Buddhism" at a radical, transdisciplinary college in the Pacific Northwest, I was drawn back to the upper Midwest, more conscious of both my racial embodiment as a white queer cisgender woman, and my "first-generation college student" status. I wanted to teach other Euro-American first-generation students because as superficially "one of them," I would have more credibility in helping these students cultivate awareness of their own embodiment, emotions, and repetitive mental narratives—as well as the ways these mental narratives shape their attitudes and relationships with different others, exploring how U.S. culture might afford them unearned privilege and attitudes of entitlement. Primarily an undergraduate institution drawing students from small-town western Wisconsin (50%) and eastern Minnesota (45%), the University of Wisconsin–River Falls (UWRF) enrolled 5,862 students for the Fall 2020 semester: of these students, 72% received financial aid, and 40% of incoming freshmen were first-generation college students; 24% of UWRF students major in animal science, and just 1 in 10 are students of color, while 9 out of 10 faculty are white (UWRF Quick Facts, 2019). How could these students benefit from practicing mindfulness? I decided to explore the possibilities.

This chapter describes a path of practice using contemplative pedagogies across a diversity of courses and student standpoints: between the years 2014 to 2020: Human-Animal Studies, Advanced Composition, and a second-year writing course with the theme, "Sustainable Happiness." Of course, I thought I had invented this theme, linking the Dharma through pedagogies of climate justice and socially engaged writing praxis—but others came before me. I later learned about an edited volume (van Gelder, 2014) and both an online course and a book (O'Brien, 2016).

DOI: 10.4324/9781003201854-8

Specific research questions drove my inquiry for each course:

- In the Human-Animal Studies course, could mindfulness pedagogy help students cultivate awareness of their own multispecies embodiment, and thus activate their capacities for multispecies empathy?
- In the Advanced Composition course, could contemplative practices support students in cultivating greater creativity, patience for the creative process, and self-compassion for that process in its many iterations?
- In the Reading and Writing Across the Disciplines course, could Buddhism's understanding of true happiness—cultivated through positive psychology—support and ground students as they grapple with the linked crises of climate, species extinctions, and a rigged economy?

Since I was planning to analyze student data from these courses, I applied for and received Institutional Review Board (IRB) approval for a multi-year study. Data collection began with qualitative reporting after each contemplative practice and developed to include the more standard instruments of social science research: informed consent forms, pre- and post-tests assessing skills I hoped our contemplative practices would cultivate (empathy, self-compassion, stress reduction, multicultural awareness, and appreciation), and happiness. After discovering research on "Fidelity of Implementation" (Gould et al., 2016), I obtained measurements in my second-year writing courses for both Fall and Spring semesters: given our harsh winters, it seemed possible that environmental contexts (weather) could skew the data collection.

Human-Animal Studies: Empathy Across Species

In the 2014 academic year, I first explored mindfulness pedagogy in my Human-Animal Studies course for both Fall and Spring semesters, using only qualitative self-reporting gathered via written responses after mindfulness practices. Prompted by Daniel Goleman's work on *Emotional Intelligence* (1995), studies of human-animal relations (Kalof & Fitzgerald, 2007; Gruen, 2015) have noted the "logic of domination" (Warren, 1990) that keeps human-centrism in place, justifying the production, confinement, slaughter, and/or consumption of other animal species for human benefit through practices such as zoos, circuses, laboratories, industrial food production, breeding, the "skin trade" (fur and leather), pet-keeping, and more.

Aimed at augmenting the university's multidisciplinary offerings, Human-Animal Studies explores multispecies relationships between humans and therapy dogs, interspecies animal friendships, horse-racing, dog-fighting, and animals in science. Counting on the empathy that animal science students still had for other species, I wondered if mindfulness could serve as a pedagogy for staying present with empathy as we gradually shifted topics from therapy dogs to intensive animal agriculture.

Companioning research and ethical arguments that challenge the human-centric logic of domination, contemplative pedagogies cultivate mind-body awareness, creativity, interpersonal skills, and, most important for anti-oppression pedagogies, empathy (Barbezat & Bush, 2014; Zajonc, 2016)—the ability to imagine and resonate with the feelings and experiences of others, and to respond with compassion. To date, explorations of oppression and privilege appeal to the intellect, providing history, workplace statistics, environmental health research, and other data—but prejudice (i.e., anthropocentrism, white supremacy, toxic masculinity) operates on a cultural level, concealed in our emotional and physical bodies until we expose it through mindful awareness.

As a form of contemplative pedagogy, mindfulness practice can be a vital complement to critical reasoning, rebalancing liberal education to include head and heart, mind and body. It is "a technique that functions to increase awareness but is not itself a doctrine or ideology" (Orr, 2002, p. 494). My course objectives for Human-Animal Studies were to

- introduce mindfulness practice as a strategy for cultivating calm, focused attentiveness, and decreasing stress;
- facilitate greater awareness of body-based sensations and emotions, as distinguished from thoughts;
- encourage conversations connecting experiences of our human embodiment with the embodied experiences of other animal species; and
- cultivate awareness of trans-species empathy, investigating connections between empathy and action.

In *The Age of Empathy*, de Waal (2010) defines empathy as the capacity to be affected by and share the emotional state of another, assess the reasons for the other's state, and identify with the other, adopting their perspective.

In-Class Mindfulness Practices

To cultivate empathy and practice mindfulness, I gave instructions at the start of each class. After each five-minute practice, students wrote a reflection describing their embodied experiences: intellection, sensations, thoughts, emotions.

Mindfulness of Breath

For our first practice with mindfulness of the breath, I introduced the pedagogy as part of a research project on Mindfulness in Higher Education. As suggested in Berila (2014), I explained the benefits of mindfulness but also the reasons people might not want to participate: stored bodily memories of trauma of many kinds (war, domestic abuse, sexual violence) (Treleaven, 2018). I created an opening for people to leave at the end of the class's final 10 minutes if they wanted to, asking that they e-mail me afterward with more information.

After giving some instructions on sitting and watching the breath, I led a guided meditation inviting students to count the breaths up to five, and then begin again. At the end, I asked them to write about their experiences of mindfulness; when students seemed to have completed that reflection, I put up an image on the screen that might allow them to apply their mindfulness to seeing in new ways relevant to our course—"Wolf Kisses Man"—and asked them to write about their immediate response to the image. In reviewing these first-day writings, I saw a correlation between those who had difficulty with the mindfulness practice ("boring" or "couldn't focus") and those who had an aversive response to the wolf-man image ("gross" or "scary"). Those who responded with more curiosity about the image had some experience in mindfulness, either as a relaxation exercise before sleeping, or as a part of their yoga practice.

Mindfulness of Sounds

For the second practice, I invited students to listen to the bell as the sound fades away and then bring their attention to their ears to listen to whatever sounds arise. I advised them not to follow the sounds or try to control them. If they discovered themselves telling stories about the sound, diagnosing the sound, or creating an image that corresponds with the sound, to simply notice that, and then return to perceiving the sound simply as sound—near or far, loud or soft, internal or external. After the sitting, I asked them to listen to some sounds from Banksy's "Sirens of the Lambs" (2013) without offering information about the video production or its images, and to write about their responses. Most people described or named the sounds—"a dog's squeaky toy," or "the video I used in my paper." Only a few continued the mindfulness practice when the video image of the truck with the heads of stuffed animals peeking through slats in the truck, crying as the truck brought them through New York's meatpacking district to slaughter, remarking on how they responded to the Banksy video—"I found it annoying," etc.

Mindful Eating

Our third session was to follow a discussion of "Livestock's Long Shadow" (UNFAO, 2006). Arriving five minutes early to class, I announced that we would be doing eating meditation and asked that anyone who hadn't washed their hands recently to please exit and do so (half of the class did so). When we were all together, I explained we would practice mindfulness of eating, beginning with a few minutes of silent mindfulness, followed by a bell and instructions for eating.

The first few minutes were very silent. After ringing the bell, I gave instructions for passing around the bags of raisins and M&Ms, using the spoons by the handles only, and taking only four pieces. As people passed around the bags,

94 Greta Gaard

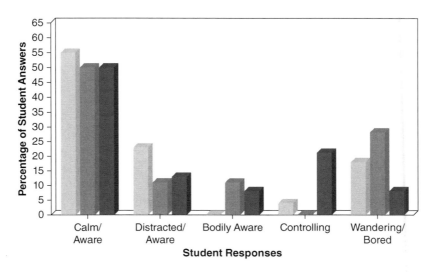

FIGURE 6.1 Responses to Mindfulness Practices 1 (breath), 2 (sounds), 3 (eating)

I asked those waiting to notice how they were feeling as they waited. We picked up one item, observed it, smelled it, then placed it in our mouths and noticed how it felt. I asked them to roll it around with their tongues and finally chew it. I waited a long time, then repeated the lesson with the second one. After that, I asked students to write about their experiences, curious if they would connect contemplative eating with the common cultural practice of eating other animal species. The class then shifted to discussing *Livestock's Long Shadow* (2006), with no overt connection made to the mindfulness practice.

Figure 6.1 depicts student responses for each of the first three practices, being mindful of (1) breath, (2) sounds, and (3) eating. These three awareness practices cultivated familiarity with mindfulness so that the fourth practice would measure not just proficiency with mindfulness but, rather, students' capacity to be mindful of bodily feelings and thoughts while watching a short documentary on pig farming in China (Yi, 2009). This embodied response to the suffering and violence inflicted on others can produce empathy—but would it do so for students socialized into human dominance, particularly through its various manifestations of hunting, trapping, and industrial animal farming common in rural Wisconsin culture?

Mindfulness of the Body

For our fourth mindfulness practice, we began class by reviewing student portfolios, summarizing the arguments of the past two weeks, and proposing a research paper topic with a list of key resources. Afterward, we watched 20 minutes of

"What's for Dinner?" a documentary about increased pork production in China from "Brighter Green" (Yi, 2009). As I watched the film, I noted my body was contracting, pulling away from the images of bloody meat, the overview of the slaughterhouse, the rough handling of the pigs, their confinement, their eyes, the way the pigs were shoved into a crate two by two, their ears unceremoniously pierced with a tag/number, then pulled by their ears and tails onto the truck bed for slaughter. Noting my body contorting in empathic identification, I decided to offer a spontaneous writing opportunity.

With ten minutes left of class, I stopped the film and asked students to take out a piece of paper and fold it in half vertically. On the left side, I asked them to write down a list of all the bodily sensations, movements, feelings they had noticed while watching the film. I gave them five minutes to do this. After five minutes, I asked students to write on the right column their mental narratives or responses to the film as they were watching it. If these mental narratives corresponded to the bodily sensations, they were to write the mental narrative next to the bodily sensation. If the mental narratives were something else, these were to be put lower down. Every student who watched the film had a physical response of pulling away, cringing, squirming, not wanting to look, trying to avoid, feeling disgusted, or "checked out" when the images were too disturbing (see Figure 6.2). These physical responses are manifestations empathy in the body, but there was also the inability to empathize with extreme suffering, as indicated by intellectual defenses such as "Is this film dated?" and "American farming is much different."

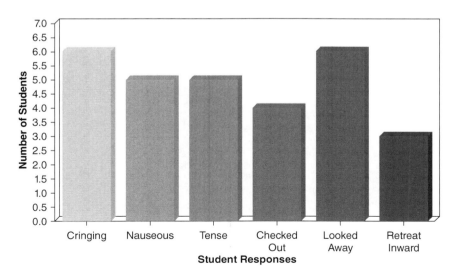

FIGURE 6.2 Mindfulness reflection on pig farming

Students reported strong emotional responses to the pig farming documentary:

- Of the total, 55% reported feelings of empathy ("cringing," "nauseous," "tense").
- Of the total, 45% reported a kind of inverse empathy or avoidant coping through their inability to be present to the suffering of others ("checked out," "looked away," "retreated inward").

I was curious about whether this awareness of others' experiences would lead students to wish an end of suffering, compassion, for other beings when we practiced loving-kindness.

Loving-Kindness

For this first practice of multispecies loving-kindness, we simply practiced the steps for loving kindness to humans. In the class period before the practice, I had asked students to write about a time when they had "broken the species barrier" between themselves and another animal, and experienced a kind of connection, understanding, or communication. They had kept these rush-writing pieces and then used them to write their reflections on the back after the loving-kindness meditation. We followed the traditional sequence of practicing first for a human or multispecies benefactor, then oneself, a dear human/multispecies friend, a neutral being, and a difficult being. For the second loving-kindness practice, we observed two student presentations on canned hunts and on the devastating assaults against elephants. We then began our loving-kindness practice with an invitation to think about the animals we had just viewed and focus their practice on other species.

While some students used the prompt of "a difficult animal" to think of snakes or mosquitoes and experienced aversion, most reflections showed how very hard it is for these students to relax the barriers or differences between themselves and an other of any species (see Figure 6.3). Their brief experience with mindfulness practice was not yet sufficient for cultivating multispecies empathy. Preston and de Waal's (2001) distinction between empathy and emotional contagion may offer one explanation:

- *Emotional contagion* lacks the self/other distinction; the subject experiences distress, vicarious emotion, or emotional transfer.
- *Empathy* maintains a self/other distinction; cognitive empathy accurately perceives the situation or predicament of the other and is capable of prosocial behaviors (actions taken to reduce the distress of another).

Following these distinctions of human self-identity, if student responses to the pig farming documentary or the images of slaughtered elephants and lions shot in

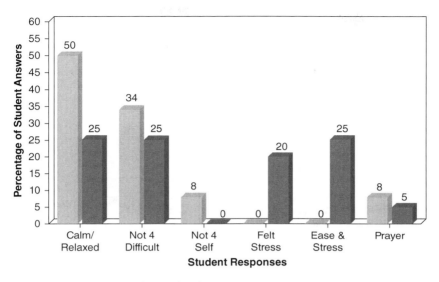

FIGURE 6.3 Responses to loving-kindness practice

canned hunts were those of *emotional contagion* rather than *empathy*, then the only way to end suffering is to move away from it—increasing the distance between self and other. An established selfhood capable of empathy—what Gruen (2015) calls "entangled empathy"—recognizes both difference and continuity of self-identity (i.e., a more Buddhist perspective of *interbeing*) and provides a ground for both compassion and action to end the other's suffering. More frequent mindfulness practice—particularly in offering loving-kindness to the difficult parts of oneself, which then serves as a foundation for offering loving-kindness to others—may help these students cultivate trans-species empathy. To safeguard future students in loving-kindness practices, I decided to integrate self-compassion into my next exploration of contemplative pedagogies.

Advanced Writing: Mindful of Stress, Self-Compassion, and Creativity

Students who enroll in Advanced Writing are majoring in fields such as English literature, English education, and creative or technical writing. Frequently earning high scores in their first- and second-year Composition classes, these students still have room to grow in their writing skills. Because this course is a regular component of my teaching, I was familiar with students' common barriers to writing: the self-judgment and procrastination, the stress of balancing coursework with wage-earning jobs, and the barriers to connecting with their own creativity. I scaffolded a variety of contemplative practices, linked to the

TABLE 6.1 Mindfulness Practices in Advanced Composition

Week	Mindfulness Practice	Course Content
1	Breath awareness	Course introduction, meeting peers
2	Breath and body scan	A 500-word rough draft and peer review on "Why I Write."
3	Listening	Prose analysis of meter and style Peer conferences
4 & 5	Loving-kindness	Introduction: "Biographical Essay"
6	Gratitude	Essay draft and peer reviews
7	Compassion and movement	Introduction: "Visual Argument" essay
8	Self-soothing	Identifying the topic & viewpoints
9	Self-compassion	Developing argument organizations
10	Mindful walking	Intro.: "Environmental Writing" essay
11	Mindfulness of our good qualities	Style analysis and practice
12	Listening: Giving and receiving Compassion	Style analysis Peer reviews
13	Mindful of tastes, body scan	Introduction: "Critical Reviews" Student-led workshops
14	Listening: Gratitude	Final papers, course conclusion

course topics and the skill development over the semester. To measure outcomes of our practice, I invited qualitative writing responses post-mindfulness practice, and gathered pre- and post-course measurements of stress and empathy using the Perceived Stress Scale (Cohen et al., 1983) and the Toronto Empathy Questionnaire (Spreng et al., 2009).

After introducing mindfulness practice as an integral but optional part of our writing class and discussing what nonparticipation could look like—from "invisible" nonparticipation, such as staying in class but shifting one's thoughts to ordinary activities such as doing laundry or grocery shopping, to active nonparticipation in leaving the classroom during practice—we began with breath mindfulness, and later included breath and body-scan mindfulness. Already in week two, the majority of students' reflections reported feeling calmer and more relaxed, yet alert, focused, and ready to learn. A few students became more aware of difficult feelings they were trying to avoid. One reported an awareness and phobia of "bodily things flowing"—blood, breath, heart. Two students came to my office to discuss anxiety, depression, suicidal ideation, or difficult family circumstances—an affirmation of the fact that mindfulness involves turning awareness toward our whole selves, including those parts that are more difficult. For each student, I spent a good hour listening and affirming the student, as well as linking them to campus resources, including the Counseling Center.

Mindfulness Practices

Mindful Listening

To support students in their first peer review and rough draft feedback session, I introduced a practice of mindful listening: a body-based music of summer rain. To start the practice, we listened for one minute to the ambient sounds in the room, and then I divided the class into three groups, inviting students to follow my lead in creating body-music of an escalating and subsiding thunderstorm. We began with rubbing hands together to create the "ssh" of light rain, then finger-snapping for light rain, slow clapping for the heavier raindrops, followed by thigh-slapping, adding stomping for the full pounding rainstorm, and then moving backwards through the sounds back to the "ssh" and then silence. This exercise of embodying ecological sounds is not universally exuberant (in fact, nothing is so, as one discovers in contemplative pedagogies): one student spoke to me after class about nonparticipation for the entire set of class practices but later decided to choose participation on a case-by-case basis. In one listening practice, we began with the sounds of ocean waves piped through the computer to the room's audio system; these waves were then used like a mindfulness bell during peer reviews, prompting a mindful pause to bring people to their bodies and to their own intentions for listening to one another.

Loving-Kindness

We began with a benefactor or dear friend and used this practice as grounding for beginning the Biographical Essay with intentions of kindness toward someone who might become the subject for their essays. Student reflections reported feeling grateful, calm, centered; some focused the meditation on their family, partners, and even the other class members. When our mindfulness turned toward the benefactor also wishing us happiness and ease, students reported feeling calm, grateful, and "good about myself." As the research predicts (Germer, 2009; Neff, 2011), it's often easier to feel compassion for a good friend than it is to befriend oneself with compassion.

Gratitude and Listening

These practices joined in the Biographical Essay unit, on the day we prepared to discuss Alice Walker's (1983) biographical sketch of her mother, *In Search of Our Mothers' Gardens*. Our contemplative practice began by watching Nikky Finney's acceptance speech for the 2011 National Book Award in Poetry, a two-part speech that begins with the 1739 South Carolina slave codes forbidding the teaching and learning of literacy for slaves and calls those ancestors into the room where the award is being given. It describes Finney's promise to her "girl-poet-self" that if her name were ever called out, she would "call out their names too." The second part of the speech names Finney's benefactors during her lifetime: parents, teachers, friends, mentors. For our contemplative practice, I asked students to listen carefully, and then to write what they had heard Finney say; next, I asked them to make connections between Finney's racial embodiment and experiences of literacy and inheritance, and their own; finally, I asked students to reflect on the connections between Finney's speech and Walker's essay. Their responses ran the gamut from white liberalism, individualism, and tolerance to solidarity and appreciation of the way both Finney and Walker trace their present achievements back to the fierce resistance of enslaved, raped, whipped, overworked, dismembered, and drowned ancestors who fought to learn, to write, and to be free. As one student reflected, the connection between Walker's essay and Finney's speech is "how people had to suffer greatly so that the road could be paved for someone to be in her honorary position, for her to be able to live her dreams and be accepted for them." Another student interpreted Finney's speech as

> one massive *thank you* to all those who had suffered or sacrificed themselves in the past in order to bring about the literary freedom she has today. . . . These people of the past (and those already in her life) are the reason for her success.

Contemplative listening practice that paired a speech and an essay by two Black women writers gave students context for exploring their own racialized assumptions about identity and individualism and to consider their biographical subjects in larger webs of relationship and racial history.

Walking Meditation

This practice was introduced for the environmental essay, as many students associate environments with outdoor activities involving walks, and this practice facilitates a greater sense of embodiment and mindful movement. Student reports noted that the practice helped in "paying attention to my body" and "getting out of my head"; some felt their bodies "moved like a wave" rocking backward and forward with each step, and many paid attention to the "soles of the feet" as well as the leg muscles and rolling hips that make walking possible. Some students experienced walking meditation as their "favorite mindfulness activity"—"it felt good to move without purpose, without the weight of my backpack, without a destination"—while others noticed how they "hurried to get to the end and turn around" even though they were simply pacing a lane, and recognized how that behavior shows up in other parts of their lives. This practice gave us ground for discussing embodiment and environments, and how to write about these intersections in their essays.

Quantitative Measures

To companion student reflections and other qualitative self-reports after mindfulness practices, I used both the Perceived Stress Scale (PSS-10) and the Toronto Empathy Questionnaire (TEQ-16) to obtain pre- and post-course measurements of the mental states and affects to investigate how mindfulness practices would influence stress and empathy. I hypothesized lowered stress, due to more effective stress management skills, and increased empathy, due to practices of loving-kindness, gratitude, and compassion (Cohen et al., 1983; Spreng et al., 2009; Neff, 2003). But it appeared that the contexts of obtaining a pre-test at the end of summer vacation and a post-test in the week before final exams might have had an influence on the outcomes, hence, the value of repeating the practice in different semesters for comparison.

The PSS-10 includes 10 items, scored on a scale of 0 ("never") to 4 ("very often"): thus, a student's total score can range from 0 to 40, with higher scores indicating higher perceived stress. Low (0–14), moderate (15–27), and high stress (28–40) scores were tabulated for both pre- and post-course outcomes. Because minimal clinically important differences (MCID) for the PSS-10 have not been established, the best approach is to consider how many students reported reduced, increased, or consistent levels of perceived stress. To view the data in light of gender socialization, student responses are coded as (F) for female and (M) for male. As Figure 6.4 shows, only 2 students (F3, F5) reported the same levels of perceived stress both at the start and the conclusion of the course; 7 students (F1, F2, F4, F8, F10, F12, M2) reported lowered levels of perceived stress at the end of the course, and 12 students reported moderate (1- to 4-point increase) to significantly higher (16 points) levels of perceived stress, with three students (F6, F20, M1) moving from ranges of moderate to high levels and one student (F9) shifting from low to high levels of perceived stress.

Students with high levels of perceived stress (F6, M1, F9, F20) were sent follow-up notes alerting them that their scores indicated self-care and a visit to the Counseling Center would be important in their well-being and potentially

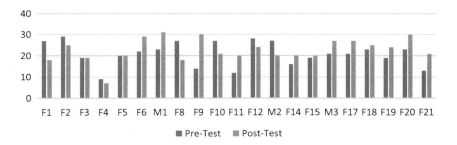

FIGURE 6.4 Perceived stress scale pre- and post-test scores

FIGURE 6.5 Toronto Empathy Questionnaire pre- and post-test scores

important in their ability to perform well on their final exams. With 9 students maintaining or decreasing their perceived stress by the semester's end, and 12 students increasing in perceived stress, it's difficult to link these shifts to our once-weekly mindfulness practices, when multiple factors outside of our classroom affect students' overall perceived levels of stress. Instead, the qualitative self-reporting after each of the practices seems more reliable, as does the research suggesting that daily mindfulness practices will have more lasting effects than a once-weekly practice.

The second measure used was the Toronto Empathy Questionnaire (TEQ), a 16-question measurement offering statements for agreement/disagreement on a zero- to four-point scale ranging from "never" to "always," with eight straightforward statements about empathy and eight statements lacking in empathy that are reverse-scored in the tallies. In Figure 6.5, total points range from 0 to 64, with males' empathy score averaging from 43.46 to 44.45 and females tending to score between 44.62 and 48.93. Such gender differences are reported as being moderate (Spreng et al., 2009).

In fact, these gendered generalities did not hold for our class, as all Writing students had empathy scores exceeding expectations: the three male students' scores averaged 47.66 for the pre-test and 49 for the post-test, and the 18 female students scored on average 51.33 for the pre-test and 51.38 for the post-test, suggesting that the mindfulness practices more significantly affect the empathy experienced by males. Due to the small sample size, I chose to use only descriptive statistics. Once again, the weekly practices and their immediate effects need more consistent, daily reinforcement to cultivate the equanimity and compassion that contemplative practices can offer.

Reading, Writing, and the Disciplines: "Sustainable Happiness" in Second-Year Writing

Recalling my experiences with students outside of the College of Arts and Sciences at this particular university, I chose for my final contemplative research project the second-year Writing course that is part of a General Education requirement for all undergraduates at the university. Apart from three standard course objectives, the course content and readings are left to the instructors. Accordingly, I chose what the Dalai Lama, Thich Nhat Hanh, and others have called the deepest purpose of the Dharma—happiness—and envisioned it as "Sustainable Happiness," a social, environmental, and economic concept (the three branches of sustainability) and an outcome of what Thich Nhat Hanh calls our *Interbeing*, variously termed "no-self" (*anatta*) or in today's vernacular, "no separate self." My course theme was well suited to the four written rhetorical assignments and the research, critical thinking, and persuasive argument that both the English Department and the University required; moreover, this theme could present timeless Dharma concepts through a secular framework.

For resources, I began with the positive psychology course syllabus my co-editor Bengü Ergüner-Tekinalp had developed, and utilized the 12 happiness practices developed by Sonja Lyubomirsky (2010) along with her co-authored *Positively Happy* (Lyubomirsky & Kurtz, 2013) workbook. In the opening module for essay one, "Defining the Anthropocene," I companioned selections from our standard second-year Composition reader (Seyler, 2015) with short online articles about youth-led climate activism, the science of extinctions and of climate change (Hawken et al., 2017), reports on "The New Happiness Studies" (Kafka, 2018) and critiques of the U.S. neoliberal economy (Stiglitz, 2018). This unit introduced tools of author analysis (standpoint, rhetorical appeals, audience), organization, and the features of reliable sources. To fortify students for exploring these difficult issues, I invited students to offer their own theories about how to increase their own happiness.

Unlike other semesters, in Spring 2020, I was assigned two sections of the same writing course enrolling 22 students per course, allowing me to compare outcomes across these two courses for the fidelity of implementation (Gould et al., 2016). Students in both sections listed ways they thought their happiness could be increased, and just as Lyubomirsky predicts, most people focus on tangible objects rather than the actual practices of nourishing connection with self and others—practices of *interbeing*—that support lasting happiness. Table 6.2 shows the baseline of practices that students already had in alignment with Lyubomirsky's happiness practices (shown in italics) versus those that focused on acquiring objects or specific circumstances. Clearly, some students already had developed non-material happiness practices such as gratitude, avoiding overthinking, nurturing relationships, practicing enjoyable activities, committing to goals, developing coping strategies, and taking care of their bodies. No students mentioned forgiveness, savoring life's joys, cultivating optimism, or practicing random acts of kindness; only one student across both classes listed spirituality. Because the exercise held an open door for students to generate their own happiness practices, rather than listing Lyubomirsky's 12 practices and thereby restricting the students' responses, statistics for this baseline of happiness practices are not available.

104 Greta Gaard

TABLE 6.2 Student Views of Happiness vs. Lyubomirsky's Happiness Practices

Students' Views on Ways to Increase Happiness		Lyubomirsky's 12 Happiness Practices
(200: 23)	(200: 24)	
• Buying things that make you feel good • *Being grateful* • Steady income	• Being healthier • Being prepared for every day • Getting a good job	1. Gratitude 2. Cultivating optimism
• A new 2020 Ford F150 Platinum	• *Not fearing judgment from others*	3. Avoiding overthinking and social comparison
• More $ at work • No student loans	• Better living situation	4. Practicing random acts of kindness
• *Time with friends* • *Family close by* • *My mother's happiness* • *Being creative* • *Time to relax and reflect*	• *Time with family* • *Family and friend time* • *Finding love* • More time, less stress • *Doing things I enjoy*	5. Nurturing relationships 6. Doing more activities that truly engage you
• Seeing the big picture	• Thinking about my family / friends	7. Replaying and savoring life's joys
• *Opening my own business* • *Traveling* • *Sleep as much as I need!*	• *Getting good grades* • *A steady job, good salary* • *Paying off bills/loans* • Being prepared each day for class • *Stop worrying*	8. Committing to your goals 9. Developing strategies for coping
• Warm weather	• Summer	10. Learning to forgive
• Being in nature • More land • More time with animals • Faith-filled community	• Having my dog at college	11. Practicing religion and spirituality
• *Exercising more often* • *Losing weight*	• *Getting good sleep* • Being healthy	12. Taking care of your body

Each of the 12 practices was taught for a week in the 14-week semester. To incentivize participation, all 12 happiness practices had small points-earning capacities so that together these practices could boost student grades by half a point, based not on their content but simply on their completion. The first few weeks were spent linking the first module's themes with the practices of gratitude and optimism—not obvious linkages with climate change or the sixth extinction, but clearly linked to happiness (Noland et al., 2017).

Learning from past courses using contemplative practices only once a week, in this class I linked each week's happiness practice to discussions or practices throughout the week. For gratitude, I began by inviting students to list things in their lives they are grateful for. For each class, I compiled a one-page handout listing all the items they had named and returned it to them during the next class period. Students noted the range of gratitude, from family to favorite pens, and I advised them to keep this collective Gratitude List posted by their computer workstations at home, so that when they felt low energy or lack of motivation, they could review the list and remember the many ways they could build the skill of shifting their awareness to the good things in their lives (Table 6.3). Their final practice that week was to write and send a Gratitude Letter to someone they had never thanked or hadn't thanked recently; their assignment was to report "how it went" when they sent the letter, whether they learned how the letter affected the recipient, and in turn, how that response affected them—all in terms of happiness.

For the optimism practice the following week, students wrote a description of their "best possible selves" (Meevissen et al., 2011) ten years in the future, and afterward were invited to add how that vision of their future selves could be used to energize or motivate their current outlook on life as it is for them right now. As predicted, students reported enjoying these practices and experiencing positive outcomes.

The second module introduced skills for researching diverse and reliable standpoints on a course topic of students' own choosing, reporting but not arguing for a specific standpoint. Along with readings on climate refugees, a climate change food calculator, redefining Gross Domestic Product (GDP), and a time

TABLE 6.3 Student Gratitude Lists

Clean Water	Winter Jacket and Boots	My Car	SUN! SUN!
Healthy food	Hot showers	Extension cords	Music
Family love	Healthy, able body	Soap	Cheese
Chocolate	Good education	My dog!	Heat
Health insurance	Cell phone	Teammates, roommates, friends	My determination
Coffee! Coffee!	My boyfriend / girlfriend	Theater!!	The outdoors
Toothbrushes	Good friends	Intuition	Music
Animals. All of them.	Corrective lenses (glasses, contacts)	Ice cream	Living in the Midwest
Laughter	Ice skates	Windows	My faith

management calculator, this longer module explored five weekly happiness skills of releasing rumination, performing acts of kindness, nurturing social relationships, being in "flow" states, and taking care of your body. To support the weekly introduction, practice, and reflection for these happiness skills, I created a one-page handout for each that compressed analyses from Lyubomirsky's book, my online research, and a practice from Lybomirsky and Kurtz's workbook (see the sample at the end of this chapter). We also started reading selections from the *World Happiness Report* (WHR) (Helliwell et al., 2019) described as "a landmark survey of the state of global happiness that ranks 156 countries by how happy their citizens perceive themselves to be." The report focuses on happiness and community, and students read "Happiness & Community" (chapter 1) and "Changing World Happiness" (chapter 2). Toward the end of this unit, we read about the Cantril Ladder (Cantril, 1965) measuring one's sense of happiness as a ladder with rungs on a scale of one to ten, and students used a worksheet to place themselves on that ladder, now and in the future. Almost without exception, students saw their past happiness as less than their present happiness and their future happiness greater than the present.

Building on the foundations of the first two essays, the third paper was a researched argument, inviting students to go full force and identify an audience that could be persuaded to change their views on some aspect of climate change, economics, species extinctions, and happiness. The alleged "money = happiness" connection was challenged by readings about Bhutan's Gross National Happiness, Hayes (2014) "The New Abolitionism" linking the profitability of slavery with fossil-fueled capitalism, and chapters 5 and 7 from *WHR* 2019, "Happiness in the U.S." and "Addiction and Unhappiness in the U.S." In the span of a 14-week semester, this third quarter is always the most challenging, so I had planned the four happiness practices of savoring life's joys, committing to one's goals, cultivating healthy coping strategies, and practicing forgiveness in this third segment.

The students' fourth rhetorical assignment was to "create a five-minute PowerPoint presentation reviewing a documentary film of their own choosing, outlining a problem of sustainable happiness and exploring its solution." Their PowerPoint was to explore the film's viewpoint, evidence-based argument, and target audience, as well as any challenges to the argument that the student could raise. In this final module, we explored happiness practices of cultivating one's own spirituality and revisited taking care of your body and practicing forgiveness (always relevant at the end of the term, when students and professors alike compare their initial goals with their actual achievements over the semester).

Quantitative Measures

At the course conclusion, I used SurveyMonkey to gain information on the students' views of the 12 happiness practices. Most important was the final question: "Which happiness practices will best help you cope with the climate changes you

Mindfulness and Sustainable Happiness **107**

will experience in your lifetime?" Figure 6.6 provides tabulations of the responses for each class: in section 24, the response rate was 50% (11 out of 22), with the practice of remembering and savoring life's joys earning the status of most popular practice (81.82%), followed by developing coping strategies for stress (63.64%), and a tie between taking care of one's body and practicing acts of kindness (45.45% each); practicing gratitude and religion/spirituality were tied at 36.36%.

Section 23 had a response rate of 67% (16 out of 22), with the top-scoring happiness practices of avoiding overthinking and social comparison, along with practicing acts of kindness both gaining 68.75% responses, followed by a tie

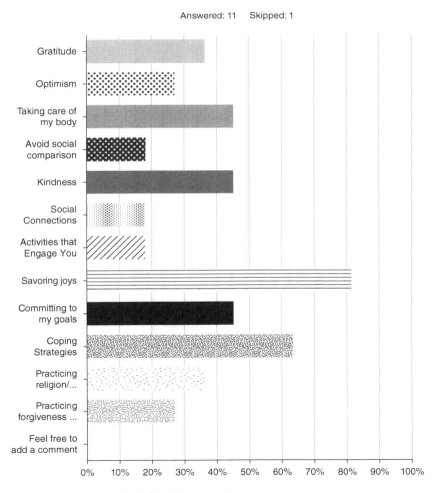

FIGURE 6.6 ENGL 200: 24 happiness practices outcomes

108 Greta Gaard

between remembering and savoring life's joys, and taking care of one's body (62.5%); practicing optimism (56.25%) and gratitude (50%) came next (see Figure 6.7). Comparing these choices with the happiness free-form lists, it seems students prioritized those practices that were newest to them. Chödrön (2000) especially talks about the eight worldly dharmas of pleasure/pain, praise/blame, fame/ill repute, gain/loss; in contrast, the happiness practices are stabilizing, as avoiding social comparison disarms the praise/blame dualism, and practicing acts of kindness disarms gain/loss through generosity and an affirmation of interbeing (i.e., your happiness is not separate from mine; increasing your happiness also increases my happiness). Students in both courses favored savoring life's joys, a

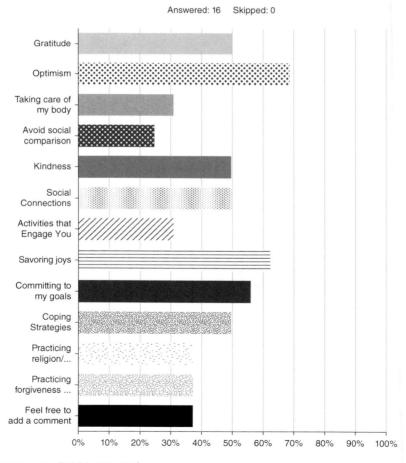

FIGURE 6.7 ENGL 200: 23 happiness practices outcomes

strategy that is useful in creating space between experiences of pleasure/pain or fame/ill repute for the ways that savoring joy also recalls one's goodness.

Conclusions

Through each of these courses, I learned as much about teaching contemplative pedagogies as my students learned from practicing these pedagogies. I continue to teach the Human-Animal Studies course with more attention to "living the questions" and supporting students in working out the multispecies ethics that can reinforce or dismantle oppression of all animals, for humans have animal bodies, though Cartesian dualisms would have us believe otherwise. My Advanced Writing students continue to adapt most easily to contemplative pedagogies, not entirely attributable to my good teaching but to the fact that Writing and Literary Studies are gendered fields, and women more than men tend to benefit from mindfulness and college-based contemplative practices (Furlan Stante, 2016; Neff, 2021; Rojiani et al., 2017). My Sustainable Happiness course also continues to teach happiness practices of interbeing, culminating in the final question: *Which happiness practices will best help you and your community cope with the climate changes you will experience in your lifetime?*

In each of these courses, contemplative pedagogy functions as an anti-oppressive pedagogy: by teaching empathy, the illusion of speciesism, and the not-separate selves of humans from diverse humans as well as from other plant and animal species; teaching advanced writers to turn towards their inner critics with curiosity and compassion; and teaching second-year students the arts of Sustainable Happiness that cultivate intentionality and care for oneself, one's body, and promote the co-arising happiness of selves-and-others that undermines the disconnection, competition, scarcity, and grasping of white patriarchal capitalist colonialism, a system profiting only by making Hungry Ghosts out of us all.

Happiness Strategy #7: Savoring Life's Joys

The benefit of this activity is that it plays right into the "HOW" of positive emotions. You are always noticing and becoming more aware of things that give you a jolt of positive emotions: beauty, love, empathy, and so on.

It also helps us as "stress-out-and-way-too-busy-people" to live in the moment. You can't savor something "in passing." You have to stop and take that moment out of life and fully engage in the savoring. This is practically the definition of "living in the moment".

Here are some ways you can try this activity for yourself:

- *Relish the Ordinary*—take the time to savor something you usually rush through or ignore. Often it's a meal, someone's smile, a hot bath, or walking to work. When you've chosen your ordinary activity, really get into that moment and make the pleasure from it last as long as possible.
- *Practice With Others*—make others a part of your savoring. Enjoy a cup of good tea or coffee, walk through a garden, whatever works for you and your friends, but remember, the point is to be fully in that moment, not just talking about "life" as you ignore the beauty of the rain or the trees.
- *Get Nostalgic*—with friends or family or on your own. Remember a particularly good or happy moment in life and take the time to savor it and *relive the happiness* you got out of it.
- *Use Imagination*—transport yourself to another time and place, or simply an image of something you admire: a beautiful mountain vista from that trip to the Rockies, a summer lake at sunset, whatever works.
- *Happy Days*—when you have a particularly good day, keep it in mind as something you can always savor later, if times are difficult.
- *Celebrate*—whether it is good news or getting a big project done at work. Far too often we do not take the time to celebrate our own accomplishments, large or small—instead, we start on the next thing right away. Take the time to STOP and savor this moment of achievement. Let it soak in and let it lift you up. If you keep doing this you'll really start to look forward to these little "self-celebrations" for completing almost anything.
- *Take a Sense-and-Savor Walk*—linger on the smells and sights—you can savor for just 10 minutes and it will make an impression. On my walk today, I noticed the beauty of the rain on the river as I crossed a bridge. I almost kept going, but instead I took the moment to stop and revel in the everyday beauty of nature.

Be open to any experience of beauty or excellence, build awareness of these things, and then take the time to savor them.

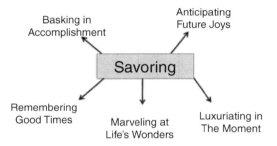

Assignment: What two savoring strategies will you use this weekend? Describe them! What were your results?

References

Banksy. (2013, October 13). *Banksy's 'Sirens of the Lambs' Sees Cuddly Toys Taken for Slaughter—Video.* https://www.theguardian.com/artanddesign/video/2013/oct/13/banksy-sirens-of-the-lambs-cuddly-toys-slaughter-video.

Barbezat, D. P., & Bush, M. (Eds.). (2014). *Contemplative Practices in Higher Education.* Jossey-Bass.

Berila, B. (2014). Contemplating the Effects of Oppression: Integrating Mindfulness into Diversity Classrooms. *The Journal of Contemplative Inquiry*, 1(1), 55–68.

Cantril, H. (1965). *The Pattern of Human Concerns.* Rutgers University Press.

Chödrön, P. (2000). *When Things Fall Apart: Heart Advice for Difficult Times.* Shambhala Pubs.

Cohen, S., Kamarck, T., & Mermelstein, R. (1983). A Global Measure of Perceived Stress. *Journal of Health and Social Behavior*, 24, 386–396.

de Waal, F. (2010). *The Age of Empathy: Nature's Lessons for a Kinder Society.* Broadway Books.

Finney, N. (2011). *National Book Awards Acceptance Speech for Poetry*. https://www.giarts.org/article/national-book-awards-acceptance-speech-poetry.
Food and Agriculture Organization of the United Nations. (2006). *Livestock's Long Shadow: Environmental Issues and Options*. United Nations Pubs.
Furlan Stante, N. (2016). Mindfulness as a Path of Women's Empowerment. *Asian Studies*, IV(XX), 2, 109–120.
Germer, C. (2009). *The Mindful Path to Self-Compassion*. Guilford Press.
Goleman, D. (1995). *Emotional Intelligence*. Bantam Books.
Gould, L. F., Dariotis, J. K., Greenberg, M. T., & Mendelson, T. (2016). Assessing Fidelity of Implementation (FOI) for School-Based Mindfulness and Yoga Interventions: A Systematic Review. *Mindfulness (N.Y.)*, 7(1), 5–33.
Gruen, L. (2015). *Entangled Empathy: An Alternative Ethic for Our Relationships with Animals*. Lantern Books.
Hawken, P., et al. (2017). *Drawdown: The Most Comprehensive Plan Ever Proposed to Reverse Global Warming*. Penguin Books.
Hayes, C. (2014, April 22). The New Abolitionism. *The Nation*. https://www.thenation.com/article/archive/new-abolitionism/.
Helliwell, J. F., Layard, R., & Sachs, J. D. (2019). *World Happiness Report 2019*. Retrieved June 4, 2021, from https://worldhappiness.report/ed/2019/.
Kafka, A. (2018, July 25). The New Happiness Studies. *Chronicle of Higher Education*. https://www.chronicle.com/article/the-new-happiness-studies/.
Kalof, L., & Fitzgerald, A. (Eds.). (2007). *The Animals Reader*. Berg Publishers.
Lyubomirsky, S. (2010). *The How of Happiness*. Little Brown/Piatkus.
Lyubomirsky, S., & Kurtz, J. (2013). *Positively Happy: Routes to Sustainable Happiness*. CreateSpace Independent Publishing Platform.
Meevissen, Y., Alberts, H., & Peters, M. (2011). Become More Optimistic by Imagining a Best Possible Self: Effects of a Two-Week Intervention. *Journal of Behavior Therapy and Experimental Psychiatry*, 42, 371–378.
Neff, K. (2003). Development and Validation of a Scale to Measure Self-Compassion. *Self and Identity*, 2, 223–250.
Neff, K. (2021). *Fierce Self-Compassion: How Women Can Harness Kindness to Speak Up, Claim their Power, and Thrive*. Harper Wave.
Noland, C. M., Talgar, C., Speed-Wiley, J., & Depue, J. (2017). Practicing Contemplative Gratitude in University Classrooms: Student Learning and Happiness Outcomes. *Journal of Contemplative Inquiry*, 4(1), 87–105.
O'Brien, C. (2016). *Education for Sustainable Happiness and Well-Being*. Routledge.
Orr, D. (2002). The Uses of Mindfulness in Anti-Oppressive Pedagogies: Philosophy and Praxis. *Canadian Journal of Education*, 27(4), 477–490.
Preston, S. D., & de Waal, F. B. M. (2001). *Empathy: Its Ultimate and Proximate Bases*. http://cogprints.org/1042/1/preston_de_waal.html.
Rojiani, R., Santoyo, J. F., Rahrig, H., Roth, H. D., & Britton, W. B. (2017). Women Benefit More Than Men in Response to College-based Meditation Training. *Frontiers in psychology*, 8, 551. https://doi.org/10.3389/fpsyg.2017.00551.
Seyler, D. (2015). *Read, Reason, Write: An Argument Text and Reader* (11th ed.). McGraw-Hill Education.
Spreng, R. N., McKinnon, M. C., Mar, R. A., & Levine, B. (2009). The Toronto Empathy Questionnaire. *Journal of Personality Assessment*, 91(1), 62–71.

Stiglitz, J. E. (2018). The American Economy is Rigged—And What We Can Do About it. *Scientific American*. https://www.scientificamerican.com/article/the-american-economy-is-rigged/.

Treleaven, D. A. (2018). *Trauma-Sensitive Mindfulness: Practices for Safe and Transformative Healing*. W. W. Norton & Co.

UWRF Quick Facts. (2019, Fall). Retrieved May 19, 2021, from https://www.uwrf.edu/Research/upload/UWRF-Quick-Facts-Fall-2019.pdf.

van Gelder, S. (2014). *Sustainable Happiness: Live Simply, Live Well, Make a Difference*. Berrett-Koehler Publishers, Inc. and YES! Magazine.

Walker, A. (1983). *In Search of Our Mother's Gardens: Womanist Prose*. Harcourt Brace Jovanovich.

Warren, K. (1990). The Power and The Promise of Ecological Feminism. *Environmental Ethics* 12(2), 125–146.

Yi, Jian. (2009). *What's for Dinner?* Brighter Green, prod. Icarus Films, dist.

Zajonc, A. (2016). Contemplation in Education. In K. A. Schonert-Reichl & R. W. Roeser (Eds.), *Handbook of Mindfulness in Education* (pp. 17–28). Springer.

PART III

Contemplative Pedagogies Across the Disciplines

7
INNER TRACKING
A Reflective Practice for Transformative Learning

David J. Voelker

Integrating anti-oppression work into higher education demands that we go far beyond the mere transmission of knowledge. If we seek to change how students see and understand the world and their place in it—a shift necessary for anti-oppression—we need to realize the potential for learning to affect students deeply and on multiple levels. Berila (2016) states this point strongly:

> Creating a more just society requires institutional and collective change, but it also requires the individual work of unlearning the messages internalized in an oppressive society and relearning more compassionate ways of being with ourselves and others. That work cannot be done at a merely analytical level. It MUST be done at the level of our hearts, bodies, and our minds.
>
> (p. 22)

To be sure, a transformation of this order is a long game, and teachers must also be committed to transforming themselves. This is not the work of a single course or a semester, yet the work must begin somewhere, and integrating reflective practices into the regular learning process of a course is one place to start.

The Roots of Inner Tracking

In that spirit, I developed an inner tracking mindfulness practice to help students integrate their affective lives and evolving identities with their learning. Inner Tracking guides students through the process of "paying attention on purpose, non-judgmentally" (Kabat-Zinn, 2005, p. 104) to their experiences as learners.

DOI: 10.4324/9781003201854-10

The initial inspiration for Inner Tracking came from the nature-connection movement, especially the work of Young (2015), who writes:

> When we apply our tracking skills on the inner landscape, and we search for our inner light, we learn some of the most important lessons of our lives. We can learn to understand the ecological conditions of our inner landscape and understand what feeds our inner fire so that it burns bright.
>
> (p. 2)

My implementation of Inner Tracking is distinct from Young's, though it shares a sense of connecting with one's purpose within the larger human and natural communities. Crucially, Young attributes this practice to "traditional people worldwide," and he specifically cites Mohawk elder Jake Swamp as one source for this process (Young, 2015, p. 1).

As I developed an inner tracking practice for use in courses, I realized that the "spiral journey" of the Work That Reconnects (WTR) could provide an organizational framework rooted in principles of interconnectedness. Joanna Macy, the root teacher of WTR, has worked with many collaborators over several decades to bring a deep ecology framework to bear on personal and social transformation (Macy & Brown, 2014). The four-part spiral offers a series of practices to support the (re)creation of a "life-sustaining world" (Macy & Brown, 2014, p. 3) that honors our interconnectedness with other humans and with all life on Earth and seeks to "transform the foundations of our common life" (p. 9) by addressing the misguided beliefs and structures that generate warfare, inequality, and ecological degradation. Macy and Brown identify "the deadening of heart and mind" as "the greatest danger" (p. 19) and barrier in the way of transformation; by repressing pain, "we cut the feedback loop and block effective response" to the critical challenges of our time (p. 22). There is ample evidence, for example, that white Americans have frequently denied, minimized, and turned away from the pain suffered by African Americans, First Nations people, and other people of color because of systemic racism. Likewise, the realities of human-caused climate disruption (Ray, 2020) and the sixth great extinction (Kolbert, 2014) can be overwhelming. Albrecht (2019) has documented a lengthy list of "negative Earth emotions" (p. 72), supporting Macy and Brown's analysis of the many ways that "blocking our pain for the world" (p. 31) reduces our capacity for feeling, empathy, and inspiration. Clearly, we must accept the realities of these harms and process the associated pain to address the underlying structures of injustice and ecological devastation.

In the Work That Reconnects, gratitude and grief are recognized as partners. The spiral movement thus begins with "Coming from Gratitude," with the idea that "gratitude will hold us steady" (p. 68). Through gratitude, we expand our awareness of our interconnectedness with all life—human and more-than-human. We may become more aware of how social injustices and ecological degradation anywhere affect all life everywhere. As Macy and Brown (2014) explain, gratitude "opens us all to our pain for the world, because knowing what we treasure triggers the knowing of how endangered it is" (pp. 93–94). "Honoring Our Pain for the World" is thus the natural second phase of the spiral. In the dominant culture, pain is almost always seen as something to be avoided and minimized, but this collective numbing must be overcome to reorient our social and economic structures around life. In educational contexts, when we ignore this pain, we effectively deny the possibility of transformation.

These first two steps prepare participants for "Seeing with New Eyes," which is "a shift in perception" (Macy & Brown, 2014, p. 303) that allows us to experience our "relatedness to all that is" and to "taste our power to change" (p. 68). This step seems especially salient in an educational context, but it goes well beyond simply absorbing new information to grasping the world in its profound interconnectedness (p. 303). The final step, "Going Forth," allows participants to explore "the actions that call each of us" as we "work for social change" (p. 68). Here again, this step is often neglected in higher education, as our current institutions focus so much attention on how students will achieve success by fitting themselves into the framework of the status quo. "Going Forth," as with the other steps of the spiral, invites us to bring mindfulness to the roles we might play in social and cultural transformation.

WTR facilitators use the spiral to organize highly interactive workshops that can be as brief as a couple of hours but typically span a few days. These practices include a wide variety of embodied activities that are designed to open both heart and mind. For example, in the "Systems Game," a large group of participants stand in a circle and are instructed to "Mentally select two other people, without indicating whom you have chosen" and "Move so as to keep at all times an equal distance between you and each of these two people" (Macy & Brown, 2014, p. 140). The game has no predetermined outcome; sometimes equilibrium emerges, and everyone stops moving, but typically the movement continues in complex patterns. Various interventions in the game demonstrate how quickly change (whether harmful or life-supporting) can happen in a system. A debriefing conversation after the game can cast light on the reality "that life is composed not of separate entities so much as of the relations among them" (Macy & Brown, 2014, p. 140). Another WTR activity, the "Council of All Beings," is a "colorful, sometimes solemn, and often high-spirited communal ritual [that] allows us to step aside from our human identity and speak on behalf of other life forms" (p. 160). Participants can be deeply moved to both laughter and tears.

Many of these practices require trust and emotional expression levels that are difficult to achieve in a traditional classroom setting. Moreover, the intensity of WTR workshops would be all but impossible to reproduce within a class that meets for a couple of hours per week. Nonetheless, as I was developing Inner Tracking, I saw the potential to apply the spiral in a limited way through written reflection. I developed prompts for undergraduate history and humanities classes, but they are general enough to be used in any course. I chose to use written reflections because I suspected that most students would be able to focus more effectively on their inner life in a private context than the classroom context, and because written reflections provide a window into student experiences and perspectives.

Transformative Learning

Although WTR emerged outside of higher education, it is consistent with "Transformative Learning" (O'Sullivan, 1999, 2002), which "involves experiencing a deep, structural shift in basic premises of thought, feelings, and actions. It is a shift of consciousness that dramatically and permanently alters our way of being in the world." Thus, "Transformative learning has an individual, and a collective dimension, and [it] includes both individual and social transformation" (Ontario Institute, 2016). Certainly, any educational approach that aspires to address social and environmental justice must work with students as whole human beings, as mere knowledge about the facts of injustice is insufficient to transform an individual, much less a society.

An exclusively objective approach to knowledge, in fact, may lead us to externalize problems that are, in fact, the result of deeply internalized patterns of oppression, and this may be true for both privileged and oppressed people. For example, African American scholar Kendi (2019) has argued that the widely deployed claim "I'm not a racist," while it might allow a person to acknowledge that racism exists as a problem, also functions as a tool of denial that allows white people to externalize racism in such a way that "allows racial inequities to persevere" (p. 9). Moreover, as Whitt (2016) has argued: "Distancing is pedagogically problematic because it prevents students from understanding important social facts, and because it prevents them from engaging with perspectives, analyses, and testimonies that might beneficially challenge their settled views and epistemic habits" (p. 427).

One function of Inner Tracking is to help overcome this tendency to distance by inviting affective experience into the learning process, evoking not only mindfulness but also heartfulness, which Murphy-Shigematsu (2018) defines as "a way of being in mindfulness, in compassion, and in responsibility" (p. 14). Heartfulness, he explains, "emphasizes purpose through connecting to something larger than the individual self" (p. 16). Understood this way, mindfulness practices can improve "our ability to realize our deep connectedness with others through empathy and kindness" (p. 33). As a process that begins by turning inward and then turns outward, Inner Tracking brings together individual and collective aspects of transformation.

The open invitation to reflection that characterizes Inner Tracking is consistent with Annalouise Keating's (2016) description of invitational pedagogies, which do not attempt to force students to change but rather "introduce students to a wide range of additional perspectives and invite students to self-reflect on their existing beliefs and other dimensions of their worldviews, to examine them from additional points of view" (pp. 25–26). The assignment helps students reflect intentionally on how their learning is affecting them. As one of my students said about Inner Tracking: "I get to express my feelings about the course, which is nice; none of my other classes do this."

An abbreviated version of the Inner Tracking practice is provided in Table 7.1. Classroom handouts of the complete assignment are freely available via a Creative Commons license on my website at https://davidjvoelker.com/inner-tracking/.

TABLE 7.1 The Inner Tracking Practice

The premise behind the practice of Inner Tracking is that your education is most likely to be transformational if it touches you deeply—not exclusively on an intellectual level. This self-awareness practice, adapted from the spiral structure of the Work That Reconnects (Macy & Brown, 2014, pp. 67–68), is designed to help you turn inward to reflect on the question: How is your learning affecting you as a person?

Each part of Inner Tracking described in this table refers to the "content, community, or learning process" of the class. "Content" here means the knowledge of history, culture, nature, etc., that is explored in the course. "Community" refers to the learning community of the class—the students, peer mentor (if applicable), instructor, guests, etc. "Learning process" means your own experience of learning in the class. You may, for instance, be struggling with some aspects of the class or learning new things about how to learn.

Preparation: To complete the Inner Tracking practice, you will need a quiet space (if possible) and some time to reflect (about 30 minutes), as well as a way to write down your thoughts.

Centering: Before you respond to the four questions that follow, please take a moment to center yourself as you begin to turn inward. First, check in with yourself: what's your emotional tone, or how would you describe the quality of your awareness in this moment? Second, if it would feel comfortable to you, close your eyes and take three deep breaths. When you feel ready, continue with the four questions below.

1. *Giving Gratitude*: What is something from this course (content, community, or learning process) that you are grateful for? (Write 125–200 words.)
- Gratitude is a fitting place to start your reflections because it may help you connect your learning to values you already hold or aspirations you have for yourself or others.
- Giving thanks restores awareness that we depend on other people and the larger Earth community for our very lives. A powerful example of a gratitude practice is the Haudenosaunee (Iroquois) Thanksgiving Address, which has been used for centuries to give gratitude for "the full circle of Creation" and to cultivate a spirit of "one-mindedness" in preparation for important ceremonial, political, or diplomatic work (Thomas, 1992, pp. 10–11).
- Consider finding gratitude for the opportunities you have had to learn, for ways your understanding was expanded by classmates, for people you have studied who worked on behalf of a value you hold dear, or for something you appreciate that has been passed down or preserved over the generations. Choose something meaningful to you.

(*Continued*)

122 David J. Voelker

TABLE 7.1 (Continued)

2. *Honoring Pain*: What is something from this course (content, community, or learning process) for which you feel sadness, grief, anger, frustration, or disappointment? (Write 125–200 words.)
- Macy and Brown (2014) have written that "pain is the price of consciousness in a threatened and suffering world" (p. 21). To study history, the humanities, or the natural world is to come face-to-face with tremendous loss and suffering, as well as with astounding beauty and resilience.
- Expressing grief does not mean "getting over" a loss, whether personal or collective. We often continue to hold sadness after expressing grief. Expressing grief is a way to acknowledge what has happened—not to deny or forget it. Part of learning deeply about the past is accepting what happened within human communities (and the community of life) in the past—communities with which we are still connected today.
- Consider acknowledging how some past injustice caused suffering or loss and how that suffering or loss may still have repercussions today. Or, you might recognize a frustration that some of the things you previously learned have turned out to be incomplete, misleading, or untrue.
3. *Seeing Anew*: How has something from this course (content, community, or learning process) helped you see the world in a new way? (Write 125–200 words.)
- The idea of "seeing anew" reminds us that learning is not simply about accumulating knowledge. Learning can bring us new ways of seeing and thinking.
- Give a specific example (or examples) of something that you see or think differently about than you did before taking the class.
4. *Going Forth*: What's something from this course (content, community, or learning process) that you want to carry forward in your life? Is there something here that will help you be the kind of person you would like to be or make the impact you want to make? How might you act on the insights you have shared here? (Write 125–200 words.)
- This question gives you an opportunity to take ownership of and responsibility for some aspects of your learning. What do you take away from the class that will help you be the person you are becoming?

Closing: Take a moment to notice, again, how you are feeling right now. Without judgment, notice any changes from when you started the practice.

Two Examples of Inner Tracking

I have used Inner Tracking in various courses with several hundred students at the University of Wisconsin–Green Bay (UWGB) between the Fall 2017 and Spring 2021 semesters (and plan to continue to do so). In Fall 2019, I surveyed about 50 students in two courses to learn more about how they experienced this reflective practice. In both courses, students completed the Inner Tracking assignment twice: once, about a third of the way through the semester, and again in the last week or so of the semester. These were graded assignments, which I evaluated based on how well each submission completed the assignment and displayed thoughtful engagement with the prompts rather than based on the students' specific views. It works well to have the students try out this practice early in the semester, to prime them for a more expansive kind of learning than they might normally encounter in an introductory course; engaging in Inner Tracking again at the end of the semester provides an effective way to support students in reflecting on what they want to take away from the course.

UWGB is a midsized, access-oriented comprehensive university with a predominantly white student body. In 2019, when the data discussed here were collected, 15.2% of students overall came from underrepresented minority groups, with 22.9% of new, degree-seeking undergraduate students coming from underrepresented minority groups. About 57% of incoming undergraduates in 2019 were first-generation college students (University of Wisconsin–Green Bay, 2019). In the American history course, nearly 78% of the students were white, while 10% were Hispanic and 7% were African American. In this class, 45% of the students were first-generation college students. In the humanities course, which was part of a first-year student success program called Gateways to Phoenix Success (GPS), 40% of the students were white, 19% were Hispanic, 17% were African American, and 15% were Asian or Southeast Asian. In this class, 77% were first-generation college students.

Given the demographic composition of UWGB and my specific courses, I seek to accomplish two related goals. First, I seek to create a welcoming and inclusive learning environment for all students. I attempt to use diverse, culturally relevant course content to support this goal; additionally, the First Nations cultural values of the "4Rs" (Relationship, Respect, Reciprocity, and Responsibility) (Christensen, 2013, pp. 21–23) provide an important framework for respectful collaboration. Second, I seek to engage all students with real-world examples of social and environmental justice struggles, especially racial justice. Because of my discipline (history), I often focus on historical examples, which may seem distant, so Inner Tracking serves as an important tool for helping students make connections between the past and the present. The two examples of courses that follow suggest that Inner Tracking is helpful in a content-driven course (in this case, an American history course), but it may be even more impactful within a more holistic course (in this case, an interdisciplinary humanities course) that has additional supports for mindful learning.

American History to 1865

This course is often seen as a "survey" of American history (focused on the region that became the United States) through the Civil War, but I aim to transcend mere coverage by working with the students to explore critical questions through sources that represent diverse perspectives, including not only the dominant European and Euro-American men, but also First Nations people (including oral traditions), African Americans, and women. For example, students discuss First

Nations creation beliefs alongside Christian beliefs; read Abigail Adams alongside John Adams on the status of women in the 1770s; learn about Elizabeth Freeman, an enslaved woman who sued for her freedom and helped bring down slavery in Massachusetts in the 1780s; and explore the roles that African Americans and women played in generating the crisis that became the American Civil War. The course's learning outcomes focus on historical thinking, interpreting historical documents and analyzing historians' arguments, and formulating historical arguments based on evidence. About half of the class time is used for small-group or whole-class discussions, which provides students with an opportunity to build knowledge collaboratively, based on diverse perspectives—both within their groups and within assigned course materials—rather than individually memorize fixed historical interpretations (Voelker, 2020).

I open the course by introducing students to Langston Hughes's 1936 poem "Let America Be America Again" as a way to begin our critical investigation of the American past. Hughes's great-grandmothers were enslaved Black women, and his great-grandfathers were white slaveholders. Given the white supremacist system of racial segregation in the United States, Hughes experienced life as a Black man. Students recognize the poignancy of Hughes's declaration that "America never was America to me" juxtaposed to his "oath" that "America will be!" (Hughes, 1936/1994). In this poem, we can see the myth of the United States as a land of liberty both exposed as a lie and invoked as a vision. Throughout the course, I invite students to reflect on and critique mythical versions of the American past—all in service of connecting the past to the present.

Helping students make this connection is a challenge, given that the discipline of history places emphasis on maintaining analytical distance from the past to understand it on its own terms. Human social conventions, economic systems, and language vary tremendously across both time and space. For example, answering what seems like a simple question such as, "What did the 'Declaration of Independence' mean when it said that 'all men are created equal'?" is, in fact, a complex task that requires sophisticated historical thinking. Given the demands of disciplinary thinking, we necessarily spend a great deal of time in class intentionally focused on the past. To be sure, recognizing continuity between past and present is another important aspect of historical thinking, and doing so can help students connect their own lives to the past—to see how they are implicated in social and economic systems that may offer privileges or impose limitations on their own lives. Personal reflection, however, has the potential to deepen these insights.

Inner Tracking thus offers an important opportunity for history students to reflect on what their learning means to them. Although there is not much space in this course to build a contemplative practice, Inner Tracking does have some support within the class. First, to help build capacity for collaboration, I share Sobonfu Somé's teachings on community, which she brought to the United States from the West African Dagara people. Somé (2000) emphasizes the importance of community as "that grounding place where people come and share their gifts and receive from others" (p. 22). Second, to help introduce First Nations cultures and worldviews at the beginning of the semester, I share the "4Rs" of First Nations education, which I have adapted, with guidance, from UWGB's First Nations Studies program (Christensen, 2013, pp. 21–23). We discuss the specific meanings of relationship, respect, reciprocity, and responsibility within First Nations cultures, and we also think together about how we might apply these values in our work together within the class. Third, I structure the course to require collaboration in ways that are low stakes, as far as course grades go, but are essential to learning and doing well in the course. Together, and in concert with Inner Tracking, these strategies help build a learning community in which students can develop their own understandings of the past and their relationships with it.

Living the Humanities: "Humans & Nature"

This course is an introduction to the humanities course that I co-developed with my First Nations Studies colleague Lisa Poupart, and co-taught in 2019 with Sarah Schuetze, my late colleague from the English Department. The course offered an introduction to the study of environmental issues using perspectives from the humanities, including First Nations studies, history, philosophy, literature, animal studies, and religious studies. Topics included the relationship between humans and the rest of nature (from various cultural perspectives), relationships between humans and (other) animals, the historical and cultural roots of contemporary environmental problems, and insights from the humanities into the challenges and solutions associated with creating a sustainable and just society.

To guide the exploration of these topics, we worked with several fundamental principles articulated in the syllabus:

- *Interconnectedness*: This is a concept, but it is also a guiding principle and something to experience. In order to experience connection with other people and earth others, a person must also experience self-connection.
- *The 4Rs* (Respect, Relationship, Reciprocity, and Responsibility): These First Nations core values are offered in the course as content and as an experience.
- *Reflection*: Cultivate a habit and practice of reflection on the meaning and significance of learning in a dynamic relationship with personal experience and values.
- *Multiple Perspectives*: Cultivate a habit and practice of seeking out and considering multiple perspectives beyond the "default" perspectives of the dominant culture.
- *Sustainability*: Sustainability is not simply a technical problem to be solved by science and technology. Our un-sustainability problems are rooted in culture, values, and worldview, as well as dominant behaviors. Addressing these

TABLE 7.2 Living the Humanities: Humans & Nature

Building Classroom Community:
- Sobonfu Somé's teachings on community
- The 4Rs (First Nations values)

Exploring Diverse Perspectives:
- Cordova, Viola. (2007). "How it is" and "A new reverence" from *How it is: The Native American philosophy of V. F. Cordova*. University of Arizona Press.
- Suzuki, David. (2009). Restoring balance, from *The sacred balance: Rediscovering our place in nature* (2009). Greystone Books.
- Macy, Joanna & Brown, Molly. (2018). Choosing the story we want for our world. From https://workthatreconnects.org/choosing-the-story-we-want-for-our-world/
- Kimmerer, Robin Wall. Reclaiming the honorable harvest. (2012). TEDxSitka.

Experiences and Reflections:
- Silent Nature Observation and Reflection
- Mindfulness Meditation
- Ecological Mapping and Reflection
- The Systems Game
- Small-Group Dialogues
- Inner Tracking Reflection

problems requires engaging the heart and spirit and asking: What are we trying to sustain?

At the beginning of the semester, to build capacity for collaboration, we introduced Somé's definition of community and discussed the "4Rs," along the lines described in the preceding list. On several occasions, we began class with guided meditations. We regularly engaged students in small-group and whole-group discussions based on short readings about the human relationship with the living planet. Students read excerpts from the World Wide Fund for Nature's *Living Planet Report* (2018); indigenous perspectives on the proper relationship between humans and the rest of nature from Leanne Simpson, Viola Cordova, John Mohawk, and Robin Wall Kimmerer; and additional reflections on environmental ethics from Aldo Leopold, David Suzuki, Eileen Crist, Pema Chödrön, Joanna Macy, and Molly Brown. They also read and discussed several journalistic pieces related to just sustainability.

While some readings directly addressed contemporary environmental problems, others explored the deep roots of those problems in culture and worldview. Students drew ecological maps to show how these issues showed up in their ecosystems, kept journals to reflect on experiences such as a silent outdoor walk, and participated in a service-learning activity (often with the local wildlife sanctuary). For example, students completed an ecological footprint calculation and responded to this prompt:

> Make a note of your "overshoot day." This is (an estimate of) the day of the year when you go beyond consuming your fair share of the Earth's

resources in a sustainable way. How many Earths would we need if everyone consumed resources at the rate you do? (Make a note of this number.) Write a reflection on your ecological footprint calculation. Start your reflection by sharing the overshoot day and "how many earths" number from your calculation. What do you make of this information? Were there factors that you had not considered that went into the calculation? Do you think that having this information might affect how you choose to live?

This reflection served as a rather gentle gateway to discussing environmental justice, especially regarding the disproportionate effects of current and future human-caused climate disruption for developing nations. As a final project, students organized small-group reflective dialogues connected with the course fundamentals described earlier. Despite various bumps in the road, students demonstrated that they could work together, prepare for, and engage respectfully and in meaningful ways around the big questions we had been exploring all semester.

Student Responses to Inner Tracking

Students' survey responses from these Fall 2019 courses, along with their reflections, suggest that Inner Tracking supported their learning, giving them an opportunity to both think and feel the significance of their learning, working not only with the intellect but also with emotions, identities, and their sense of how they fit into the world.

Most students responded very favorably to the Inner Tracking practice and saw its value. Some students in the humanities class explicitly recognized the usefulness of reflection. One student described the practice as "A chance for internal reflection that helps to process what you have learned." Students in the history course tended to orient their reflections around course content, but a number of them pointed to the value of reflection. One student wrote:

> It's a really good way to reflect on yourself and how you have learned and progressed through the class. Sitting back to complete the inner tracking and reflecting on how I've learned, what I've learned from others and my overall experiences through the class has really helped me realize how much I've progressed throughout the semester and not just focus on what I learned, but how I felt about it as I learned it.

The fact that students offered these comments in an optional part of the survey suggests that they sincerely valued the opportunity to reflect.

Many students explicitly valued the opportunity to express gratitude related to the course, often focusing on the classroom community. One humanities student noted: "I appreciate that the class is able to sit together and even talk about personal stories and struggles because this can help everyone get closer and make meaningful relationships with each other." Another wrote: "This class has taught me how to open up and trust people again." Many students likewise expressed the importance of learning from each other.

As they reflected on the painful parts of their learning experience, students in both courses noticed how the course content increased their awareness of social injustice or ecological degradation, or both. This practice allowed them to grapple with the moral implications of history and even, for some students, with their own complicity in injustice. Inner Tracking, with its focus on feeling and meaning, can help students break through the façade of objectivity so that they can confront the reality that they live in the world that we have been studying and that it is their world to respond to and help shape. For example, a student in the history course connected their own behavior to ongoing injustices:

> This course has reinforced a deep sense of disappointment in me for my own country and my society's past actions. While I know that I personally did not partake in any of the atrocities that we have discussed I cannot help but feel incredibly attached to the stories and events that we have explored. . . . [I]n the end, I often feel that I am perpetuating the cycle of hate through inaction and complacency to the contemporary events that will one day be looked upon as our era's great injustice.

The student expressed ambivalence about their own role in allowing injustices to continue, but there is a strong sense here of how historical injustices continue in the present. A small number of students in the American history course acknowledged racism primarily as a phenomenon that existed in the past, perhaps distancing themselves from contemporary racial injustice. This problem specifically affects white students, who may come from relatively homogenous communities or social enclaves. Although I discuss contemporary racism while teaching about the past, white students may still be able to overlook, deny, or compartmentalize this information. Additional opportunities to reflect more specifically focused on racial justice might be used to foster a deeper orientation toward social justice. For example, I could ask students to find evidence of and discuss how systemic racism in the past continues to shape the present and to afflict the United States today.

Recognition of injustices helped many students set intentions about how they wanted to participate in the world. One student in the humanities class, for example, elaborated on a desire to contribute to social and environmental change:

> Something that I want to carry forward in my life is the idea of caring for something that is bigger than myself. I want to help make a difference on this planet and help it start moving in the right direction for the betterment of humankind and what we stand for. I want to give my time to organizations that need my help pushing forward in the impacts that they are trying to make on the world and help them move forward.

While fewer history students set such activist intentions, some discussed the importance of constructive dialogue. For example, one student wrote: "I want to be a person who is able to look at everyone's perspective and learn from them, even if I do not necessarily agree with their position." Another student reflected on what they had learned from participating in class discussions:

> I really want to carry forward the sense of open-mindedness that the class has taught me to have and reciprocate. I've heard many opinions that differ from mine but made me see things in a new way that I perhaps wouldn't have ever thought of before.

While open-mindedness can go in many directions—not all of them positive within the context of disinformation and expressions of hatred—the idea of being able to listen to different perspectives seems essential for creating social change.

Although the overwhelming majority of students seemed positive about the assignment, a tiny number of students reacted quite critically, explicitly rejecting the idea that the assignment had any value for them. In some cases, this perspective seemed to emerge from their position that the course could not (or perhaps should not) affect them as a person. When students have difficulty seeing the connection between reflective practices and course content, instructors can offer to talk with students about the purpose of the assignment. During an earlier semester, I had a very productive face-to-face conversation with a student who had criticized the assignment. The reflection thus served as an entryway to building my relationship with this student and seemed to increase his capacity to learn in the course. Even students who were critical of the assignment often wrote thoughtful reflections.

Conclusion

Inner Tracking plays an essential role in the learning experience that I aspire to create for students. It opens a space for reflection that can help increase their awareness of their interconnectedness with human and natural communities, including their awareness of social injustices and ecological problems, and it offers them an opportunity to set an intention about how they relate to the world. Moreover, student reflections give me insight into their experiences as learners and how their education connects to their aspirations. The practice honors students as whole people and invites them to both think and feel their way into the significance of their learning—often in areas that go well beyond the course content.

The reflective practice described here is just one piece of a broader approach to course design that utilizes critical thinking, dialogue, and reflection to engage students wholly in their learning. The Inner Tracking practice seems most meaningful within a course that supports integrative learning. As Keating points out in *Transformation Now!* (2013), transformational learning cannot be scripted as a mechanical process:

> Transformation is optional and always exceeds our conscious intentions and efforts. I can invite transformation into my own thinking, but I can't accurately pinpoint exactly what this transformation will look like or entail. . . . Transformation in the context of the classroom is even less within my control. . . . All I can do is set the intention, carefully self-reflect, thoughtfully organize each activity, and remain open to my students' reactions. . . . Transformation can't be known in advance, dictated, orchestrated, or in any way fully controlled, and there are absolutely no guarantees that transformation will occur.
> (p. 185)

Transformation is not something that instructors can or should try to control. We are not transforming students according to our own designs. What we can do, rather, is create learning experiences that encourage and support students as they engage in their own ongoing transformational processes. With greater attention to these processes, perhaps more students would end a course with an appreciation for both reflection and entanglement, as this student did:

> The freedom allowed during this class for personal investigation and reflection is a time that is invaluable in this hectic world, and I cherish it. If for nothing else, I feel grateful that this class has given me a chance to slow down and be truly engaged with a topic which is so intimately intertwined with my personal history and culture.

Notably, this student recognized "freedom," which indicates that they accepted invitations but did not feel compelled.

As I noted at the outset, I believe that instructors who teach with transformation as a goal must themselves be open to transformation. We need to be open to being changed by our engagement with students. When I read students' Inner Tracking reflections, I am often gratified and humbled (and only very occasionally disappointed) by what they have learned and chosen to share with me. I frequently experience "heartfulness" as I hear how students are taking in their learning. I find myself restored by this process and emboldened to be more authentic in my presence with students. Over time, this experience has allowed me to trust students and explore more difficult value-infused questions with them. In that sense, Inner Tracking may hold the potential to transform teaching as well as learning.

Acknowledgments

I am grateful to many people for the varied roles that they played in the development of the Inner Tracking practice and this chapter describing it, including but not limited to Gretchen Sleicher, Alex Britzius, Alison Staudinger, Lisa Poupart, Sarah Schuetze, Sam Cocks, Nicole Bickham, Greta Gaard, Bengü Ergüner-Tekinalp, and countless students. I thank Samantha Surowiec of the UWGB Office of Institutional Strategy and Effectiveness for providing course-specific demographic data.

Data collection for this study was approved by the Institutional Review Board (IRB) at the University of Wisconsin–Green Bay. Participation in the study was completely optional, and all students who participated gave their informed consent for me to use their responses as data.

References

Albrecht, G. A. (2019). *Earth Emotions: New Words for a New World*. Cornell University Press.
Berila, B. (2016). *Integrating Mindfulness into Anti-Oppression Pedagogy: Social Justice in Higher Education*. Routledge.
Christensen, R. A. (2013). Connective Pedagogy: Elder Epistemology, Oral Tradition, and Community. In R. A. Christensen & L. M. Poupart (Eds.), *Connective Pedagogy: Elder Epistemology, Oral Tradition, and Community* (pp. 13–32). Aboriginal Issues Press.
Hughes, L. (1936/1994). *Let America be America Again*. Poets.org. Academy of American Poets. https://www.poets.org/poem/let-america-be-america-again/.
Kabat-Zinn, J. (2005). *Wherever You Go, There You Are: Mindfulness Meditation in Everyday Life*. Hachette Books.
Keating, A. (2013.) *Transformation Now! Toward a Post-Oppositional Politics of Change*. University of Illinois Press.
Keating, A. (2016). Post-oppositional Pedagogies. *Transformations: The Journal of Inclusive Scholarship & Pedagogy, 26*(1), 24–26.
Kendi, I. X. (2019). *How to Be an Antiracist*. One World.
Kolbert, E. (2014). *The Sixth Extinction: An Unnatural History*. Picador.
Macy, J., & Brown, M. Y. (2014). *Coming Back to Life: The Updated Guide to the Work That Reconnects*. New Society Publishers.
Murphy-Shigematsu, S. (2018). *From Mindfulness to Heartfulness: Transforming Self and Society with Compassion*. Berrett-Koehler Publishers.
Ontario Institute for Studies in Education, University of Toronto. (2016). *About the Transformative Learning Centre*. Retrieved June 13, 2021, from https://www.oise.utoronto.ca/tlcca/About_The_TLC.html.
O'Sullivan, E. V. (1999). *Transformative Learning: Educational Vision for the 21st Century*. Zed Books.
O'Sullivan, E. V. (2002). The Project and Vision of Transformative Education: Integral Transformative Learning. In E. V. O'Sullivan, A. Morrell, & M. A. O'Connor (Eds.) *Expanding the Boundaries of Transformative Learning: Essays on Theory and Praxis* (pp. 1–12). Palgrave Macmillan.
Ray, S. J. (2020). *A Field Guide to Climate Anxiety: How to Keep Your Cool on a Warming Planet*. University of California Press.
Somé, S. (2000). *The Spirit of Intimacy: Ancient African Teachings in the Ways of Relationships*. Harper.
Thomas, J. (1992). Words That Come Before All Else. In José Barriero (Ed.), *Indian Roots of American Democracy* (pp. 10–11). Kon Press.

University of Wisconsin—Green Bay. (2019). *UW-Green Bay Fact Sheet: Fall 2019*. https://www.uwgb.edu/UWGBCMS/media/ise/files/FactBook-Fall-2019.pdf.

Voelker, D. J. (2020). Beyond Coverage: Tackling Student Success in the Introductory History Course. *Journal of American History*, 106(4), 1012–1015.

Whitt, M. S. (2016). Other People's Problems: Student Distancing, Epistemic Responsibility, and Injustice. *Studies in Philosophy and Education*, 35, 427–444.

Worldwide Fund for Nature. (2018). *Living Planet Report: 2018: Aiming Higher*. https://www.worldwildlife.org/pages/living-planet-report-2018.

Young, J. (2015). *Quick Guide to the Renewal of Creative Path (ROCP)*. https://s3-us-west-1.amazonaws.com/8shields-online-courses/ROCPtoolkit/ROCP+Quick+Guide.pdf.

8

A MINDFUL APPROACH TO TEACHING ART AND YOGA AS A MEANS OF LIBERATION

Jan Estep

I start with a personal story. In 2015, after two years of heightened stress at my university position, I suffered a major depression that required me to take a leave from teaching. Depression was my body's way of forcing me to stop what I was doing and reevaluate my choices. Throughout most of my academic career, I was primarily focused on work. From the time I entered a PhD program in philosophy and got my first job in that field, then a second graduate degree in studio art, leading to a tenure-track position in a visual art department until I became a full professor 11 years later, I pushed single-mindedly to move up the academic ladder, which demanded from me a singular focus on a life of the mind. Writing and publishing art criticism and exhibiting conceptual art for a hybrid creative research practice, teaching studio and non-studio art-theory courses, participating in and leading various committees—the usual trifecta of research, teaching, and service—commandeered my attention in a distinctly intellectual way. Pushing, striving, proving my worth, I internalized the conventional academic values of productivity, performance, and overintellectualizing. I followed the program happily until that focus no longer worked. For better or, in my case, for worse, the message I unconsciously understood was that I was never doing enough for an institution that always wanted more. As I later discovered, scholarship on the phenomenon I experienced was already in the publishing pipeline, describing an alternative in "slow scholarship," but this concept and community were not available to me at the time (Berg & Seeber, 2017; Mountz et al., 2015). Academia prizes those who internalize the message of "high performance" and deliver ceaseless work and productivity. I certainly have been rewarded for these efforts, financially and professionally, and for a long time wasn't interested in questioning my choices.

DOI: 10.4324/9781003201854-11

My specific location as white, able-bodied, and cisgendered afforded me access to the system. Since I was then primarily identified with my analytical, rational side and ignored my embodied, emotional, and intuitive side, I fit the model—that is, until a major depression stopped me in my tracks, giving me the space and time to assess my expectations and behavior. Not coincidentally, a few years prior to going on medical leave, I enrolled in a Mindfulness-Based Stress Reduction (MBSR) course to address the high levels of stress and anger I was experiencing in my job. Meditation turned out to be highly effective, encouraging a gap of awareness between my thoughts, emotions, and actions and helping me dis-identify with the stress and emotional reactivity. Mindfulness inserts a pause in the chain between thought and action, slowly creating the buffer I needed to consider the unconscious thinking and beliefs fueling my behavior and ultimately to make different choices. Unconscious assumptions started to become conscious. But honestly, in my case, I wasn't going to give up my academic training and the comparative status it provided until poor health forced me to. The way individuals are disciplined and socialized in academia can make it difficult to unlearn norms and conventions from within an academic context; systems are set up to perpetuate themselves, and the reward system is strong. While select people thrive in such conditions, those of us who want a different definition of success, one that allows for more aspects of self, greater inclusiveness, and a better work/life balance, need to incorporate an alternative value system. My personal journey involved exactly that.

The medical leave from university gave me the space and time to reevaluate. As a part of recovery and other forms of psychotherapy and medication, I turned to mindfulness, meditation, and yoga to heal the separation between mind and body. Still under the thrall of productivity, I also embarked on an intense six-year period of professional training to slowly re-tool and turn directions. These healing modalities allowed me to return to the physical body, reconnect with the emotional body, and integrate my thinking mind from its formerly separate, dissociated position. These are the same principles that began to feed my pedagogical approach when I prepared to return to campus.

I've streamlined this story to quickly contextualize how my personal experience motivated a new course I developed when I returned to teaching. I didn't want to perpetuate the same coping mechanisms I had used earlier or put myself under the old value system that favored the intellect and productivity over mind-body integration and balance. I also assumed that my students were as sensitive to mainstream academic messages and the pressure to perform and produce as I was, and they too would benefit from a different approach to learning and achieving. What was needed was an approach that valued the whole person: body, mind, emotions, and spirit. My students and I needed a curriculum that highlighted the ways we are socialized along particular paths in culturally specific ways, along with training for how to identify that socialization so we could make more conscious choices. Specifically, I wanted an approach that helped students to become aware of their unconscious habits of mind (the assumptions, beliefs, and thought patterns influencing their actions) and habits of the body (the automatic emotional and nervous system reactions based on our conditioning and lived experience), so they could learn to question whether those habits aligned with their highest values, and ultimately be able to make choices that freed them of assumptions that no longer served them or others. Because the culture of overwork is part of a racialized (white) and gendered (toxic-masculinized) system defining success, challenging and refusing the markers of this internalized mandate for ceaseless production becomes a liberatory project. It's this liberatory aspect that leads to anti-oppression within and outside of the university.

Arts 1202: Art and Yoga

Until recently, I taught in a large, midwestern public research institution that is predominantly white. Out of a desire to try something new after my leave, I created an intro-level art and yoga course to integrate mindfulness and creativity within an academic setting. The subtitle of the course—"Combining Somatic, Contemplative, and Creative Practices"—speaks to the pedagogical approach of the course. To teach this content, since 2015 I have earned 720 YTT (Yoga Teacher Training) in Kundalini Yoga and Prana Flow Yoga and become certified to teach MBSR (Mindfulness-Based Stress Reduction), plus participated in a number of other somatic-based training courses. In this section, I describe the course in detail, examining the liberatory impact of the teachings, analyzing the potential for cultural appropriation and what I do to resist that potential, describing the role that self-reflective writing plays in encouraging mindfulness, and the relationship between a focus on personal spiritual healing and the wider social community.

First taught in the fall of 2017, this experiential course offers a dynamic mix of art and yoga to tap into students' creativity, cultivating a strong sense of embodiment and intuitive intelligence and developing self-awareness and a fuller, more soulful sense of self. Each class opens with yoga, chanting, and meditation and then leads into guided creative exercises with various art materials. During class we occasionally meet in small groups and also have structured time to share our explorations. I've taught the class successfully in person for three semesters and once remotely, the latter as a mix of synchronous live sessions (on Zoom) and asynchronous teaching videos delivered on a course Learning Management System (LMS).

This yoga-then-art sequence helps us selectively calm and energize the body and mind prior to experimenting with art. Highlighting Kundalini Yoga during the first part of the class, students learn a mixture of pranayamas (breathing techniques), kriyas (postural asana sequences), and meditations (silent and guided) with mudra (hand positions) and mantra (repetition of primal sounds and chanting of sacred phrases). Working with the physical body in this way, students connect more deeply to their mental and energetic bodies, illuminating and becoming more conscious of their emotions, intuition, and spirit. These practices also have dramatic effects in calming and relaxing the nervous system, aiding the release of tension, anxiety, and distracted mind states. With this greater self-presence and calm, in the second half of the class, students then explore a guided creative prompt, typically using either oil pastels, water-based paints, and other mixed media for drawing and painting, or pen and paper for creative writing. Periodically we explore sound and expressive movement as the creative component. The emphasis throughout the creative portion is placed on trusting the process and experiencing creative flow rather than focusing on the final outcome. This yoga-then-art sequence (meditation and yoga coupled with overt art or creative writing practice) is also used for weekly creative home practice assignments that, along with additional reflective writing assignments, receive timely feedback.

Why yoga and art? Calming the body-mind and centering into self-presence at the beginning of class lets students shift from the outer turmoil and stresses of ordinary life, awakening the natural calm and ease within. Yoga and meditation cultivate mindfulness: moment-to-moment nonjudgmental awareness of one's thoughts and sensations. From this place, students explore creative expression—through drawing, painting, image-making, writing, sound, and movement—connecting with themselves in a deeper, freer way. Throughout both halves of the class, students are encouraged to track their experience on multiple levels. The intention is to cultivate a mindful, nonjudgmental attitude toward the body and towards creative expression. Together, students and I create a supportive community that encourages each person to learn, explore, and grow and accept our physical and creative uniqueness while learning to respect the differences within the group.

The course objectives are numerous and varied:

- Experiment with a variety of artistic media, including drawing, painting, writing, sound, and authentic movement.
- Practice accessing creative flow, and what (for the individual) blocks such access.
- Practice breathing and self-care exercises to relieve stress, calm anxiety, buffer against depression, and revitalize the body.
- Foster mindfulness—nonjudgmental, present-moment awareness—towards one's body, emotions, thoughts, and creative expression.
- Soften self-judgment and learn ways to work with the inner critic and heightened self-consciousness/self-criticism.
- Cultivate an appreciation for diverse perspectives concerning personal, physical, spiritual, and cultural norms.

This course overtly encourages innovation and imagination as well as enhanced creative flexibility. With an emphasis on process over product (Cassou & Cubley,

1996), the course helps students tap into their intuition and unique creativity, outside the conventions of academic aesthetic judgment and definitions of who gets to be an artist. For example, when engaging visual art practices, I don't teach a rote aesthetic standard (that is, I don't present artists from the Western art-historical canon as examples). Instead, I introduce students to various art materials and encourage them to follow their own creative energy while exploring those materials. The approach is a mix of process-based art practices and expressive arts, where the engagement in the direct processes of creativity and using art as a means of personal expression outweigh the final results of that engagement and expression. This shift in focus is disconcerting to many students who assume there is a "right" and "wrong" way to draw or paint, for example. Since most of the students who enroll in the class do not self-identify as artists or major in art, it's enlightening for them that creativity can be experienced outside of art-historical canonical norms or a binary judgment of "good" and "bad."

Students learn to trust creative processes without preconceived ends and to express original ideas and vision without automatically comparing these views to what others have done before them. The freedom from a set standard is initially perplexing, as it asks people to question their preconceived ideas of art, good art, legitimate art, mastery, inherited definitions of success and failure, and, behind these ideas, how dominant culture has solidified around a narrow range of Western/European, white, male artistry (Guerilla Girls, 1998; Berger, 1990; hooks, 1994). Students are typically socialized into inherited art canons that don't allow much variance and don't value creative expression if it doesn't hit those marks. The course encourages them to undo inherited expectations and definitions. The emphasis on process and personal expression removes the pressure to conform, freeing energy into more flow-like, playful, and experimental states.

Contemplative Decolonial Pedagogy and the Skills of Unlearning

Students often come into the course expecting one set of skills (here, in terms of art, the traditional proficiency-based ones) but learning another. I have to be very explicit early on in describing the differences, so we're all on the same page and can negotiate our mutual expectations fairly. As an instructor, I found the rote teaching of technical proficiency is not enjoyable, and over time I expanded my priorities. Certainly, I had the luxury of developing my own course when instructors bound to predetermined content and departmental requirements may struggle to insert alternative skills into their course flow. The acquisition of these broader skills fascinates me, keeps me engaged as a teacher, and allows the course to have broad consequences.

For example, focusing on process and the concrete physical qualities of the materials and the flow of energy during creative exercises frees students from having to make their images look like something referentially or having to defer to a predetermined standard. Simultaneously, incorporating mindful practices of art and yoga cultivates other skills: it's a skill to remain connected to one's body and emotions (and listen to the information they give us) while also eliciting our analytical thinking and reasoning. It's a skill to be flexible and creative in one's response to materials, to be able to remain engaged in the process, and to let the image emerge in the making rather than be overtaken by the expectation of a "perfect" end-product or predetermined agenda or plan. It's a skill to let go of judgment and any tendency to compare self to others. It's a skill to be forgiving rather than harshly critical of one's or another's efforts. And it's a skill to tolerate difference without projecting one's own norms onto others. All of these can be learned using a scaffolded and mindfulness-based process of observation, reflection, and conscious awareness. In Art and Yoga, the unlearning begins when students are asked to let go of their inherited ideas about art, aesthetic judgment, and creativity. It continues when students are asked to expand their sense of yoga.

Beyond Cultural Appropriation: Decolonizing Yoga

The decision to avoid monoculturalism—by not defaulting to Western, patriarchal, white knowledge systems and frames of reference, and not prioritizing a pedagogical methodology that emphasizes the thinking mind, rationality, and reason above embodied and emotionally informed learning—is central to the course (Lee, 2017). Drawing on the rich history of Eastern yoga introduces a radically different knowledge system and frame of reference. However, I need to balance the act of diversifying the knowledge bases I pull from, on the one hand, with the potential threat of cultural appropriation, on the other. As Barkataki (2015) explains,

> yoga means liberation from every construct, including that of race, gender, time, space, location, identity and even history herself. However, in the current cultural context where there is a billion-dollar industry profiting off taking yoga out of context, branding and repackaging it for monetary gain, we need to address this.

This is a generalization, but in the United States, many yoga studios have usurped ancient south Indian yogic traditions in a piecemeal fashion, and with various motives: for profit, as a commodity, to claim ownership and cultural capital, in ways that disrespect the complex cultural history from which it stems, and/or in ways that disadvantage one culture and privilege another. Especially in the current political climate of Black Lives Matter and decolonization, I am sensitive to ensuring students understand this tension.

Most students, if they have prior yoga experience at all, come to my course with an exposure to a distinctly Western form of "Power Yoga," a vinyasa-based flow yoga with an emphasis on workout and the physical body. The audience has been distinctly white, thin, able-bodied, financially secure, and young. For many, yoga is a form of exercise, which may also have the benefit of releasing stress, and a form of self-care that emphasizes the individual over the collective. This reductive model extracts the physical asana practice out of the original cultural context of the full suite of yoga practices and traditions, which includes an interconnected system of ethics, philosophy, spirituality, seva or service, pranayama, mantra, and meditation. Yoga, in the original sense, comprises a whole life path that integrates body, mind, and spirit. According to Barkataki (2015), there are at least five ways to decolonize yoga practice:

1. Learn the full honest integrity of an authentic yoga practice, aligned with Gandhian self-rule and inquiry, in which one's own awakening is connected to the whole.
2. Cite cultural references and learn the cultural history of this tradition.
3. Ask the hard questions about yoga's accessibility today, and address past injustices through our teaching practices and our lives.
4. Share and practice not just asana, but all eight limbs of yoga—ethical conduct, personal practice, breathwork, awareness of the senses, meditation, concentration and insight, nonjudgmental presence with whatever arises, interconnection with all that is.
5. Be humble, honoring your own and other people's journey.

To ensure we honor the broader cultural context of yoga, an integrated approach is used in my class. We don't select out the physical asana alone but always present it within a set of practices that include chanting, pranayama (breathwork), and meditation. References to the ancient Vedic texts give the historical context of the practices, and respect for the wisdom collected and passed down from the ancient yogis are running touchpoints, as is the critical question of how yoga's history connects to contemporary practice. For any mantra not in English, we learn the meaning and correct pronunciation of the original Sanskrit or Gurmucki/Punjabi language, and students are asked to actively reflect on how it feels to borrow these global languages. I overtly recognize the dislocation of yogic practices from one culture to another and the potential for appropriation, misunderstanding, and exploitation. There is always much to learn from the ancient yogis, and this course is an introduction. It's a revelation for students when they realize yoga's wide reach.

Just as the course does not teach yoga primarily as a decontextualized form of physical exercise, it does not offer it as a form of spiritual bypassing (Welwood, 2000; Masters, 2010) either. Spiritual bypassing is the act of using spiritual ideas and practices to hide from critical areas of one's life: "blissing out" to distract oneself from pain and suffering; using yoga to divorce oneself from stressful problems, difficult emotions, spiritual growth, and social justice issues (Magee, 2019); using spiritual ideas to turn away from the rest of the world and concentrate solely on oneself. The way yoga is taught in the course, it is not a means to escape one's conditioning and reactivity or to numb out to social issues, but just the opposite: we use yoga as a means to confront social conditioning (biases, expectations, assumptions), become aware of how this conditioning shapes and limits one's perspective on the world, and choose consciously to expand and release these limiting beliefs. Yoga is a way to become more conscious of one's unconscious patterns of thought and behavior; this includes issues of privilege and oppression. Through increasing self-awareness and self-presence, yoga is a liberatory path toward greater self-knowledge and greater connection to the whole, shifting our view from seeing self as separate, isolated, and individual to recognizing the interdependence among diverse people, groups, and the cosmos. As Batacharya (2018) has explained, the issue of cultural appropriation requires us to recognize the threat of appropriating something to serve one's own needs and the value of learning from different perspectives. "Good intentions" alone are not enough to protect dominant group members against perpetuating harm, and "intent" doesn't excuse the impact of our actions. Care, thoughtfulness, and respect matter.

Practicing yoga and personal creative expression are not ways to avoid social or personal problems but rather ways to observe one's conditioning, regulate reactive emotional states, build resilience, and build resources, so one can go back out into the world. What self-care looks like is an affirmation of self-love in the moment of recognizing culturally produced and internalized self-hatred. It's deciding to shift from judgment into acceptance, to reconnect to the whole of who you and others are. It's a moment of breath and noticing the physical sensations in the body to remind yourself that you are safe. It's not only a formal meditation practice isolated on the mat; it's being mindfully aware while riding the bus or doing the dishes or changing diapers in the stream of life, not separate. Regular attempts are made to name the relevance of what we learn in the classroom to the health and well-being that extends beyond the classroom.

With the consistent mixing of artistic and yogic disciplines, students in the course grow their capacity to make connections between seemingly unrelated ideas and disciplines (art and yoga) and states of being (mental, physical, emotional, intuitive, analytical, creative). We repeatedly magnify the effects of yoga, meant in its broadest sense, by linking it with creative artistic activities, and further by linking it with the way we function in everyday life. As part of the course, these linkages are articulated in the act of writing. The interconnectivity between mind, body, and emotion is encouraged through an intentional written reflection activity before and after the art and yoga practices.

Writing as Inquiry

To underscore the self-reflective gains in the course, students regularly engage in writing as a means to explore their thinking and assumptions, to observe their inner experience, and as a means of communication. The writing takes different forms: (a) short informal responses to weekly Inquiry Prompts; (b) contemplative Written Reflections that accompany their weekly Home Creative Practice; and (c) formal Self-Assessment Learning Reports spread throughout the semester. Here, I focus on the weekly Inquiry Prompts and Written Reflection notes.

Inquiry Prompts

Self-reflective writing supports students in cultivating greater self-awareness and comprehending the yogic and creative principles shared in class. The Inquiry Prompts guide students to discover their beliefs, values, assumptions, and personal worldview and trust their intuition; often, a person doesn't know what they believe until they voice it out loud in writing (or speech). Table 8.1 lists the 15 prompts offered during the semester, following along these themes; some are tied to specific somatic practices, though most are stand-alone questions.

TABLE 8.1 Inquiry Prompts for Self-Reflective Writing

- What helps you feel welcomed? And that you belong?
- Create your own personal mantra and describe in what contexts it could be helpful. [This is tied to a video about the yogic history of mantra practice.]
- What strengths do you bring to this course?
- Experiment with either the Sound Chakra Practice or Drawing Chakra Practice and then report on what you experienced. [This is accompanied with guided sound and creative practices that focus on the Chakra system.]
- What is your relationship with your voice? [This is connected to a specific chanting meditation that moves through silence, a whisper, and an out-loud voice.]
- What do you love?
- What supports you? Where do you need more support?
- What does creativity mean to you?
- What do you do to comfort yourself? What soothes your body, mind, and soul?
- What is one limiting belief you hold, and how could you rephrase it in a way that expands the limitation? [This is connected to a longer reflective practice with guided instructions.]
- What small act of kindness were you once shown that you will never forget? What small act of kindness can you do for another?
- What does your relationship to nature and planet earth look like?
- What would you do if you weren't afraid? If you could say anything, do anything, what would it be?
- What problem did you used to have but now have overcome? What shifted within you to allow that change?
- List ten things or people you are grateful for. Now select one of those and describe in more detail.

Many students report that they've never been asked such questions at the university. Their responses give them an opportunity to name what is important to them, share their experience and what they know about themselves and the world, and discover their goals and values in life. The greater awareness afforded by these reflections is situated to inform how they embrace the yoga and art practices within the course—no part of them is unwelcome (Selassie, 2020)—and the way they carry these learnings into their lives outside the formal frame of the course.

Home Creative Practice

The stated intention of the Home Creative Practice instructs students to mindfully observe their reactions in mind, body, and emotions and to track the connection between yogic and creative activities and their effects. The addition of recurring self-guided home practice to the live class we do together encourages them to develop a regular habit of meditation, yoga, and creativity that will serve them well once the class is over. The Home Creative Practice follows the same basic yoga-then-art sequencing as our live class sessions, but students decide which meditations and art modalities to explore with the addition of a self-reflective writing component. At least twice per week, using art materials purchased for the course, students follow a structured format: they creatively express themselves in the modality of their choice following 11 minutes of meditation and/or pranayama of their choice, and also keep a written record of how they feel before and after the practice in a separate notebook or Word document. They upload documentation of one of these sets of practices to the course LMS each week for feedback.

Two kinds of expressive activities are required for submission in their Home Creative Practice: creative work and a written reflection piece. The creative work can be in any artistic media (e.g., oil pastels, pencil, watercolor, collage, creative writing) and can vary from week to week. Students can use prompts I share with them during class, they can make up their own prompts or give themselves time and space to intuitively explore the materials without following a guide. Artistically, students are encouraged to consider the home practice a form of creative play, focusing more on the process than the end product. This approach asks them to trust the process, trust their intuition, and learn to listen to and follow the energy of their natural creative impulses. Not knowing the outcome is part of the creative experience.

The goals of the creative portion are:

- To grow comfortable expressing oneself creatively, especially with new materials and forms.
- To grow more comfortable with not knowing and feeling uncomfortable in that uncertainty.

- To cultivate a habit of creative expression so that it becomes a regular part of one's self-care.
- To observe and learn which creative activities engage one the most and the specific impacts they have on one's well-being.

The written reflection component of the Home Creative Practice follows a template (described in the next section) asking students to check in emotionally, physically, and mentally before and after the yoga and art practices, along with writing a summary note. Their notes record the day and time, the meditation or pranayama they choose to do, and comments about the impact of the session, including a short description of their physical, emotional, and thinking states before and after, and a summary of any insights they learn from the session that day. These notes are specific and detailed enough for them to track the impact of the selected art and yoga practices. In effect, they are experimenting with art and yoga, closely observing the effect of certain activities on their mind/body, and building a repertoire of reliable resources. For example, certain breath practices such as Long Deep Breathing have a calming effect, where others such as Breath of Fire energize (Lumpkin & Khalsa, 2015), and certain creative practices release pent-up emotions or help process and make visible unconscious worries (Khalsa, 2011). Learning which practices are best suited to which conditions is a personal endeavor and one that takes shape in the doing. From week to week, students expand their literacy for tuning in and describing their experiences. When students might default to surface generalizations over time, they are asked to notice when they repeat similar words for each session and then to explore a little deeper. Expanding their vocabulary, how else could they describe what they feel and notice within themselves? And, deepening their awareness, can they notice what is underneath the surface description? When students tend to rush through the process, especially when this level of intimate observation is new to them, I encourage them to be curious and patient, using self-reflective writing to connect with themselves on all levels, noting the ways their physical and emotional bodies and their thinking mind habitually react and then how yoga and art influences those reactions.

The goals of the template-based writing reflection are:

- To develop greater literacy and a richer vocabulary to describe one's physical sensations, emotions, and thoughts.
- To grow one's capacity to observe one's reactions without judgment, noting the content and not identifying with it.
- To understand the connection between cause and effect of the various practices, what brings one greater ease and helps expression, and what doesn't.
- To cultivate a new habit of self-presence and self-reflection as a regular part of one's day.

Home Creative Practice Written Reflection Template

Students copy the italicized sections into their notebook and fill in responses for each session.

- *Date/Start time*: list the date and time of day that you start your practice.
- *Meditation/Pranayama*: name the practice(s) you do and duration time(s).
- *Optional*: list any additional warm-ups and/or a full kriya if you add them.
- *Check-in Before*
  - *Physical state*: How do you feel physically? Where are the strongest sensations in your body right now? Any areas of tension or holding? Are you tired, sick, energized? Any knots, pangs, muscular soreness, tightness, or other strong physical sensations? Describe your sensations.
  - *Emotional state*: What are you feeling? Anything needing attention today? Is it a mix or a solid state? Do you know the source of the emotion? If so, what's causing it to arise now? Do your best not to get lost in the story, and bring the catalyst or source of the emotion forward in consciousness to help you connect to the emotion itself. Notice and name the emotions.
  - *Mental state*: What's on your mind? What are the dominant thoughts, worries, and concerns in this moment? Anything preoccupying you? Any story going on in your head? Beliefs? Expectations? Name your thoughts.
- *Check-in After*
  - *Physical state*: How do you feel physically after the practice? Any differences? Be specific.
  - *Emotional state*: What are you feeling after the practice? Did anything shift or change regarding your emotions or the way you are relating to them? Did the emotion grow or stay the same?
  - *Mental state*: How did this transform during and after the practice? Is the mind clearer or still confused and preoccupied?
- *Summary, overall impact, and insight*
  - Reflecting on your overall being, what did you learn about yourself today in this session? What are the major takeaways or gifts, if any, of today's practice? Note the circumstances when you don't have any major insights to glean.

The impact of this reflective piece can't be understated. As contemplative practice confirms, naming one's internal states creates a small gap of awareness between oneself and one's reactions, so one isn't overwhelmed or overidentified with them (Brach, 2020; Salzberg, 2020). This is important because often things happening in one's system block access to creative flow: by distracting or preoccupying one, sucking up one's energy, or hijacking one's nervous system. For example, maybe when someone sits down to make art, they have a strong inner critic that berates their efforts, robbing them of joy and filling them with fear of taking risks. Or perhaps when someone begins their practice, they are reeling from an angry exchange with a friend earlier in the day and can't seem to focus. Being able to name what's happening, if/when it prevents full presence, allows one to release those energetic blocks and get things moving again, freeing up access to natural creative flow. Like yoga and process-based arts, self-reflective writing is an action that helps keeps things moving. Writing becomes a contemplative tool to reconnect with the creative flow. As a bonus, it affects one's relationships with others.

Self-Assessment Learning Reports

At the beginning, middle, and end of the course, students reflect on their learning to date, in a more formally written paper. The early report gives them a chance to identify any blocks to access or understanding that might prevent full engagement with the course material, be it on a digital, psychological, cultural, or physical level. The mid- and end-term reports summarize the successes and challenges and how they meet those. Students name their own growth, resilience, and learning.

Connecting Body, Mind, Emotion

Throughout their engagement with the art and yogic material, with a heavy emphasis on self-reflective writing, students develop skills in somatic, mindful, and emotional intelligences, while earning the wisdom to apply those skills via direct experience. This comprises an expanded definition of "critical thinking," in which emotional and somatic intelligence (and even social intelligence) are just as important to education and living a good life as intellectual intelligence (Ng, 2018). The aggregated goals of this self-reflection and practice are:

- To help students track which practices help or hinder their given condition when they sit down to practice. Some pranayama practices are energizing, purifying, or calming. Some kriyas and chanting meditations are activating, raising energy, or restorative; some focus on flexibility in the spine or release in the lymphatic axes. All have a different and selective impact, and students learn the real-time effects on their particular body and mood.
- To create a record of cause and effect that students can refer back to.
- To develop awareness of how breath and yoga impacts the creative process. The creative exercises are more than just momentary play and flow: they, too, affect the students in distinct ways. Watercolor with the breath, slow and process-oriented, calms the body and helps them connect to themselves. The quick expressive movement of paint or crayon on paper can release anger, agitation, or other emotions.
- And in turn, to understand the impact of various creative processes on one's internal emotional states: for example, painting an abstract pool of color that can express and release sadness, grief, and loneliness. Creating symbolic forms and images can increase courage, focus, and commitment. Or it can temporarily bring joy and peace and renew a person's sense that everything is going to be okay.

These structured activities help students to be present with their emotions and sensations with less overwhelm. The simultaneous distancing and presence-ing also allows students to be with their thoughts—for example, anxious concerns about the future or past—without further fueling those thought loops. The invitation is for students to become aware of their unconscious habits (of emotion, actions, thoughts) and to distance themselves enough to think critically about whether or not those habits serve them and align with their goals.

Moving Into Relationality

In both the Inquiry Prompts and Home Creative Practice Written Reflection Template, students are writing primarily for themselves as a means to self-understanding. This self-reflective process brings their unconscious assumptions, expectations, and beliefs into conscious awareness so they can evaluate whether or not they align with their best self. However, their increased awareness of their values, beliefs, and reactions (thoughts, sensations, and emotions) means they will also become more aware when interacting with others relationally. As they learn to listen to themselves with greater empathy, understanding, emotional intelligence, and compassion, they become a better listener to others. As they watch the happenings of their own internal landscape, they appreciate the ways another person's internal experience may not be visible on the surface outside. So, while also teaching specific practical skills of art and yoga, the way these activities are framed conceptually and structurally, with the before and after check-in template and the Inquiry Prompt responses, underscores the other levels of learning taking place. For example, just as students learn that their mind and body are interdependent, so too is the connection between self and other.

All of this reflective writing means there is a strong emphasis on communicating clearly. In this interdisciplinary class, participants combine two different modes of expression: yoga, which affects the body and transforms the mind, and art, which uses different material means to express a person's inner experience. Students learn from each aspect: ways to move the body through physical asana and gesture and ways to utilize various artistic materials, including writing.

A prime objective of the course is to externalize, through movement, mark, and image, one's internal thoughts, beliefs, emotions, and sensations. For instance, moving the body into unfamiliar poses and actions, students are asked to remain aware of sensations in their body, developing an expanded vocabulary to track and identify changes happening within. When we then shift to our art practice, students are asked to translate that awareness into an artistic medium. And at the end of the yoga-art sequence, students are invited to describe their experience verbally and/or in writing. Throughout the class, a multimodal approach to enhanced communication and self-awareness is developed.

Conclusion

A central tool of the course is heightened self-awareness and sensitivity: of one's particular body and its capabilities, one's emotional reactivity and intelligence, habits of thinking, preconceived ideas and expectations of self and others, one's creativity, and social/historical conditioning. Just as yoga asanas look different on each body—some of us are more or less able, larger and smaller, older and younger, darker- and lighter-skinned—the way each person expresses their creativity is utterly unique. Attention to and acceptance of the differences among the group creates a more diverse understanding of the whole, encouraging freedom of thought and expression, an appreciation for different worldviews, respect for others, greater empathy, compassion, and a nascent commitment to social justice (questions of access, rights, and equity).

Resisting dichotomies of mind vs. body, theory vs. practice, reason vs. emotion, secular knowledge vs. spirituality, *Arts 1202: Art and Yoga* supports students in cultivating artistic skills and training in specific yoga techniques and asana postures. The learning environment asks students to engage in these practices while also opening up to intense self-awareness and reflection. This "decolonizing" combination aims to free students of limiting beliefs, old patterns of thinking and acting, unconscious ingrained expectations, and habitual assumptions learned through their particular socialization, all with the idea of change, healing, and transformation. Students may walk into the course expecting to "make art" and "do yoga" but end up also embarking on a self-discovery journey of their very person.

References

Barkataki, S. (2015, February 7). How to Decolonize Your Yoga Practice. *DecolonizingYoga.com*. https://decolonizingyoga.com/decolonize-yoga-practice/.

Batacharya, S. (2018). Resistance and Remedy Through Embodied Learning: Yoga Cultural Appropriation and Culturally Appropriate Services. In S. Batacharya & Y.-L. R. Wong (Eds.), *Sharing Breath: Embodied Learning and Decolonization* (pp. 161–198). Athabasca University Press.

Berg, M., & Seeber, B. K. (2017). *The Slow Professor: Challenging the Culture of Speed in the Academy*. University of Toronto Press.

Berger, M. (1990). Are Art Museums Racist? *Art in America*. https://www.artnews.com/art-in-america/features/maurice-berger-are-art-museums-racist-1202682524/2/.

Brach, T. (2020). *Radical Compassion: Learning to Love Yourself and Your World with the Practice of RAIN*. Penguin Publishing.

Cassou, M., & Cubley, S. (1996). *Life, Paint and Passion: Reclaiming the Magic of Spontaneous Expression*. Tarcher Perigee.

Guerilla Girls. (1998). *The Guerilla Girls' Bedside Companion to the History of Western Art*. Penguin Books.

hooks, b. (1994). *Teaching to Transgress: Education as the Practice of Freedom*. Routledge.

Khalsa, H. K. K. (2011). *Art & Yoga: Kundalini Awakening in Everyday Life*. Kundalini Research Institute.

Lee, A. (2017). *Teaching Interculturally: A Framework for Integrating Disciplinary Knowledge and Intercultural Development*. Stylus Publishing.

Lumpkin, N., & Khalsa, J. K. (2015). *Enlightened Bodies: Exploring Physical and Subtle Human Anatomy*. Kundalini Research Institute.

Magee, R. V. (2019). *The Inner Work of Racial Justice: Healing Ourselves and Transforming Our Communities through Mindfulness*. Tarcher Perigee.

Masters, R. A. (2010). *Spiritual Bypassing: When Spirituality Disconnects Us from What Really Matters*. North Atlantic Books.

Mountz, A., Bonds, A., Mansfield, B., Loyd, J., Hyndman, J., Walton-Roberts, M., Basu, R., Whitson, R., Hawkins, R., Hamilton, T., & Curran, W. (2015). For Slow Scholarship: A Feminist Politics of Resistance through Collective Action in the Neoliberal University. *ACME: An International Journal for Critical Geographies*, 14(4), 1235–1259.

Ng, R. (2018). Decolonizing Teaching and Learning Through Embodied Learning: Toward an Integrated Approach. In S. Batacharya & Y.-L. R. Wong (Eds.), *Sharing Breath: Embodied Learning and Decolonization* (pp. 33–54). Athabasca University Press.

Salzberg, S. (2020). *Real Change: Mindfulness to Heal Ourselves and the World*. Flatiron Books.

Selassie, S. (2020). *You Belong: A Call for Connection*. HarperOne.

Welwood, J. (2000). *Toward a Psychology of Awakening: Buddhism, Psychotherapy, and the Path of Personal and Spiritual Transformation*. Shambhala Publications.

9
CONTEMPLATIVE PRACTICES FOR TEACHING THE SCIENCES

Franklin M. Chen

Roth (2014) defines contemplative practice as the sustained, focused attention that leads to deepened states of concentration, tranquility, insight, and contextualizing orientation. Much research has shown that contemplative techniques like meditation can help students go beyond a merely cognitive understanding of their responsibilities as global citizens and find an authentic motivation to serve (Harshman & Augustine, 2015; Walsh, 2014; Zajonc, 2006). Contemplative pedagogy empowers students to integrate their own experience into the theoretical material they are being taught to cultivate and develop attention, deepen their understanding, foster greater connection to and compassion for others, and engender engaged inquiry into their most profound questions. In science, contemplative practices cultivate sustaining attention and contemplative insights of knowing (Zajonc, 2014), which are key ingredients of creativity.

I teach beginning and upper-level chemistry, beginning mathematics, and introductory environmental science courses. Although contemplative practices can be applied to all of these, the environmental science course was my first attempt to apply contemplative practices in class. My purpose was to engage students in reflective thinking to be more aware of contemporary environmental issues and become mindful of their consumption habits. Gradually, I introduced contemplative practices in all my other science classes.

While some educators are eager to include contemplative practices in their teaching, others find the introduction of contemplative practices—particularly in science classrooms—as somewhat controversial. This range of standpoints was initially present among my students, who saw the value of meditation and spirituality, yet considered these practices in the classroom as artificial, nonauthentic, and diluting the teaching and learning of course contents. Many scholars (Keiser & Sakulkoo, 2014) in the field have also reported this range of perspectives in

DOI: 10.4324/9781003201854-12

their classrooms and have used diverse tactics to assist students and colleagues in recognizing the value of these contemplative practices—especially in science classrooms. Through many years of contemplative experiences in the classroom, I have found that the sense of the *teacher's presence* as seen by students is critical for students' "buy-in" to these practices.

In this chapter, I describe the evolution of my contemplative practices, both in my courses and in my own daily practice, and share the qualitative results of these practices. From one-minute mindfulness to community service learning, mindful readings of environmental science, contemplative music, gratitude, storytelling, and poetry, my contemplative pedagogy uses many branches of the "Tree of Contemplative Practices" offered by the Association for the Contemplative Mind in Higher Education (CMind) (2014). But the trunk and roots of that tree are grounded in the contemplative practices of the teachers themselves.

Contemplative Practices and Training: Foundations for Teaching

Miller (2014) indicates successful teaching involves three essential elements: (1) the content of the material; (2) the strategy and practices, which include students' learning evaluation; and (3) the teacher's presence. According to Miller, this third element—the teacher's ability to show up and be present to his or her students—can have major impacts on students' learning and lives.

While faculty may complain about students' distraction by various technology gadgets, the faculty member's life is often fragmented because of pervasive cultural mandates for busyness and techno-saturation. Alderman (2014) remarks that her daily calendar was divided first into days, then hours, then 20-minute segments, and now 10. We see how time compression contributes to the constant sense of stress. When faculty do not pay attention to this onslaught of time fragmentation and stress, it is challenging for them to be present and show up for the students.

I began my own contemplative practice in 2010. My decision grew out of my personal experiences during my sabbatical in Taiwan. After 60–70 hours/week working while living alone without taking care of myself, which included poor diet, lack of exercise, lack of social and spiritual connections, I was gravely ill. After returning to the United States, despite the state-of-the-art medical care in this country, I was still not well. On several occasions, I attended free healing summits sponsored by Hay House Publishing. During the summits, prominent speakers like Wayne Dyer and Deepak Chopra addressed the spiritual components of healing. Inspired by their words, I started my healing journey that includes a healthy diet, regular exercise, and daily meditation.

My contemplative practices in my healing journey include 30 minutes of sitting meditation in the morning when I wake up. Then, I write my intentions of the day in my daily journal. After rigorous exercises, I do qigong and yoga to cool off. After lunch, if time permits, I have 20–30 minutes of sitting meditation.

Before going to bed, I write in a gratitude journal. Besides those daily contemplative routines, I also read books and listen to podcasts from various luminous scholars. Every week, I attend two sangha meetings held regularly in my area. These sanghas follow the tradition of Thich Nhat Hanh and include sitting meditation, walking meditation, dharma talks, and discussions that emphasize deep listening. Mindfulness practices permeate my daily life through activities such as eating, cooking, dishwashing, and conversations. Deep listening practices help me to improve relationships with my family, my friends, and colleagues. These practices and other dietary changes and exercise routines gradually healed my body. Today, I believe I have better health than I had 12 years ago. Contemplative practices enabled my healing journey, and I am eager to share those experiences with my students.

Along with these contemplative practices, I have undertaken many trainings in contemplative pedagogy through various organizations. My first contemplative pedagogy training with Joanne Gozawa (2014) resonated with my heart, and I became determined to try out contemplative pedagogy in my environmental science classes. Over five years, I explored and tested the research foundations for the practices I use today.

In 2017, I attended the CMind summer session at Smith College. One of the sessions I participated in during that weeklong gathering was "Soulfulness," presented by Steven Murphy-Shigematsu (2018), fluent in English and Japanese. The most impressive part of his presentation was his interpretation of busyness in the Chinese pictograph, 忙. This pictograph, 忙, consists of two radicals: the one on the left, 忄, means the heart; the radical on the right, 亡, means death—the word "busyness" in Chinese means the death of the heart. When a teacher is too busy in life, they will not be present to their students. As a result, such teachers will lose their authenticity and lose their teaching effectiveness because teachers' authority derives from their authenticity (Spurlin, 2018). Although Chinese is my first language, I had not paid much attention to radicals until Murphy-Shigematsu mentioned it. Then, I began to notice busyness in my life and this pervasive busyness culture.

Another takeaway from CMind summer school was the mindful walk led by another attendee (Johnson, 2017). The walk started with 15 minutes of meditation. Then the group of approximately ten people walked in silence along a wooded trail at Smith College. The leader provided mindfulness prompts at different stops, for example: (1) find where the animals live; (2) find out how many shades of leaves are in a tree; (3) pretend you are a tree that dances with the wind; or (4) make a coyote howl in the woods. The mindful walk was an excellent exercise for connecting us with nature and training our minds to pay attention to our surroundings, and I decided to use that technique in my own science classrooms.

In 2018, together with 19 other faculty from 18 disciplines and six institutions, I participated in a Mind and Life think tank on "Mindfulness as a Strategy for Anti-Oppression Pedagogy: Preparation, Implementation and Assessment" convened by co-editor Greta Gaard. Our think tank opened with reminders of the painful facts that one in four college students have diagnosable illnesses, 40% of them do not seek help, 80% of them feel overwhelmed, and 50% of them have become so anxious that they struggle in school (NAMI, 2012). Their diagnosable illnesses include depression, anxiety, suicide, eating disorders, sexual violence/stalking, self-injury, panic attacks, sleep disorders, post-traumatic stress, and unresolved/acute grief (Gaard, 2018). Those numbers are shocking, and they call for mindfulness practices to be offered at universities through our pedagogies, counseling centers, and topic-specific courses.

During the academic year of 2018–2019, I participated in monthly dialogues with my colleagues in various disciplines in my university, discussing strategies for teaching with transparency. I began to realize that one of my courses, Introduction to Environmental Science, was exploring sustainability education in the context of Western culture's global set of beliefs and values (Eaton et al., 2017). These beliefs and values place a heavy emphasis on "progress, reason, competition, individualism, and materialism. This tacit and often unconscious collective understanding profoundly influences how we treat the earth and how we treat each other" (Eaton et al., 2017, p. 7). Pressing sustainability issues such as mitigating climate change and improving human health requires new thinking and problem-solving methods. Characterized as the presence of relaxed yet concentrated minds, contemplative pedagogy holds a space in silence, allowing intuition and creativity to flourish.

Contemplative Practices in the Classrooms

CMind's Tree of Contemplative Practices shows the many forms of contemplative practice besides meditation and yoga. Here, I discuss my uses of six different contemplative practices in teaching sciences.

One-Minute Meditation

Regular meditation practice has been known to have beneficial mental health results since ancient times, and now contemporary research confirms the health benefits of meditation practice. Accordingly, in 2014, I used the one-minute guided meditation practice in both the Introduction to Environmental Science and the upper-level Thermodynamics and Kinetics classes. At the end of each chapter or the end of each conceptual explanation, I asked students to close their eyes as I read through the summary of the concepts while their eyes remained closed. After the meditation and listening to the summary, students then opened their eyes and asked questions. The practice gave enough space for students to reflect, absorb information, and generate new ideas. At the end of the semester, I took a survey asking for the students' reflection on the one-minute experience in these words: "Do you feel that short meditations in class when we are moving from one chapter to another help you become more reflective about the materials we have learned, and more mindful on the material we are about to learn?" Results indicate that approximately 58% favored this type of contemplative practice, while 26% disliked the practice. Approximately 16% of students neither favored nor disfavored the practice. Selective students' comments on these experiences are as follows:

> Gave time to process the information.
> I honestly think it is kind of strange.
> I am indifferent with meditation. I have never done meditation before. I am not for nor against it. If that is what Dr. Chen likes to do then there is nothing wrong with it. Also, if a student has any problems with meditating during and between chapters in class then he or she doesn't need to participate and I feel that Dr. Chen has made it clear that the students are not required to participate in meditation if they do not want to.
> The meditation was helpful to imagine how our life [would be] if we were in those situations. It was fun too. It gives me a great refresher on everything we learned. Also, it feels good to relax and take a breath and focus now and then in this fast pace of life.

Since then, the one-minute meditation exercise has evolved due to the need to cover course materials and make the practice less awkward in the middle of classroom problem- solving. Instead of providing guided meditation, I now simply ask students to close their eyes, listen to their breath for one minute, and then ask if they have any questions.

Community Service Project

I also started offering a six- to eight-hour Community Service Project in my Introduction to Environmental Science courses, explaining the purpose and intended outcomes in my syllabus and providing resources for students to contact various community organizations for potential service-learning opportunities. In the syllabus, I stressed the importance of interrelatedness, explaining that we need to care for the environment not just from the head but also from the heart. Communities that welcomed students' services include Habitat for Humanity, Domestic Abuse Shelter, Homeless Shelter, and House of Hope.

While comparable to the Service Learning many instructors have employed, the Community Service Learning Project differs in that the "Students' Instructions" emphasize two additional aspects of the project: Interrelatedness and Deep Listening. For Interrelatedness, I quote a Departing Gatha written by Thich Nhat Hanh;

> We are related to each other.
> By taking care of you, I take care of myself.

> By taking care of myself, I take care of you.
> Happiness and Safety are not individual matters.

I also provide instructions for students in practicing deep listening while interacting with others during their service-learning project. A simple method for "deep listening" is to pause before responding to others and to reflect on three questions: (1) Is it true? (2) Is it kind? (3) Is it necessary? When we practice deep listening while others are speaking, we help create a calm and receptive environment. Our listening contributes to the collective insight and understanding of humanity. In this way, deep listening enacts and nourishes the health of our interrelatedness.

In their reflection papers, community service learning students wrote,

> As a community, we do not realize how lucky we are to have environmentally friendly organizations helping recycle unwanted materials while at the same time helping underprivileged people in the community have affordable housing and do home improvement projects within their budgets. The Green Bay Habitat for Humanity ReStore and Habitat for Humanity do both of those things. . . .
>
> The over-consumption of non-renewable resources makes our environmental quality a lot lower than it should be and one way of fixing this is to reduce the amount of resources consumed. The ReStore contributes to this cause by reusing building materials in the community and by serving as a recycling center for aluminum cans and other metal products.

End-of-semester quantitative survey results are shown in Figure 9.1.

The question: The eight-hour community service helped me become more aware of the environmental issues we are facing today.

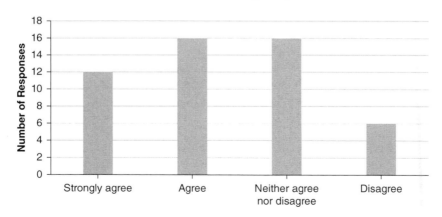

FIGURE 9.1 Survey results of students' responses to community service

Students' approval for the Community Service Project was 56%, with 12% of students disapproving, and 32% of students having no opinion. For those who did not support service learning, the feedback had more to do with their approach to the service:

> I feel like doing service projects doesn't help me think about the environment. It only feels like I'm doing it just for the grade and not for the environment. Therefore, there is very little motivation for me to do something like that.

But for those who reaped the benefits of service learning, the feedback was clear:

> I was very involved.
>
> This was a good thing to include since it gave you first-hand experience in the issues that the environment faces. It allowed you to have a better grasp of those issues and I feel like this project should be included in the future courses of this class.
>
> I feel that the Environmental issues volunteer project was very beneficial. It helps us focus on others rather than being self-centered. It is very rewarding to feel like you are helping and changing the world.

While there is room for improving students' mindfulness practice in the Community Service Project, this project still has a lot of students' support. Student feedback shows that environmental sustainability requires students to become mindful of our society's vast problems of poverty and overconsumption as part of our classroom content in Environmental Science.

Environmental Awareness: Reading Rachel Carson's Silent Spring

I use Carson's (1962) *Silent Spring* in my Introduction to Environmental Science course. This poetic and contemplative book details Western science's mechanistic view of nature that disposes us to produce pesticides and other related chemicals with very harmful environmental effects. The purpose for asking students to read this additional text was to expand students' awareness, which is one of the goals of contemplative practice: in the words of Thich Nhat Hanh, "to be a buddha is to be awake." Reading *Silent Spring* enhanced students' understanding of the interrelatedness among the processes of environmental life support systems such as the atmosphere (air, carbon dioxide, ozone), hydrosphere (water in lakes, rivers, oceans, in frozen ice), geosphere (rocks and soils) and biosphere (human and all other species). The teaching objective was to embed this interrelatedness into regular course examinations, with test questions that specifically encourage students' awareness of the interrelatedness among different life-supporting processes.

Carson's text also allows students to recognize and evaluate assumptions that human interference with Earth's life-support systems is natural and right. *Silent Spring* has many examples illustrating the consequences of Western science's implicit assertion of authority and the ecological and human effects of scientific interference. One example is in Chapter 2: "Obligation to Endure," where Carson asks,

> How could intelligent beings seek to control a few unwanted species by a method that contaminated the entire environment and brought the threat of disease and death even to their own kind? Yet this is precisely what we have done.

In another example from chapter 3, "Elixirs of Death," Carson mentions the common mindset of modern humanity:

> The desire for a quick and easy method of killing unwanted plants has given rise to a large and growing array of chemicals that are known as herbicides or, less formally, as weed killers.

Students at the end of the semester wrote an essay reflecting their awareness of the interrelatedness of humans and environments and completed an end-of-semester survey. I especially asked students to capture specific paragraphs reflecting the mindset of modern humanity that had helped create modern environmental problems. Quantitative results and the question: Reading Silent Spring helped me become more aware of the environmental issues we are facing today are shown in Figure 9.2.

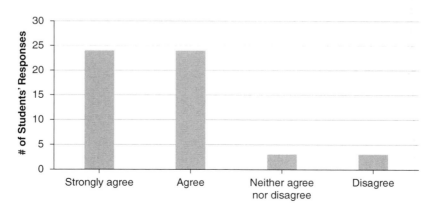

FIGURE 9.2 Students' responses to reading Carson's *Silent Spring*

The survey indicated 96% of students reported that their environmental awareness increased; 2% believed their awareness did not increase, and 2% had no opinion. Those students whose awareness increased provided very positive comments:

> Carson's [book] caused me to have more awareness of my surrounding environment and what chemicals are in everyday products. It was an overall good read. Very interesting and informative.
>
> The book affected me a lot about environmental issues, and it gave me a chance to think about environmental issues too. The book was written about 50 years ago, but it must have shocked everyone who was in that era.
>
> The book explains environmental issues, therefore, leading me to think about them while reading it.

Meditation Music Interlude

During my personal healing journey, I had explored Weil and Arem's (2004) sound healings. Andrew Weil is a physician practicing integrated medicine, while Kimba Arem is a music therapist. Their research, clinical experiences, and publications have shown many health and learning benefits of using music as a tool enhancing mental health and well-being. These findings are corroborated by wider research. For example, Mastnak (2016) explains music's preventive and therapeutic effect in stress-associated disorders and burnout using a triadic model encompassing neuroendocrine, psychological and aesthetic facets. Daykin and colleagues (2018) report that music has been associated with reduced anxiety in young adults, enhanced mood and purpose in adults, mental well-being, quality of life, self-awareness, and coping in people with diagnosed health conditions. Music and singing are effective in enhancing morale and reducing risk of depression in older people.

More recent research shows the clinical and educational benefits of music. Sugaya and Yonetani (Kotala, 2016) have taught "Music and the Brain," exploring the impacts of music on brain function and human behavior. They indicate music familiar to the listener will have positive impacts on the brain, a finding that suggests any music that is familiar to students can be used.

To investigate these benefits during both Spring 2015 and Spring 2016 semesters, I taught two Principles of Chemistry sections back-to-back: section 2 ran from 11:40 a.m. to 12:35 p.m.; section 3 started at 12:45 p.m. Both sections were in the same classroom, giving me the opportunity to explore the effects of using contemplative music on students' mental clarity and capacity for learning. During the ten-minute interlude between sections, I played Arem's Self-Healing with Sound and Music and other YouTube-available meditation music such as Nada Himalaya. The section that started with music had increased student attendance and performance, as shown in Figure 9.3. For section 2, the Final exam average grade was 56.76% with grade distribution spread from 17% to 110%.

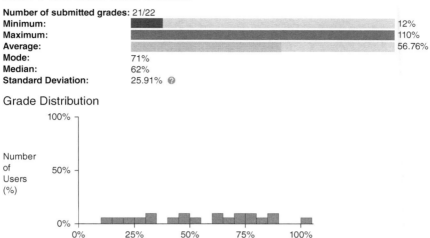

FIGURE 9.3 Students' 2015 final grade comparison, section 2 (class without meditation music at the beginning of class)

For section 3 (shown in Figure 9.4), the final exam average grade was 65.6% with grade distribution mostly clustered between 48% and 85%. A similar test result trend was also observed in 2016: students with the music interlude had almost 10 points higher in grade averages (65.6% versus 56.8%) than those students without the music interlude. The grade distribution charts also indicate that while students' grades in the section without the music interlude were spread from a low of 10% to 80%, students' grades in the section with the music interlude clustered between 50% and 80%.

In their end-of-semester reflection papers, many students expressed how welcome those contemplative practices were for them in the chemistry class, even though I did not solicit students' comments on the meditation music interlude:

> I really enjoyed the few seconds we would take out of class each day to listen to some meditation music and read an inspiring quotation. It was a nice refresher to my hectic schedule.
> I also learned about just slowing down, breathing, and relaxing. I truly enjoyed the inspiration that you provided each and every day in class, along with joke time to break up the lecture. I learned that sometimes you could study all you want, but you will not test well if you don't get enough sleep the night before. I had learned so many things in chemistry that were not chemistry-related that I wound up really enjoying the class even when

Exam 4-Test Class Statistics

Number of submitted grades: 25/25

Minimum: 34%
Maximum: 85%
Average: 65.6%
Mode: 83%
Median: 65%
Standard Deviation: 13.34%

Grade Distribution

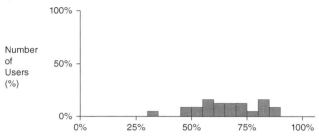

FIGURE 9.4 Students' 2015 final grade comparison, section 3 (class with meditation music at the beginning of class)

I was lost and frustrated with not understanding the material. I realize that this reflection is generalized, but if I were to go into detail about this it would be a very long essay.

I just want to thank you Dr. Chen for making this semester fun and teaching me valuable lessons that will apply in every aspect of life. Also thank you for believing in me. You truly are the Zen master.

Although I cannot make a hard case that the meditation music before the beginning of the class helps students improve their test grades, many students seemed to welcome the contemplative practice in the chemistry classroom especially before the class starts. The benefits of students' learning in my practice are consistent with the research findings.

Nature or Mindful Walk on Campus Trail

In the conventional sit-in classroom with almost 130 students, allowing everybody to spend a whole class time to walk in nature provides a good break in the routine and cultivates intuition and creativity. Albert Einstein often walked into the woods and played his violin after intense math work in his Princeton office (Clark, 1971). There are numerous reports on both physical and mental health benefits of walking in nature (Frumkin et al., 2017; Cox et al., 2017).

In the Fall 2016 semester, during one meeting of the Introduction to Environmental Science class, we walked on the prairie. Students were asked to identify five different animals and five different plants using sketches, descriptions, and photo-shoots to report their findings in an online discussion forum. Students collected photos and posted their photos. Although students did not elaborate on what they saw and collected during their process, they found this activity extremely interesting.

In the Fall 2017 semester, I modified the nature walk into the Mindful Walk on the campus trail. The difference between a mindful walk and a nature walk is the extent of awareness of the walker during walking. Here is a Gatha for Walking Meditation in our sangha, which I also shared with my class:

> The mind can go in a thousand directions
> But on this pathway I walk in peace
> With each step, a gentle wind blows
> With each step, a flower blooms.

In addition to this walking meditation Gatha, I also quoted a few verses from Thich Nhat Hanh. Here are the examples of the verses:

> The miracle is not to walk on water but to walk on the Earth
> Walk as if you are kissing the Earth on every step.

In my syllabus, I explained the purpose and practice for the Mindful Walk:

> We will gather initially at the classroom and walk on foot to the prairie. The objective is to be mindful while you are walking on the trail. Be attentive to what you see, what you hear, what you smell, what you touch while walking on the trail. You do need to report a *collection of 5 senses* from your team in your report. Each team leader will get a book of prompts from the instructor prior to the mindful walk; these prompts will heighten your 5 senses in embracing the beauty of the nature.

The prompts used in this Mindful Walk are to

1. Observe how many shades there are in the greens.
2. Pick up a handful of soil and smell the odor of the soil. What do you see in the soil?
3. Find out where animals live.
4. Take off your shoes and feel the contact of the Earth on your feet.
5. Pretend that you are a tree dancing in the wind.

The walking itself symbolizes how we care about the Earth and the environment. At the end of the walk, I had students write reflections. Here are samples of their reflections:

> Once I set off on the trail and got to look at all the trees and the stream I began to relax. I felt calm and collected again as I felt the grass and the leaves on the trees, the mosquitos were horrible, but I tried to ignore them. I smelled the flowers and the lingering scent of fresh cut grass as I got closer to campus again.
>
> When I first stepped outside I had some classmates ask me "are you seriously going for a walk"? I replied "Why not?" As I started for the nature paths they decided to follow along. We walked through the prairie and I showed them the little bug houses inside withered Queen Anne's Lace and how the still green leaves smelled like carrot. We did bring out our phones but only for a moment to look up the name of some bright yellow prairie flower. We think it was Goldenrod. A little further down the path we came across an abandoned gazebo covered in vines. The wood of the benches was covered in various mosses and lichen. I wonder how long it's been since the benches had someone sitting on them. I've seen the vines that were wrapping around the posts in various places around the school. I'm pretty sure the same ones are invading one of the gardens at home. Is it an invasive species? This is the first year it stood out to me.

The difference between the Nature Walk and Mindful Walk is the degree of attention that students paid during their walk. With a class of almost 130 students, I cannot guarantee students will follow the protocol of mindful walking. Even in the Mindful Walk protocol, students are more interested in knowing the plants' names than in observing the plants more closely. Nonetheless, I am fully convinced that a walk in nature—whether it is a Nature Walk or a Mindful Walk—is a good way to break up the routine and increase students' awareness of interrelatedness with nature.

Gratitude Reflection, Storytelling, Poetry, and Quotations

Numerous published research studies confirm the benefits of gratitude practice (Emmons & Stern, 2013; Tala, 2019), poetry (Clark, 2009; Gao & Guo, 2018), storytelling (Tanaka et al., 2019; Mannell et al., 2018) and affirmations (Cohen & Sherman, 2014). Chemistry and mathematics classes require extensive use of the rational minds. Most of the class times, students and instructor are engaging in math drills either in lecture or in note taking, or in whiteboard problem-solving and practices. A break from this routine of less than five minutes, with careful selections and skillful delivery of the gratitude reflection, storytelling, poetry, and quotations, is often well-received by the students. These contemplative practices can be considered in the science classroom setting.

Starting in the fall semester of 2017, I added gratitude reflection, storytelling, poetry, and inspirational quotations in all courses I teach. Usually, I ask to see if any student in the class would like to share something to be grateful about for the day or for the past few days. Although it is not common for students to openly share their story to the whole class, I do get a few students sharing gratitude from time to time. Typical students' gratitude sharing involves going home to see their parents, getting good grades on the tests, or getting new cars. While I do not want to discourage students telling the class that they were happy because they got "something" (car, or good grades), I emphasize that they can be grateful and happy for anything that has happened in their lives. To make such attitude changes in students, I share my gratitude or tell stories to the class. The gratitude messages that I give to my class demonstrate that gratitude can be practiced regardless of one's circumstances. For example, I share my personal story in 2018 during an ice storm in Wisconsin. My two-month-old new Prius car was hit by a car behind me, causing a lot of damage. Even in such unfortunate accidents, I said to the class, I was grateful because the police came to the accident site and braved the cold weather preparing the paperwork for both drivers so that the car could be quickly repaired.

Storytelling is another contemplative practice to break classroom routine. Human beings are creatures of storytelling. In contemplative education, storytelling is an example of creative and artistic contemplative practices (CMind, n.d.). Le Guin (1979) has once said that "there have been great societies that did not use the wheel, but there have been no societies that did not tell stories." Most stories we tell, however, are often negative-biased, which is not useful. In contemplative education, storytelling is intended to evoke positive emotions such as love or compassion among listeners. In my classroom, storytelling consists of a mix of my personal stories, stories retold from great Zen Masters such as Thich Nhat Hanh and Jack Kornfield, and inspiring fairytale stories. One of my favorite stories I share involves a highway incident, when a guy with road rage showed the middle finger at me and tried to insult me while driving. I tell students that no one can insult you without your consent. Another story I have shared was from one of the dharma talks by Kornfield (n.d.) describing a couple walking out a doctor's office at the Mayo Clinic, where the husband had just been diagnosed with a deadly ALS disease. In the lobby, a pianist was playing music that happened to be the music played when the couple was married. The husband put down his briefcase containing all the medical tests and diagnosis, and grabbed his wife's waist and danced on the floor. Other couples joined in with beautiful spirit, demonstrating that we can be joyful no matter what the circumstances.

Besides gratitude sharing and storytelling, I have also used mindful poetry reading, and inspirational quote reading. Harper (2018) said that poetry writing has always been a process of what she sees and experiences in the world:

> The playfulness with language, the brevity of using as few words as possible to get to the heart of something, helps me understand things more deeply. In this regard, I think it was a natural progression for my poetry to become a tool of contemplation, an essential part of my spiritual practice.

For poetry reading, I tell the class that poetry is the language of the soul. I select poems from both ancient and contemporary poets including Jaluluddin Rumi, Thich Nhat Hanh, Mary Oliver, Annabel Laity, Barbara Crooker, Ellen Bass, Naomi Shihab Nye, and John O'Donohue.

Inspirational quotes are often taken from books of Thich Nhat Hanh (1999b) and Wayne Dyer (1998). Among all the quotes, the one I like best and have shared often to my class is Thich Nhat Hanh's quote (1999a), "Waking up This Morning"

> Waking up this morning I smile,
> 24 brand new hours before me.
> I vow to live fully in each moment,
> and look at beings with eyes of compassion.

In science classes, covering the required course materials is still considered as the most important expectation for instructors and students in the classroom. The timing and duration of time spent by the instructor on contemplative practices such as gratitude sharing, poetry reading, storytelling, and other mindfulness practices is critical. It is most effective when both students and instructors do not have time pressure to "rush" through course materials—or midway through a class session, when a new problem or material has just been covered, and both students and the instructor need time to decompress and digest. Also, the selection of the materials for storytelling, poetry, and more is also important. I often avoid any religious and political overtone but focus on uplifting thoughts such as loving kindness, gratitude, resilience, and forgiveness. Students know what is right and what is wrong. A less-than-five-minute contemplative practice often improves students' moods and helps them continue to be "good listeners" for the rest of the class period.

Outcomes

Students' responses to these types of contemplative pedagogy are quite positive. While I did not quantitatively measure the impact, I did receive many positive comments from students through many channels: semester course evaluations, unsolicited feedback from students and students' parents, Student Nominated Teacher Award narratives. For example, an excerpt from a student email in May 2019, reads:

> Having a moment of gratitude has inspired and impacted me in such a way that it has changed my life forever along with the stories you shared.

That same semester, an email from a student's parent describes the effect of the class on both the student and her family:

> Every Friday night our family . . . goes out to eat to celebrate the week and talk. I cannot tell you specifics about many of Emily's classes at UWGB, but I can tell you that every week we talk about your class. . . . The topic is always regarding how you have the class talk about for what they are grateful. . . . My wife and I are grateful you are Emily's professor. (Also 'thank you' for your teaching in math. Emily's grades are improving!!!!)

I conclude with an excerpt from a student's narrative in his course evaluation, describing how gratitude and mindfulness practices supported his healing from combat:

> So many life lessons learned from your stories and poems. I was not one for compassion and gratefulness prior to your class. I was an emotionless shell, ... My wife knew me before and after my last deployment and really noticed my emotionless short-tempered grouchiness. . . . I figured it was caused by deployments for the military and learning to block emotions as I lost friends over there, seeing and doing things that are primal, not meant for modern life, but its war. . . . I can say that now as you taught me about being grateful and thankful for everything around us. I am finding my old self again. My true self I used to be, the one my wife married. I reflect on this semester and can see how I am happier; appreciate the time I have on this earth. I now start most mornings off with gratefulness, and mindfulness. I will now pause a few times a day to work on mindfulness and breathing.

Concluding Reflections

The ultimate goal of contemplative education in science-centered classrooms is to cultivate a classroom climate that fosters reflection and creativity. For contemplative practices to be effective in the classroom, there are many factors, including the class size, the degree of difficulty for students' learning the course materials, and the receptivity for students to contemplate those kinds of practices. To be successful, it is essential for the students to see the instructor as someone who is present and authentic.

Since 2014, I have been using contemplative practices both in my daily life and in my classrooms, with clear and positive outcomes. Practicing mindfulness in my personal life is essential for me to be "present" to my students and to be authentic in the presence of students.

The receptivity of students for contemplative practices depends on the mutual relation between an instructor and a student. One cannot overemphasize that being authentic and being present during student-instructor interactions is critical for the success of any contemplative practice in the classroom. Much of what we teach about mindfulness is through our own authenticity, and this is why our daily mindfulness practices, as instructors, are critical. If we ask students to reflect during a moment of the gratitude in class, as instructors, we too should use that moment of reflection to write a note of daily gratitude.

As a science instructor, I often have to choose time properly to interject contemplative practices in the classroom because teaching and learning core class materials is still the most important expectation for any science instructor. Many years of teaching science classes have given me confidence in choosing the proper time and proper materials to allow students to immerse themselves in various forms of contemplative practice. When the timing is right, and the materials are appropriate, contemplative practices are often experienced as a way to decompress students' heavy mental load, allowing them to be more creative in the long run.

References

Alderman, M. (2014). Kindred Spirits in Teaching Contemplative Practice: Distraction, Solitude, and Simplicity. In O. Gunnlaugson, E. W. Sarath, C. Scott, & H. Bai (Eds.), *Contemplative Learning and Inquiry Across Disciplines* (pp. 51–68). State University of New York Press.

Carson, R. (1962). *Silent Spring*. Houghton Mifflin.

Clark, R. (1971). *Einstein: The Life and Times*. World Publishing, Times Mirror.

Clark, T. (2009). Poetry, Recovery and Beyond. *Australian Psychiatry*, 1, 167–169. Doi: 10.1080/10398560902948407.PMID: 19579135.

Cohen, G. L., & Sherman, D. K. (2014). The Psychology of Change: Self-Affirmation and Social Psychological Intervention. *Annual Review of Psychology*, 65, 333–371 Doi: 10.1146/annurev-psych-010213-115137.PMID: 24405362.

Contemplative Mind in Higher Education. (2014). *Tree of Contemplative Practices*. https://www.contemplativemind.org/practices/tree.

Contemplative Mind in Higher Education. (n.d.). *Storytelling*. https://www.contemplativelife.org/practice/storytelling/all/creative-artistic.

Cox, D. T. C., Shanahan, D. F., Hudson, H. L., Fuller, R. A., Anderson, K., Hancock, S., & Gaston, K. J. (2017). Doses of Nearby Nature Simultaneously Associated with Multiple Health Benefits. *International Journal of Environmental Research and Public Health*, 14(172), 1–13. Doi: 10.3390/ijerph14080936, PMCID: PMC5580638.

Daykin, N., Mansfield, L., Meads, C., Julier, G., Tomlinson, A., Payne, A., & Victor, C. (2018). What Works for Well-being? A Systematic Review of Well-being Outcomes for Music and Singing in Adults. *Perspectives in Public Health*, 1, 39–46 Doi: 10.1177/1757913917740391. Epub 2017 Nov 13.PMID: 29130840.

Dyer, W. (1998). *Wisdom of the Ages*. Harper Books.

Eaton, M., Davies, K., Williams, S., & MacGregor, J. (2017). Why Sustainability Education Needs Pedagogies of Reflection and Contemplation. In M. Eaton, H. J. Hughes, & J Macgregor (Eds.), *Contemplative Approaches to Sustainability in Higher Education, Theory and Practice* (pp. 3–15). New York: Routledge.

Emmons, R. A., & Stern, R. (2013). Gratitude as a Psychotherapeutic Intervention. *Journal of Clinical Psychology*, 69, 846–855. Doi: 10.1002/jclp.22020. Epub 2013 Jun 17.PMID: 23775470.

Frumkin, H., Bratman, G. N., Breslow, S. J., Cochran, B., Kahn, P. H. Jr., Lawler, J. J., & Wood, S. A. (2017). Nature Contact and Human Health: A Research Agenda. *Environmental Health Perspectives*, 125(7), 075001. Doi: 10.1289/EHP1663, PMID: 28796634.

Gaard, G. (2018). *Strategy for Integrating Mindfulness and Anti-oppression Pedagogy in Your Classroom*. Think Tank Conference Presentation, November 8–10, 2018.

Gao, C., & Guo, C. (2018). The Experience of Beauty of Chinese Poetry and Its Neural Substrates. *Frontiers in Psychology*, 9, Article 1540.

Gozawa, J. (2014). Contemplative Pedagogy and Compassionate Presence. In O. Gunnlaugson, E. W. Sarath, C. Scott & H. Bai (Eds.), *Contemplative Learning and Inquiry Across Disciplines* (pp. 341–360). State University of New York Press.

Hanh, T. N. (1999a). *Twenty-Four Brand New Hours. Call Me by My True Names* (p. 182). Parallax Press.

Hanh, T. N. (1999b). *The Heart of the Buddha's Teaching: Transforming Suffering into Peace, Joy, and Liberation*. Harmony Books.

Harper, S. (2018). *How to Use Contemplative Poetry as Spiritual Practice*. Grok Nation. https://groknation.com/soul/contemplative-poetry-spiritual-practice/.

Harshman, J., & Augustine, T. (2015). Using Informal Social Studies Education Space and Mobile Technology in Teacher Education. *Ohio Social Studies Review*, 52, 7–19.

Johnson, L. (2017). *Walking Meditation*. A facilitation offered at CMind Summer School.

Keiser, D. L., & Sakulkoo, S. (2014). Fitting in Breath Hunting: Thai and U.S. Perspectives on Contemplative Pedagogy. In O. Gunnlaugson, E. W. Sarath, C. Scott, & H. Bai (Eds.), *Contemplative Learning and Inquiry Across Disciplines* (pp. 81–96). State University of New York Press.

Kornfield, J. (n.d.). *Heart Wisdom Podcast*. https://beherenownetwork.com/category/jack-kornfield/.

Kotala, Z. (2016). *Music and the Brain: A Love Story of Two UCF Professors*. https://www.ucf.edu/news/music-and-the-brain-a-love-story-of-two-ucf-professors/.

Le Guin, U. (1979). *Language of the Night: Essays on Fantasy and Science Fiction*. G.P. Putnam's Sons.

Mannell, J., Ahmad, L., & Ahmad, A. (2018). Narrative Storytelling as Mental Health Support for Women Experiencing Gender-Based Violence in Afghanistan. *Social Science and Medicine*, 214, 91–98. Doi: 10.1016/j.socscimed.2018.08.011. Epub 2018 Aug 23.PMID: 30165294.

Mastnak, W. (2016). Music in Health Promotion and Therapeutic Practice. Cultural, Theoretical and Clinical Perspectives. *Deutsche medizinische Wochenschrift*, 141(25), 1845–1849 Doi: 10.1055/s-0042-109418.

Miller, J. P. (2014). Contemplation: The Soul's Way of Knowing. In O. Gunnlaugson, E. W. Sarath, C. Scott, & H. Bai (Eds.), *Contemplative Learning and Inquiry Across Disciplines* (pp. 69–80). State University of New York Press.

Murphy-Shigematsu, S. (2018). *From Mindfulness to Heartfulness: Transforming Self and Society with Compassion.* Berrett-Koehler Publishers.

National Alliance on Mental Illness. (2012). *College Students Speak: A Survey Report on Mental Health.* https://www.nami.org/Support-Education/Publications-Reports/Survey-Reports/College-Students-Speak_A-Survey-Report-on-Mental-H.

Roth, H. D. (2014). A Pedagogy for the New Field of Contemplative Studies. In O. Gunnlaugson, E. W. Sarath, C. Scott, & H. Bai (Eds.), *Contemplative Learning and Inquiry Across Disciplines* (pp. 97–118). State University of New York Press.

Spurlin, M. (2018). Sustainability through Authenticity: A Portrait of Teaching as Contemplative Practice. In J. E. Dalton, E. H. Dorman, & K. Byrnes (Eds.), *The Teaching Self: Contemplative Practices, Pedagogy, and Research in Education* (pp. 59–70). Rowman & Littlefield.

Tala, A. (2019). Gracias por todo: Una revisión sobre la gratitud desde la neurobiología a la clínica [Thanks for Everything: A Review on Gratitude from Neurobiology to Clinic]. *Revista medica de Chile*, 147(6), 755–761.

Tanaka, E., Iso, H., Tsutsumi, A, Kameoka, S., You, Y., & Kato, H. (2019). School-based Psychoeducation and Storytelling: Association with Long-Term Mental Health in Adolescent Survivors of the Wenchuan Earthquake. *Epidemiology and Psychiatric Sciences*, 23(29), 1–9. Doi: 10.1017/S2045796019000611.PMID: 31640825.

Walsh, S. (2014). Towards Teaching with an Open Heart. *Paideusis*, 14–23.

Weil, A., & Arem, K. (2004). *Self-Healing with Sound and Music.* Sounds True Recordings.

Zajonc, A. (2006). Contemplative and Transformative Pedagogy. *Kosmos Journal*, 1, 1–3.

Zajonc, A. (2014). Contemplative Pedagogy in Higher Education: Toward a More Reflective Academy. In O. Gunnlaugson, E. W. Sarath, C. Scott, & H. Bai (Eds.), *Contemplative Learning and Inquiry Across Disciplines* (pp. 15–30). State University of New York Press.

10
ENHANCING STUDENTS' MINDFULNESS PRACTICE THROUGH PHILOSOPHY OF MIND

Sam Cocks

As any good teacher knows, there is great value in an experiment that allows us to fulfill multiple interests. In my Philosophy of Mind course, the opportunity involves a student exercise that brings together anti-oppressive pedagogy, mindfulness, and concept applications. In pursuing this project, I asked, how can a combination of student mindfulness practices and the descriptive tools from a philosophy class serve to bring awareness and to disrupt behaviors and intentions linked to bias or oppression? Further, how might this approach enhance both the course content as well as the point of focus associated with the mindfulness practice? Given the clear link between the exercise and course content, I believe that concepts from a Philosophy of Mind class provide helpful tools for describing and understanding what occurs within the space of mindfulness practice.

My 300-level "Philosophy of Mind" class is cross-listed with the psychology program and is composed primarily of juniors and seniors. The class is populated by traditional white students between the ages of 19 and 22, and is comprised of equal numbers of females and males. The majority of students are heterosexual, and are influenced by either an implicit or an explicit Western Judeo-Christian worldview. The course engages in a thorough overview of the different arguments, objections, and responses about what constitutes mental life, mind-body interaction, subjectivity and consciousness, internalist and externalist notions of mind, empathy, animal minds, and disordered minds (Heil, 2013). Although course concepts in philosophy provide assistance in understanding oppression, the theme of oppression is not the primary focus of the course, and thus the course seemed ideal for exploring the efficacy of mindfulness in raising awareness of oppression.

Because Philosophy of Mind normally requires a semester-long project, I offered both the standard philosophy project and a mindfulness project, allowing

DOI: 10.4324/9781003201854-13

students to choose, and thereby obtaining a self-selected group of 32 out of 64 students who were at least somewhat motivated to explore mindfulness. My goals for this project were to provide students with:

1. A technique that is proven to facilitate well-being and overall flourishing.
2. An opportunity to apply important course concepts to a concrete practice.
3. Helpful conceptual tools that enrich the chosen mindfulness project.
4. A reflective tool that allows them to understand how bias and institutionalized oppression unfold within personal experience.

Although the fourth project goal describes mindfulness as "a reflective tool that allows [practitioners] to understand how bias and institutionalized oppression unfold within personal experience," class discussions addressed bias (i.e., prejudice) rather than oppression. I avoided the term "oppression" both for its particularly "heavy" meaning with this student demographic and because the course description did not specify oppression as a theme. However, the notion of "bias" is a common theme in both Philosophy of Mind and psychology.

Those students who chose the mindfulness project were instructed to engage in an intentional mindfulness activity for at least five minutes a day. Students were provided with resources that offered basic guidance in a variety of contemplative practices, as well as an approximately 45-minute class overview introducing these resources. Many students willingly looked into other resources or were already familiar with a practice they wanted to continue or re-engage. This was an exercise based on trust. While the instructor was available to discuss the students' experiences, and "checked in" with the group participants two or three more times during the semester, the expectation was for the students to be self-motivated. The students who chose the mindfulness project were asked to fill out the Five-Facet Mindfulness Questionnaire (FFMQ) at the start of the project and at the end of the semester (Baer et al., 2006). The FFMQ involves a numerical ranking of different elements of mindfulness and assists in clarifying the sort of self-understanding and transformation that might occur. Finally, a substantial part of the work included a written analysis organized around the following prompts:

FIG. 10.1 Prompts for the Mindfulness Project Written Reflections

1. Explain if and in what way the mindfulness exercise led you to recognize certain biases or habitual ways of thinking.
2. Explain which Philosophy of Mind theory from the semester applies to and assists in understanding these biases.
3. Explain which Philosophy of Mind theory from the semester applies to and assists in understanding the results of the Five-Facet Mindfulness Questionnaire.

Students were encouraged to see these prompts as fluid and connected, and to explore the themes that were most meaningful to them, as long as the chosen themes remained linked to the content addressed in the prompts.

What follows are the results of this exercise: (1) the themes that emerged in the review of students' final reflections; (2) the overall significance of the course concepts as aids in framing their experiences; and (3) the significance of the FFMQ results.

Themes in Student Experiences of Mindfulness

Students embraced a wide variety of mindfulness options, sometimes intentionally exploring new practices out of curiosity, and sometimes experimenting with the intention of finding that one right practice. Some students simply felt an intuitive connection with a particular technique and stayed with it from the very beginning. The practices students explored included breath focus (vipassana and Chan), open field awareness, yoga, body scan, and 5–3–1 practice (five minutes of meditation, list of three good things that happened in your day, and one random act of kindness). Many of the students had prior mediation practice, and one had been involved in substantive mindfulness retreats. While my influence is certainly present in describing the basic theories from Philosophy of Mind, the *link* between these ideas and the students' mindfulness experience was left open for the students to investigate; it was never explored in class.

Three themes emerged in the student comments (I created clusters based on a minimum of eight students (25%) expressing similar remarks).

1. Negative emotions, negative self-talk, and ruminating upon the future ($n = 13$).
2. Significance of mindfulness of body ($n = 10$).
3. The concrete but malleable nature of personal identity ($n = 12$).

Negative Emotions, Negative Self-Talk, and Ruminating Upon the Future

When describing habits of mind, students recognized a number of experiences as negative or troubling:

- There were negative or troubling emotions that were often general, manifesting as more of a phenomenological *mood* (Heidegger & Stambaugh, 1996, p. 126). Some of these emotions were marked as buried, only to be revealed within the space of meditation.
- Several students remarked about the awareness of habitual self-talk that was negative and critical in character, sometimes becoming *heightened* during formal meditation practice.

- There were explicit remarks about emotional, often troubling rumination about the future, checking off lists, and the feeling that meditation was a waste of time.

The following student remark captures the sentiment of the former comments:

> I have noticed a lot of things about myself after I have taken the time to slow my mornings down and focus on meditation. I have noticed some habitual biases and ways of thinking that I have not explicitly acknowledged before. . . . I have struggled with depression and anxiety for a few years now, and sometimes it is really easy for me to think about all the things going wrong in my life and the things I don't like about myself. As I started to sit in silence in the morning, at first, I kept thinking about how stressed out I was and how much I needed to get done that day. I would also notice little things in my body that didn't feel right and dwell on them . . . anything from headaches to cramps to exhaustion. . . . my mind started going crazy with all sorts of insecurities about myself as a person and my relationships. All of these struggles that I felt during meditation led me to believe that I was not capable of clearing my mind and just being in the moment. I felt like I was doing something wrong because I was trying to be at peace but instead, I was being bombarded by thousands of thoughts and feelings at once. As I continued on with the practice however, I got a lot more comfortable and it honestly became my favorite part of the day.

These remarks reveal not only the phenomena of negative self-talk, but also how mindfulness might serve to bring further focus to these troubling experiences.

Mindful self-compassion (MSC) can be helpful with these experiences. MSC is a practice bringing mindfulness, self-compassion, and a recognition of common humanity to moments of suffering (Germer, 2009; Neff, 2011). In compassion-hungry cultures, we learn from a young age how to use negative self-talk and punishment as motivation, and to blame ourselves for our own suffering rather than challenge the status quo. Germer (2009) acknowledges the "backdraft" that can arise as a result of practicing a loving and mindful attitude towards oneself:

> When a fire is deprived of oxygen, it will explode when fresh air is introduced through an open door. Firefighters call that "backdraft." A similar effect can occur when we practice loving-kindness. If our hearts are hot with suffering—self-hatred, self-doubt—when we begin to practice, sympathetic words can open the door of our hearts, causing an explosion of difficult feelings. Those feelings are not *created* by metta [loving-kindness and compassion] practice; we're simply recognizing and feeling them as they go out the door. It's part of the healing process.
>
> (p. 150)

Many traditions show how sustained mindfulness and compassion practices open the door to excavating, feeling, and releasing difficult experiences.

Insight meditation can bring us face-to-face with varying embodied and conceptual tensions that are directly linked to oppressive beliefs about ourselves and others. For example, the exposure to oppressive speech and actions can generate negative self-talk or anxieties concerning our own self-image. Sometimes these oppressive actions are extended to others. Neff (2011) writes, "[m]ost people develop patterns of reacting in relationships that are unhelpful, patterns that are typically formed in response to early childhood traumas" (p. 232). Coming to understand oneself as unworthy by a family member or society (e.g., racial and/or economic oppression) can lead to an identification with such a self-concept, leading us to "project" (Germer, 2009) this same sense of unworthiness onto others. Perhaps if I am "no good," you are "no good." Sometimes this projection is a way of *avoiding* the oppressive feeling or self-understanding by disburdening oneself of such a self-interpretation and associating it with another (Germer).

Contemplative activity provides information that will help us understand the conditions that have generated the former ways of thinking of oneself and others (Tejaniya, 2016). For example, how is one's sense of self-worth impacted by structural oppression? What are the conditions that give birth to a particular thought or mood? These conditions often include the society or family in which we are raised. Moreover, what further intentions and actions do these thoughts, as conditions, generate? Noted earlier, as I begin to become more aware of critical self-talk, I can begin to notice how these ways of thinking may lead me to relate to others in a similar way. Mindfulness recognizes the benefit of *staying with* what is arising with a gentle curiosity, rather than resistance, in order to develop a fuller understanding of the dynamic of human experience. According to Germer (2009), "[f]ormal mindfulness meditation especially helps us figure out how to *live with discomfort*" (p. 52, emphasis in original), as depicted in the following student reflection:

> Another key point that I learned was that the act of meditation isn't just a relaxing thing to do, it's actually very hard work. Digging deep into your innermost emotions and thought patterns is overwhelming and at times scary. Dealing with what you find and working with it and through it takes practice and dedication. When I first started to meditate regularly, I would only do it on days where I was already feeling good—the days where my anxiety was bad or I was in a worse headspace I would find myself avoiding meditation at all costs.

In reference to Germer, the student stuck with the practice, developing the mindset necessary to remain present with these difficult emotions and thoughts.

However, access to the benefits is easily lost. How a practice is framed will influence the effectiveness. One student noted that the class project was so much more meaningful because the particular meditation instruction they investigated provided guidance for a higher quality and deeper exploration. In this case, the chosen practice involved focusing on the rising and falling of the breath. To contrast, the criticized example offered by the student was a mindfulness project from another class that was constructed for the sake of athletic improvement. Coopting mindfulness solely for the sake of concentration or positive visualization practices neglects its deep cultural roots as something that is prepared to assist with some of the more challenging, interesting, and exciting moments of human life (Batacharya & Wong, 2018; Purser, 2019). There is a growing concern that meditation is coopted as a white, upper-class, elitist practice that in many ways simply reinforces or fails to challenge certain forms of self-identity (Wilson, 2014; Forbes, 2019). It is a good sign that students are having the sort of experiences we see mentioned in their comments presented in this chapter.

Significance of Mindfulness of Body

For those students who chose a meditation practice that explicitly attends to mindfulness of the body (i.e., body scan), the reflections revealed three interrelated ideas. First, awareness of the body is significant in the sense that there appear to be experientially verified causal connections between bodily events and mental events noticed as biased. For example, something as simple as a bodily tension may lead to an attitudinal shift. Or, emotions "felt" in the body that triggered varying thought processes, often labeled as problematic, were noticed with greater clarity. One student writes, "even the simplest habituated reaction as tensing up when you see a black guy could easily be explained away by making an excuse."[1] Next, many students find that bodily events (hearts beating) and mental events (psychological occurrences) are substantively different types of events that nonetheless mutually influence one another. Hence, the clear connection illustrated in awareness of the body led many students to endorse a theory discussed in Philosophy of Mind, *interactionist dualism*. This theory attempts to account for the way two very different experiences of human life connect with each other. It draws attention to the fact that at least two sets of happenings that *appear* to be quite different and perhaps disconnected, are in truth deeply intertwined. Two different students comment,

> Through the lens of interactionist dualism, we see that complex material processes influence one's mental experience. In the case of my yoga practice, this is seen in the muscle fatigue and pain sensations that come with holding a pose, which interact with my mental state by provoking frustration or impatience. I then turn these emotions into focus through the application of breathing techniques and mindfulness.
>
> I've always been a very spiritual person, so initially I didn't like the idea of this simplification, but the act of meditating made me reflect on how

essential my body is to who I am. As I paid closer attention to what my body was feeling and how it was linked to how my mind was feeling, I began to appreciate the idea that all this was happening inside of my body, and that my body has been with me through every single thing my mind has experienced.

The motivation to view mind and body as disconnected, and in some cases the exclusive focus on the mind, emerges from Euro-Western culture's mind-body dualism. Returning to the body and recognizing our bodies as an essential aspect of identity is for many an eye-opening event in mindfulness practice.

Finally, some students came to see the body as the most real and primary feature of experience in the sense that thoughts and mental states seemed secondary, or outside of their control. For this reason, they invoked a theory known as *epi-phenomenalism*. In this theory, thoughts and mental events are other than physical events, but physical events cause these mental events; in contrast, while very real, mental events have no causal power—they can't "do" anything. Each of these interrelated responses confirms the *foundational* role that the body plays in the production of thoughts. We can augment these comments by sharing what contemporary scholars say on this matter.

As Menakem (2017) demonstrates, any thorough understanding of bias and its link to structural oppression will have to take into consideration embodied experience. There is evidence that cultural bias and institutional oppression manifest at the somatic and instinctive level and can be transferred through the actions of one body upon another, cultural institutions, and even DNA—for example, direct physical abuse—and institutional systems that generate anxiety are directly experienced at the level of the body. In many cases, those who oppress others often feel oppressed themselves. The fear that many police officers experience in coming face-to-face with what might not be in their control is deeply instinctive and habitual (Menakem, 2017). Hence, abstract, conceptual, or intellectual analysis and clarification, while clearly important, are insufficient on their own: "[i]f we only ask students to learn about oppression at a conceptual level, then we are missing two-thirds of the journey" (Berila, 2015, p. 34). Mindfulness brings focus to bodily experience as it is lived from the first-person perspective, and in so doing, brings to light a number of complex emotional and sensorial phenomena:

> That deeper layer is embodiment. Most contemplative practices invite us to reflect on our experiences, but in order to do that, we first need to become aware. How do we know when we are happy, afraid, or angry? What does that feel like in our bodies? What sensations arise that we then characterize as particular states of being? What conceptual storylines do we attach to those sensations, and how can we tease apart our labeling of those bodily sensations from the tainting ideologies of oppression itself.
>
> (Berila, 2015, p. 42)

In day-to-day experience, it is easy to ignore these cues, or neglect to raise them to explicit awareness given that our first experience of them is often pre-reflective and implicit. Only by *staying* with these felt moments can we begin to sink into their complexity. This, I would argue, is an educating moment.

On this, it is not only the complexity of said bodily experiences, but the foundational and causal role these events play that is of importance:

> So, too, when we are getting angry, it is often in a brief lag in the anger, in a moment of reflection, that we notice how tense we are, how our fists are clenched, how aroused we are, and if we are near a mirror we notice (uncomfortably) the contortions on our face.
>
> (Solomon, 2008, p. 118)

These sorts of connections become more and more visible as one engages in a consistent meditation practice. This process is similar to Husserl's (2012) "phenomenological reduction," an activity that involves tracing out *how* and why things mean what they do. To have a biased attitude involves seeing the world in a certain way, and this seeing is best understood in terms of what something *means* to us. Indeed, Husserl coined one form of the reduction "genetic" in the sense that it is possible to better understand how certain ways of thinking and understanding come to be. Mindfulness can help us *see* this connection between the body and varying formations of meaning. For example, as Menakem (2017) and Berila (2015) allude, forms of oppression that are more conceptual in nature can often be traced back to the complex somatic lived-experience. Further, the very observation of bodily experience holds the promise of dissolving the damaging chain of events. That is, the more we become aware of bodily states that give rise to aversion *as they* are happening, the less these sorts of problematic body-thought-action sequences might arise. Bias is often habitual and in many ways dependent on a lack of awareness. Simple awareness of this complex phenomenon facilitates self-development.

Finally, when thinking about embodied experience, we can see that it might not be correct to label the body, along with its sensations (including emotions) as merely physical. While neuroscience tells us about what is occurring within meditation, one of the advantages of the practices the students explored lies in how they reveal the very experience of the body as *expressive* of something: "Emotions are purposive . . . they have meaning—meaning as teleology" (Solomon, 2008, p. 123). Mindfulness brings varying stratifications of meaning, some of these submerged in bodily happenings. Hence, while interactionist dualism is useful, such a theory might miss what the body and mind have in common.

Mindfulness of the body as a complex, lived event, might very well lead to access of certain phenomena that some, due to privilege, have been encouraged to *ignore*. This can be both confusing and abnormal depending on the agent (Brunette-Debassige, 2018). Indeed, because of such discouragement, the attempt to engage in mindfulness might require extraordinary effort and courage. Relatedly, this practice can bring us to an awareness of the enormous privilege some individuals have as concerns this relationship with their own bodies. However, here I mean not only those who may have been encouraged to remain in touch with their bodily experience, but also those who are *able* to do so.

The Concrete but Malleable Nature of Personal Identity

Students reported that many of the thoughts and emotions they were mindful of were, in different ways, outside of their control. Here a theory understood as "externalism" was broached as a way to articulate the fact that much of their subjective experience and personality can be argued to be the result of concrete environmental causes. Importantly, we should understand the causes as phenomena or events that are literally *outside* the person—including their body. These are often events that arise through causes that go beyond what we have direct power to control—they affect us in direct and unavoidable ways. Oppressive frameworks of meaning that are ossified in varying cultural institutions (language, education, etc.) are an example of influences that are external or "outside" of us (Burge, 1979).

Internalist accounts typically highlight the connection between, for example, our central nervous system and identity, neglecting to take into consideration the very information the central nervous system manages. In addition, internalist accounts of mind are often aligned with theories that champion different forms of "innate" knowledge. So, instead of seeing the human subject as primarily motivated by an internal information system and varying inborn ideas, it is useful to consider externalism and how we are vulnerable to social forces. Given that the influences now being considered are often shared, it is fitting that Manuel (2018) writes, "[t]he content of our lives is not just *our* lives. Our ordinariness and oppression is collective" (p. 103). Many of these ideas are noted in the following student passage:

> [A]fter finding comfort in the voice-guided mindful practice, I found myself stumbling across thoughts and ideas that I would believe to not be my own. There were a couple of times that I literally stopped mid-meditation and took a solid couple of minutes to reflect upon the idea/thoughts that just crossed my mind. . . . I didn't personally align myself with the belief system that underlined the thought. I found that to be the most important part of the reflection, because yes they might be estranged and far-fetched but that doesn't mean I should feel shame for having that thought cross my mind. I know who I am and I know what makes up my self-identity, so these thoughts I more considered to be for my entertainment rather than a red flag that should cause concern to my-self-identity. In regard to the externalist objection, none of these random obscure thoughts were too random.

They always involved either things from my day that I never thought to think any further into or things that I know I have been personally avoiding and they slip in during these times morphed into random ideas that makes no sense without a little personal reflection. With that being said, this part had to be the most rewarding/eye opening gain I had received from completing this project.

A usual feature of a consistent mindfulness practice is becoming more aware of the nature of our thoughts, what beliefs they are bound to, what causes and conditions bring them about. One instance of this awareness will involve further clarity about presence and "impact" of external motivators, broadly understood. To recall a previous example, such an influence could be a social practice to which we are exposed. The fact that these influences often become influential as memories—internalized—does nothing to diminish their original contingent and external nature.

All of these influences can shape our habitual biases, and hence shape our identity; yet students' personal identity was seen, nonetheless, as malleable. Returning to the student passage partially quoted earlier, we note,

> even the simplest habituated reaction as tensing up when you see a black guy could easily be explained away by making an excuse. But because of the meditation and recognition of my own biases I think I would try to confront the bias. I would do this by recognizing how the "karma" from my environment, situation, and myself leads to these biases. For example, being a white male from a middle-class family living in midwestern America I should realize that from my parents, the media, my environment, friends, and myself, I'm predisposed to biases against individuals that don't fall in that category. And by not recognizing or just ignoring these biases I perpetuate them to others. I also would have to realize that I am the only reason that these biases are habituated not my situation. I must recognize that the topics of my biases come from my situation but ultimately, I am the one who habituates them. So, when I confront a bias, I can approach it as an aspect about myself that needs to change instead of a virus-like entity that is attached to me from my environment.

Students typically identified the ability or capacity to change in terms of "memory theory" the view that personal identity is understood in terms of a chain of memories, which are often generated through varying external and internal mechanisms. While the idea of identity as memory is not exotic, the fact that memory is something fluid and changing appealed to students. In conjunction with this, students expressed relief that mindfulness demonstrated the value of considering how we *react* to the habits associated with the memories that constitute our life. That is, these loose yet connected memories don't have to define exactly how we respond or move forward. Importantly, this theory resists a description of human identity as something that is fixed or permanent, and something solid or substantive that exists below the collection of changing, ever-developing memories.

Last, the former attitude about change is remarkably close to the promise Buddhists believe *impermanence* holds (Carpenter, 2014). The notion that we are not somehow fixed aligns with the real possibility of not being perpetually identified with a particular habit, or set of mental states. Certainly, we can *be* oppressed or *participate* in oppression (or some combination of both) in many ways. As for the latter habits associated with oppress*ing*, it is not only possible to imagine moving past a complex set of habits that oppress others, but in fact, this justifiably happens through the assistance of mindfulness practice. Nonetheless, students recognized that while the destructive mental habits associated with oppressing others do not seem fixed, and thus lack the sort of substantive permanence one might believe they do, the effect or emotion associated with these causes is associated with very real suffering. As for those mental habits that are associated with *being* oppressed—i.e., thinking oneself as unworthy of love or self-care (Selassie, 2020)—students also recognized that such habits needn't permanently define how they relate to themselves. For these students, there was evidence that internalized habits and forms of self-identification can change. Several times in the student comments—but not limited to any particular cluster—there was evidence of an attitude of tenderness toward oneself in the face of some difficulty or tension. The actual mindfulness practice seems to have created the space to make that possible. Students were seeing themselves for who they were, and because they were temporarily not absorbed in the mental habits, they were able to muster some self-compassion.

The Significance of Course Concepts

While it is clear that students were able to use philosophical terminology to interpret their experiences, it is useful to return to this aspect of the exercise. Several students remarked that the different theories of mind were immensely helpful in clarifying what was occurring within mindfulness practice. These concepts served as a way to give focus to the experiences they were having, and in so doing appear to have enriched the overall practice. Further, applying a concept not only provides the former focus, but also helps the student to better understand the concept itself by moving beyond a mere definition. To be sure, many disciplines can demonstrate the relevance of mindfulness practice, but being mindful is well suited to utilizing the conceptual resources found within a Philosophy of Mind class.

Further, it is evident that the choice of theoretical model not only provides general clarity but also influences the overall interpretive or metaphysical lens the student brings to the experience (i.e., their worldview). The differences that arise are often substantive. The first difference, internal vs. external conceptions of mind, concerns conscious experience as constituted by the world, or consciousness as a non-worldly, internal "something." The second focuses on what the self or person "boils" down to—an impermanent collection of memories, or something eternal and substantive. And the third difference, dualism vs. monist eliminativism, refers to whether a description and explanation of mind and consciousness requires both physical and nonphysical forms of description, or only the physical. For instance, those who defend dualist accounts find that the experience of being consciously aware cannot be fully captured by the natural sciences (the claims of eliminativism). These ways of thinking have serious implications for how we think about our connection with others and the world, change, and what we mean when we say the word "me" or "I." For example, as alluded to previously, to even say that the human person is a complex collection of dispositions and habits that are in principle malleable is to draw one into a set of questions that would soon reveal one's metaphysical commitments. For example, some people are genuinely committed to the idea that we are more than this complex collection of dispositions and habits. That is, that we have some stable, permanent, and enduring self or soul, that this self is our essence, and that this essence is the deepest and most real aspect of who we are.

In thinking about mindfulness pedagogy moving forward, it is wise for teachers to consider seriously the implications of which of these theories is operative for students as they engage mindfulness practice. Knowing this helps the instructor and student understand why the student clarifies their mindful experience in the way they do, and how they are more than likely experiencing the states of mind associated with meditation. Further, the "why" and the "how" also assist both instructor and student in better understanding the positive and negative aspects of the experience.

Significance of the Five-Facet Mindfulness Questionnaire

The Five-Facet Mindfulness Questionnaire is an instrument involving a series of descriptive statements that students rank from 1 to 5 (1, never or very rarely true, and 5, very often or always true). The questionnaire consists of 39 such statements organized under five different categories: "observe items," "describe items," "act with awareness items," "nonjudge items," and "nonreact items." A common scoring method is to total the rankings for the statements associated with each category, resulting in five scores. The first four of these categories allows for a total of 40 points (8 statements), while the last allows for 35 points (7 statements).

Twenty-eight students took the FFMQ at the beginning of the semester when they first began their mindfulness practice and did so again towards the end. A few students who committed to the mindfulness experience provided a FFMQ only at the beginning of the semester. Those students who submitted the questionnaire pre- and post-course showed an increase in score, suggesting that mindfulness practice led to some sort of positive change. For example, an increase in the "act with awareness items" typically means that the student is more generally aware throughout their day-to-day lives. The question of whether the change has become a habit remains open. The average change in the different categories across all involved students is as follows:

Observe items: +4.8
Describe items: +2.4
Act with awareness items: +3.1
Nonjudge items: +4.5
Nonreact items: +2.4

As shown, there is an increase in each category, implying a desirable change.

I suggest that these scores demonstrate the cultivation of certain habits, dispositions, and attitudes necessary for an anti-oppressive stance. In order to provide additional clarity, we can draw on four brief examples. Speaking first of the "nonreact" category, a student involved in this study noted,

> [t]hus, we see a shift in my FFMQ scores from the beginning to the end of the semester. The quality of this "mineness" has shifted through mindfulness practices as I have learned to distance myself from the immediate reactivity to my subjective experiences.

Here the student defined "mineness" in terms of habitual biases that often function in an unaware and automatic fashion, and are often damaging to both ourselves and other people. By developing a practice of observing and describing how our body and mind react in different situations, we come to better understand exactly what situations or stimuli motivate our habituated reactions, as well as these habits themselves.

Turning to our second and third examples, one statement from the FFMQ "observe category" is "I pay attention to how my emotions affect my thoughts and behavior." One gain from this is a better self-understanding: "I hope to become more aware of certain non-skillful or harmful emotions that might motivate me to act in a certain way." We can see how the statement about emotion connects with the following from the "act with awareness" category: "I find myself doing things without paying attention." The latter is reverse scored. If mindfulness ultimately leads me to pay much more attention, then my response of 1 (I rarely do things without paying attention) would be marked as a 5, contributing to a desired increase in score. Paying attention to the influence of my emotions, and how I am acting in general, would seem to provide the knowledge and space necessary to avoid perpetuating undesirable behavior.

Last, being nonjudgmentally honest with ourselves would seem to provide clearer insight and detail into exactly what motivates us to act ("I disapprove of myself when I have irrational ideas"). Here, we wouldn't burden the moment with a negative "filter" that from the very beginning influences the content of our experiences. In turn, to battle oppressive habits towards others (what we are mindful of) with an oppressive approach towards oneself ("I" am bad) would seem only to perpetuate oppression in some form (see the earlier comments about the internalization of a negative self-image).

However, the average change for *individual* students in each category is quite diverse. For example, in the non-react category, one student showed an increase of 9 points across both reports, while another student demonstrated a decrease of 5 points. In the latter case, the student reflection didn't provide an adequate account for the change. One possible reason might be that the student's initial self-assessment was simply incorrect, and it changed because of the mindfulness practice. The following statement can serve to make this point: "I perceive my feelings and emotions without having to react to them." It is feasible a student might initially choose 4 (often true), and then later 1 (never or very rarely true). As the student becomes more familiar with the quality of their experiences, recognition of reactivity can increase. To be sure, there is the understandable hope that there is an overall decrease in reactivity. However, one benefit of a sustained meditation practice is that it helps expose a variety of more subtle and sometimes harmful habits.

I end this section with two final remarks. First, as an instrument, the FFMQ is clearly influencing the mindfulness experience. It seems that certain features of experience are salient because we are directed to these contents, as noted in the following:

> One of the first things I noticed while conducting the self-study was that I didn't consider myself too emotional previously. I still wouldn't consider myself "emotional," in the sense that it is typically used, i.e. "you're being so emotional right now," but nonetheless I noticed that there is not by any means a negligible amount of feeling behind my monotone and subtle self.

Thus, the practice of mindfulness across a period of time can influence how people rank certain statements, and the FFMQ can influence what we notice within meditation. Hence, while this study is clearly valuable, it should be supplemented by a summary reflection about the scoring of the FFMQ from the student in order to acquire more information about the preceding two factors. While I prompted the students to speak more about the FFMQ, doing so was optional.

Second, the FFMQ serves as a powerful contribution to this study by how it sheds light on possible ways to interpret the clusters discussed earlier. It appears that, as a whole, students aren't only becoming more aware of negative self-talk, bodily contributions to biased perception, and the malleability of personal identity *in general*. Rather, we can speculate that these experiences include a general tendency towards self-transformation and improvement, as evidenced in the

FFMQ. Hence, the dual approach to this exercise serves as a powerful tool to assess both self-understanding and self-change.

Conclusion

One unique aspect of philosophy is its call to *vigilance* and *awareness*. At minimum, the project motivated the students to turn inward, to consider habits and biases, and to take note of the conditions and contexts that surround these habits. The course provided an extensive set of conceptual tools to assist the students in that part of the process that was ultimately descriptive. There is evidence that the students' experience led them to experience or consider difficult thoughts that gravitate around self-identity; the role of the body in habit, bias, and thought production; the origin of their cognitive habits; and whether what we are is something malleable or fixed. Finally, the recognition that one does not always have to react to different motivating factors surfaced as a theme. Articulated earlier, these factors are essential in considering oppression, and thus any exercise that begins to bring the student to these factors should be viewed as an accomplishment. In terms of our particular project's goals, a benefit of mindfulness practice lies in how it can isolate the foundational or core features that support oppressive behavior and work to *alter* these through direct observation.

In addition, this experiment offers insight into the possibility of education. Students were able to both increase their comprehension of important concepts and engage in an activity that has serious ramifications for their flourishing as human beings. By revealing the possibility of change, this exercise points in the direction of self-transformation. As noted earlier, the FFMQ also provided evidence that valued forms of self-transformation were occurring. Given that many of these students hail from locations that are homogenous and lacking in diversity, the mindfulness practice is effective in tapping into a number of oppressive biases that, while internalized, are causally bound to interpersonal and structural forms of oppression. The larger hope is that self-change will motivate corresponding structural and interpersonal change.

Two issues should be considered if and when this experiment is duplicated in the future. First, distributing more of the literature linking mindfulness and anti-oppressive behavior could arguably enrich students' experience and resulting reflections. While I was earlier concerned about "buy-in," as well as oversaturating the students with theory, it seems there is value in experimenting with both approaches. Second, it would be beneficial to extend the project so that students continue their practice beyond one semester. Then, a follow-up assessment could be used to track students in order to discern whether there were increased changes and novel reflections, and of what sort.

Last, while I believe there is evidence that mindfulness can assist in the awareness and modification of certain problematic mental attitudes and habits, by no means is something like bias and institutionalized oppression able to be "handled" by individual students through a brief daily meditation practice, or somehow be resolved within the space of one semester. It would be dangerous to assume that mindfulness "in a bubble" can resolve these problems, and troubling if we returned to the idea of mindfulness as a quick-fix, feel-good remedy. This is especially so in regard to those who perpetuate acts of bias and oppression. Nonetheless, actions stem from embodied belief, and becoming mindful of our embodied beliefs is a good first step.

Note

1 I come back to the full student comment later in the chapter. Here, it is important to know that the student recognized this as a problematic bias (Menakem, 2017).

References

Baer, R. A., Smith, G. T., Hopkins, J., Krietemeyer, J., & Toney, L. (2006). Using Self-Report Assessment Methods to Explore Facets of Mindfulness. *Assessment*, 13(1), 27–45.

Batacharya, S., & Wong, Y.-L. R. (Eds.). (2018). *Sharing Breath: Embodied Learning and Decolonization*. Athabasca University Press.

Berila, B. (2015). *Integrating Mindfulness into Anti-Oppression Pedagogy: Social Justice in Higher Education*. Taylor & Francis.

Brunette-Debassige, C. (2018). From Subjugation to Embodied Self-in-Relation: An Indigenous Pedagogy for Decolonization. In S. Batacharya & Y.-L. R. Wong (Eds.), *Sharing Breath: Embodied Learning and Decolonization*. Athabasca University Press.

Burge, T. (1979). Individualism and the Mental. *Midwest Studies in Philosophy*, 4(1), 73–121.

Carpenter, A. (2014). *Indian Buddhist Philosophy*. Taylor & Francis.

Forbes, D. (2019). *Mindfulness and Its Discontents: Education, Self, and Social Transformation*. Fernwood Publishing.

Germer, C. (2009). *The Mindful Path to Self-Compassion: Freeing Yourself from Destructive Thoughts and Emotions*. Guilford Publications.

Heidegger, M., & Stambaugh, J. (1996). *Being and time*. State University of New York Press.

Heil, J. (2013). *Philosophy of Mind: A Contemporary Introduction*. Routledge.

Husserl, E. (2012). *Cartesian Meditations: An Introduction to Phenomenology*. Klumer Academic Publishers.

Manuel, Z. E. (2018). *Sanctuary: A Meditation on Home, Homelessness, and Belonging*. Wisdom Publications.

Menakem, R. (2017). *My Grandmother's Hands: Racialized Trauma and the Pathway to Mending Our Hearts and Bodies*. Penguin Books Limited.

Neff, K. (2011). *Self-Compassion: The Proven Power of Being Kind to Yourself*. Harper Collins.

Purser, R. E. (2019). *McMindfulness: How Mindfulness Became the New Capitalist Spirituality*. Repeater Books.

Selassie, S. (2020). *You Belong: A Call for Connection*. HarperOne.

Solomon, R. (2008). Educating Emotions: The Phenomenology of Feelings. In R. T. Ames & P. D. Herschock (Eds.), *Educations and Their Purposes: A Conversation Among Cultures*. University of Hawai'i Press and East-West Philosophers Conference.

Tejaniya, S. U. (2016). *When Awareness Becomes Natural: A Guide to Cultivating Mindfulness in Everyday Life*. Shambhala.

Wilson, J. (2014). *Mindful America: The Mutual Transformation of Buddhist Meditation and American Culture*. Oxford University Press.

11
CREATING MINDFUL AND SELF-AWARE COUNSELING PRACTITIONERS

Centering Privilege and Oppression

Teysha L. Bowser, Renae Swanson, and Amney J. Harper

More and more programs are teaching counselors to utilize mindfulness in their counseling practice, both for their clients' benefit and for themselves (Reilly, 2016). Mindfulness practices encourage individuals to attend to their automatic thoughts and overall present-moment experiences without judgment or emotional reaction, thus supporting the development of empathy and compassion (Ivers et al., 2016; Lenes et al., 2020). To be effective counselors, students must develop an awareness of their own attitudes and beliefs, obtain knowledge and skills, and engage in action within the domains of counselor self-awareness, client worldviews, and the counseling relationship (Ratts et al., 2015). Magee (2019) describes mindfulness as "simply paying attention, on purpose, with the attitude of friendly, open, nonjudgmental curiosity, and a willingness to accept what arises" (p. 16). One's capacity to convey internal experiences into words ("mindfulness describing") may support counselors in developing an understanding of how their own biases, beliefs, and values are influenced by their privileged or marginalized status (Ivers et al., 2016, p. 78), as well as understanding different worldviews when working with variously privileged or marginalized clients (Ivers et al., 2016).

A competent counselor sees the client as a whole person: their development, their intersecting identities, their mind and heart, their environment, and their social and cultural context. To understand their clients, professional counselors must also understand themselves, and the process we use to help facilitate self-understanding teaches students to become reflective practitioners. Nearly all the competencies and standards for professional counselors require self-awareness (ALGBTIC, 2010; CACREP, 2015; Cashwell & Watts, 2010; Harper et al., 2013; Ratts et al., 2015). Mindfulness can assist in aiding practicing counselors to develop this self- awareness in the here and now.

DOI: 10.4324/9781003201854-14

The very nature of learning about social justice, racism, and oppression is an emotional process. Cognitive-Experiential Self-Theory (CEST) provides a compelling connection between cognition and affective learning (Tyler & Guth, 1999; Villalba & Redmond, 2008); learning consists of the rational system and the experiential or affective system (Epstein, 1994). In order to balance cognitive and affective learning in counseling courses—including social, cultural, and multicultural classes—it is essential to include reflective and mindfulness practices. Mindfulness increases the student's self-reflection, emotional monitoring, and ability to respond to new affective and cognitive information, thereby minimizing reactivity during future practice (Griffith et al., 2017; Rose et al., 2018).

This chapter explores the connections among multicultural competence, social justice, trauma-informed care, mindfulness, and the strategies we use to develop reflective counselors through experiential learning and reflective practice. We teach in a Counselor Education program housed in a Predominantly White Institution (PWI) and Predominantly Christian Institution (PCI) in the Midwest. Students are primarily from rural, working-class families. The most recent reporting of the race/ethnicity of the students in the program shows that 90.63% of students identify as White, with the remaining 9.37% of students scattered across diverse identities: 1.04% identify as American Indian or Alaska Native, 1.04% identify as Black or African American, 5.21% identify as Hispanic or Latinx, and 1.04% Multiracial. Fewer than 5% of our students are from large urban areas. The vast majority of students have been raised in a Christian background. Approximately 20% of our students are cisgender men, 75% are cisgender women, and 5% identify as nonbinary or transgender. About 20% of our students identify as lesbian, gay, bisexual, or queer. Fewer than 3% of students identify as asexual. Additionally, 1.04% identified as having a disability, and 1.04% are active military or veterans.

The background of our students impacts how we teach about social-cultural foundations, privilege, and oppression. In their early years, many of our students have had no/limited contact with people from backgrounds different from their own, and they have learned about diversity primarily through television and/or media. While learning about multiculturalism can be overwhelming to such students and lead to highly emotional reactions, students are still open to learning more when both thoughts and emotions are involved in their learning process. Mindfulness practice can help students develop the self-regulation skills needed to process cognitive and emotion-laden material that is part of multicultural education. Rose and colleagues (2018) shared that students learn difficult or conflictual information best when they are in a "workable range," which means they are not experiencing hyperarousal or hypoarousal (p. 432). In order to expand a student's workable range to allow for greater learning potential, we have found it helpful for students to develop a reflective mindfulness practice to bridge the affective and cognitive gaps, assisting students in staying open to their experience (Griffith et al., 2017; Rose et al., 2018; Tomlinson-Clark & Clark, 2010). Our program has seen success in students addressing biases and privilege by combining the content and academic learning with activities that encourage mindfulness and reflection.

Mindfulness Practice

Beginning with the introduction of Mindfulness-Based Stress Reduction (MBSR) by Jon Kabat-Zinn, secular mindfulness and mindfulness-based interventions have gained global interest, particularly in Western culture (Hyland, 2015). This learning has led to different institutions, disciplines, and individuals engaging in meditation, yoga, body scans, and other practices to encourage self-care and manage anxieties that may arise through interacting in multiple environments (educational, work, social) (Christopher & Maris, 2010). Counselor educators have incorporated mindfulness practice into their programs utilizing a similar process as including multiculturalism. Some have chosen to create a separate course, and some have chosen to use an integration and infusion model (Kagnici, 2014).

Stauffer and Pehrsson (2012) suggested 16 mindfulness competencies for counselors and psychotherapists to follow when training clients, categorized under four areas: "integrated and engaged practice, cultural competency and mindfulness use, competency limits and continuing education; and clinical considerations" (p. 233). While integrated and engaged practice underscores being well-versed in mindfulness practices, the cultural and mindfulness competencies emphasize respecting the values and cultures of clients, and having an awareness of multicultural competencies relevant to these practices and training (Stauffer & Pehrsson, 2012). The importance of knowing one's professional limits of competence in mindful practices and engaging in continuing education, developing knowledge of multiple methods of mindfulness and their effectiveness or potential harms, having the ability to discern between different mental/psychological processes related to both mindfulness and clinical psychological distress, and overall skills and experience with the techniques are the final competencies (Stauffer & Pehrsson, 2012). While focused on counselors and psychotherapists, these competencies provide a general outline for counselor educators to consider when designing mindfulness their programs to include mindfulness. To expand further on these competencies, counselor education programs must avoid cultural appropriation, incorporate a trauma-informed lens and body-based techniques to mindfulness practices, and utilize a social justice framework.

It is essential to understand how cultural appropriation is defined and the harm and impacts it has on those who are its "target" (Matthes, 2016). Cultural appropriation involves the taking of created goods from one culture by individuals from another (Matthes, 2016). An example of this would be when individuals from a dominant cultural group take from a marginalized cultural group, limiting the cultural autonomy of people from a marginalized cultural group, and further oppressing and silencing them (Matthes, 2016). Cultural appropriation removes the ability of culturally marginalized individuals to be seen as knowledgeable due to prejudice, leaving them unheard, spoken for and over, and victims of epistemic violence and injustice (Matthes, 2016). These credibility deficits and overall harm from cultural appropriation can also happen when individuals from the dominant cultural group represent knowledge about or from individuals in a marginalized cultural group. This "speaking for others" reinforces the stereotypes and prejudices defining who is an expert and who is not (Matthes, 2016). As counselor educators, it is our responsibility to recognize the potential harms caused by implementing mindfulness practices without acknowledging their origins in Buddhist and other cultural traditions. In addition, it is essential that we do not engage in reifying the social marginalization, epistemic violence, and injustice that creates credibility deficits and credibility excesses (e.g., recognizing and accepting the knowledge presented by privileged voices or making marginalized voices the speakers for the group, i.e., unwarranted credibility excess) (Matthes, 2016).

Incorporating mindfulness and mindful practices into counselor education programs requires that counselor educators approach mindfulness from a trauma-informed lens (Compson, 2014). As many students entering counseling programs are wounded healers, it is not improbable to assume that multisensory stimuli might trigger trauma reactions, which would make them less able to attune fully to the experiences of their mind, body, and feelings, and could negatively impact their well-being overall (Bodhi, 2011; Grabbe & Miller-Karas, 2018; Hyland, 2015; Treleaven, 2018). Guiding students in somatic techniques may assist them in regaining attunement and developing a better understanding of trauma responses if the educator has knowledge of trauma and knows when the student has reached a point where a referral is necessary (Grabbe & Miller-Karas, 2018; Treleaven, 2018). This also may provide students with coping strategies to utilize if they become triggered while engaging in mindfulness practice and align more with the traditional practices of mindfulness that begin with building one's awareness and understanding of the sensations in one's body in a calm and composed manner (Compson, 2014).

Body-based therapies, such as the one found in the Trauma Resiliency Model, may serve as a method to engage in mindfulness practice while strengthening students' psychological and physiological resilience while furthering their multicultural and social justice competence (Compson, 2014; Grabbe & Miller-Karas, 2018). The Trauma Resiliency Model highlights that physical sensations are connected to each emotion and assists individuals in moving from negative and unpleasant affect and physical feelings to positive or neutral ones (Grabbe & Miller-Karas, 2018). Numerous skills are utilized in this model to expand individuals' resilient zone, where we have the greatest facility in our thinking, feeling, body, and energetic awareness (Grabbe & Miller-Karas, 2018). In short, individuals perceive they can handle the highs and lows that life presents when they are within their resilient zone.

Incorporating mindfulness and body-based therapies could potentially address the concern that traditional academic courses favor intellectual learning while often ignoring the importance of understanding and learning from the body. This knowledge [body-based/body-centered] is instrumental in anti-oppressive pedagogy (Wagner & Shahjahan, 2015) through exercises illustrating the dynamics of privilege and marginalization and inviting students to observe their bodily sensations as a strategy for understanding their dis/advantaged locations in various contexts (Wagner & Shahjahan, 2015). Trauma therapist Treleaven (2018) highlights the importance of practitioners and educators recognizing the connections between systemic oppression and trauma, the limits or barriers to integration, and our biases regarding what counts as trauma or traumatic stress. Mediums such as images, skits, or body movements offer another strategy for encouraging students to reflect on dominant communication styles and the impact of privileged and marginalized statuses (Wagner & Shahjahan, 2015). These forms of embodied pedagogy assist in understanding how the body's sensations, placement in spaces, and use in communication demonstrate a different level of awareness about social positioning in diverse contexts, as well as the privileged or marginalized statuses that individuals hold (Wagner & Shahjahan, 2015).

Counselor education faculty are responsible for and often face challenges in creating learning spaces that allow for optimal learning about difficult topics such as racism, social justice, and diversity. We must make critical choices in terms of what pedagogies will be centered and techniques utilized, evaluating and diminishing influences of cultural appropriation and other forms of oppression (Matthes, 2016; Wagner & Shahjahan, 2015). Jenkins (2015) noted that students learn best when they are interested in the topic, aware of the importance of learning the information, motivated to understand more about the subject, can connect the learning to their lives outside the classroom, and feel safe and supported. To be able to achieve these conditions, students have to feel as though the professor and classmates meet their needs, and they have to be open to learning, which can be challenging when students are working through their own racial developmental processes and realizations of differences (Lenes et al., 2020). Mindfulness can both help students mitigate their anxiety and promote a safe and calm classroom (Schwind et al., 2017). Specifically, mindfulness requires individuals to develop the capacity not to be overcome by unwholesome mental states. This creates opportunities for students not only to develop an awareness of their biases, beliefs, values, and worldviews and the mental states and bodily sensations that arise with them, but also to work towards developing the calmness needed to effectively evaluate how privilege, marginalization, and historical events influence them (Compson, 2014; Ivers et al., 2016; Lenes et al., 2020). Additionally, Roach and Young (2007) noted that students working towards multicultural learning must have personal awareness and work towards personal and professional growth, connecting both qualities to mindfulness and wellness as core characteristics for ethical, effective counselors.

In addition to mindfulness practice, experiential learning and reflective practice can bring about specific outcomes in education. Mindfulness practice paired with reflective practice learning before, during, and after experiential learning can help students to ground and become more in tune with their reactions and inner dialogue, remaining aware of staying open to new experiences and what they are learning. Practicing both can help student counselors more readily to integrate their learning.

Reflective Practice

Reflective practice or reflectivity includes an intentional self-awareness of one's thoughts, feelings, and behaviors and the counselor and client/student interactions (Tobin et al., 2009), and it can be expanded to include awareness of one's intentionality in counseling as well (Griffith & Frieden, 2000). Reflective practice is considered vital to developing awareness around one's growing multicultural competence in working with clients who are culturally different from the counselor (Ziomek-Daigle, 2017). In a traditional learning environment, graduate students may be outcome-focused, meaning they are attentive to things like GPAs, learning outcomes, and scores on comprehensive exams; however, developing reflective practice is essential to developing clinical thinking and skill development (Tobin et al., 2009). Specifically, reflective practice is considered vital to completing complex analyses of client issues and concerns (Griffith & Frieden, 2000) (e.g., including multiple layers at one time like intersecting identity, development, social and cultural environment, theory, intrapsychic processes, neuroscience, etc.). Traditional methods of instruction have not been shown, to date, to relate to therapeutic effectiveness, bringing home the importance of reflective practice (Griffith & Frieden, 2000). Griffith and Frieden also explain that students could never memorize or learn responses to the myriad of possible scenarios that pop up in counseling: for the many unpredictable situations that may arise in counseling, reflective practice is needed as preparation.

Mindfulness practice and self-reflection go hand-in-hand, and how students integrate their experiences into a regular reflective practice is essential for creating self-aware practitioners. Reflective practice aids in integrating experiences, intentions, and beliefs/assumptions/awareness of self, others, and context. This is essential to creating counseling practitioners who can continue to grow and learn throughout their lifetime. Counselor educators are encouraged to help counselors-in-training to develop a reflective practice, and such practice should be encouraged to create reflective practitioners (Tobin et al., 2009). Accordingly, we employ self-reflective assignments throughout our graduate training program to support counselor development and deliberate practice.

Reflective Pedagogy

A variety of pedagogical methods and assignments can help students to develop their reflective practice. Our discussion focuses on the types of reflective writing and reflective teams or groups as some of the most effective methods in developing reflective practitioners.

One benefit of reflective writing is that it enables faculty to be able to understand students' experiences and assess students' learning (Ziomek-Daigle, 2017). Reflective writing can take many forms, such as journaling or reflective papers.

Journaling can be beneficial in processing one's clinical experiences, specifically in reflecting on biases and assumptions (Griffith & Frieden, 2000). Feedback on reflective journaling from faculty can help students build on insights and identify patterns and effective interventions (Griffith & Frieden, 2000). An example of reflective journaling is in the Relational Systems course, where the students facilitate healthy relationship groups at the Boys and Girls Club in the area, which has a diverse community of children and staff. The students complete Three-Minute Reflection Journals immediately after returning to the classroom from facilitating their group. This assignment encourages students to reflect on their children's experiences and the signs of privilege and oppression they witnessed. This is a new experience for many students, and they need to process their emotions and thoughts before talking with the class. The faculty member who teaches this class also gives extensive feedback, support, and gentle challenges before returning the journals to students. Students then use the feedback for their next experience facilitating their group.

Whereas journaling often relies solely on processing experiences, reflective essays can encourage students to integrate their processing of experiences into a document that integrates their readings and other literature. According to Ziomek-Daigle (2017), "Effective, intentional writing practices include describing meaningful learning experiences and articulating examples of how this learning is tied to broader curriculum goals" (p. 263). This allows for greater synthesis of the materials because it encourages students to take what they are experiencing and pair it with concepts and findings from the literature and their textbooks. By doing so, they can analyze how the reading fits with experiences in their practice. In order to make the most out of reflective writing practices, though, faculty must structure assignments in a way that helps in assessing the learning objectives for the course (Ziomek-Daigle, 2017). Ziomek-Daigle describes one model of reflective writing as the DEAL Model for Critical Reflection. It includes the following components: describe (D), examine (E), and articulate learning (AL) (Ziomek-Daigle, 2017). When describing, students are encouraged to provide the details of the experience, including who was present and what took place objectively (Ziomek-Daigle, 2017). The next step includes examining their learning experiences given the learning objectives. The final step is to articulate their learning by looking at how they may set goals for insight, practice, and learning in the future.

Little Acts of Advocacy

Reflective writing is used throughout our program as a means of helping students integrate their experiences into their overall learning. Students, for example, do a reflective paper on an assignment called Little Acts of Advocacy, where they must complete 15 acts of advocacy over the course of the semester. After completing the experiences, they must reflect on the experience, such as: how they learned to improve the effectiveness of their advocacy over the semester, how they were able to expand their advocacy to include a broader range of social justice issues, what barriers and challenges they faced, and how they overcame them.

Creative Writing

Another example of reflective writing is creative writing. Our faculty uses creative writing activities to invite students to examine their culture, privilege, oppression, beliefs, and biases. An exercise that the authors use in their classes is the "I Am From" activity. This activity is adapted from a poem of the same title by author Mary Pipher (2007) (from her book, *Writing to Change the World*), where students write their version of the poem, talking about the sights, sounds, words/phrases, and memories about their home and childhood that demonstrate what important values, beliefs, and culture they experienced growing up. Students then share this activity with their peers. This activity allows students to share about themselves and begin experimenting with taking risks, experiencing vulnerability, and trusting each other, which sets the stage for their program. The students start to gently become aware of their identity as they begin their journey of developing insight into their biases and racial/cultural development. This also creates the opportunity for faculty to conceptualize the students' racial identity development and craft possible future interventions to promote student growth.

Reflective Teams

Another opportunity to build a reflective practice is to use reflective teams or groups, where students can be the ones to share a challenge or, in the role of observer, be the one to provide feedback (Griffith & Frieden, 2000). The authors use teams and groups in our clinical skills courses—i.e., Counseling Process, Group Counseling, Theories, or Practicum—and other classes using "accountabilibuddy" groups. These groups come from a concept introduced by Kathy Flores (2017) at the Annual Ally March at the University of Wisconsin–Oshkosh. Accountabilibuddies are people in our lives who can encourage us to continue to grow, to fight for social justice, and to support us when it is hard, but also to hold us accountable to continuing the work (Flores, 2017). In our courses, we create groups that students meet with regularly during the semester to be accountabilibuddies for each other. It is essential to be intentional when assigning students to groups. Faculty need to pair students with others who are ahead of them and behind them in their awareness so that more learning opportunities can occur. Because the course requires students to engage in the ongoing development of their multicultural competence as well as complete 15 small acts of advocacy, this group can serve as a support and ensure accountability by providing a space where these experiences are discussed and processed. In the clinical courses, students can practice, observe, and provide feedback, allowing students to gain multiple perspectives on a single problem (Griffith & Frieden, 2000). The accountabilibuddy groups serve as an opportunity for students to share their reflections of their experiential learning with their peers and receive feedback, support, and challenges to continue to encourage their growth.

The program also uses small groups and teams to help students process their cultural immersion experiences during their study abroad experience in India. During this experience, students go to India for roughly 21 days, where they engage with counselors, counselor educators, and other students. They also spend time volunteering for different organizations with people in the communities where they visit. Before they go, our students engage in pre-trip seminars to learn about the culture of the different areas of India that they will visit, common impediments that Americans face in visiting the region, cultural rules the students will be expected to follow, and the activities they will be engaging in while they are there. The faculty member who travels with the students to India is mindful of creating experiences that support and challenge students' learning of spirituality, mindfulness, and social and cultural aspects. To guide the process, the faculty member uses the Tomlinson-Clark and Clarke (2010) seven-phase model of program development, recruitment and selection, orientation, pre-trip departure seminars and training, implementation, debriefing, evaluation, and culminating event (pp. 169–170). While overseas, students engage in regular small group discussions to process their learning and their emotions, helping them expand their workable ranges (where they are not experiencing hyperarousal or hypoarousal) sensitively and protectively (Rose et al., 2018, p. 432). For many of our students, this is the first time in their lives they have experienced being outside of the dominant culture. It is a powerful experience with multilayered learning opportunities. Throughout the trip, they also engage in different activities that encourage mindfulness. After returning home, students engage in a creative project that summarizes their learning as their culminating experience.

Each of the methods described here facilitates reflective practice, and many of them are implemented in connection to the experiential learning experiences in our program. While mindfulness is not necessarily required for reflective practice, it can enhance awareness. With a greater understanding of one's experiencing and thinking, it is easy to imagine the benefit of reflective practice. Mindfulness encourages awareness of the what, where, and when, and reflective practice fosters an understanding of the how and why. Together, they can help students to make learning more personal, meaningful, and deep.

Conclusion

Experiential learning offers a powerful tool to connect the real world to our classrooms if we can help our students employ the self-regulation skills needed to process cognitive and emotionally laden material encountered when learning about social justice (Griffith et al., 2017; Tyler & Guth, 1999; Villalba & Redmond, 2008). All activities discussed in this chapter require faculty to help students develop the skills to process strong emotions, to reflect, and to be mindful in their responses, especially when confronting information that challenges their previously held beliefs. Our goal is to assist students in expanding their "workable range" where they can still feel emotions towards new experiences while remaining in a place of response rather than reaction—which is exactly how they will need to be with clients (Rose et al., 2018). Helping our students to develop regular reflection and mindfulness practices assists our students in developing these skills at the same time they are meeting their social and cultural learning goals.

References

ALGBTIC. (2010). American Counseling Association Competencies for Counseling with Transgender clients. *Journal of LGBT Issues in Counseling*, 4(3), 135–159.

Bodhi, B. (2011). What Does Mindfulness Really Mean? A Canonical Perspective. *Contemporary Buddhism: An Interdisciplinary Journal*, 12(1), 19–39. Doi: 10.1080/14639947.2011.564813.

Cashwell, C., & Watts, R. (2010). The New ASERVIC Competencies for Addressing Spiritual and Religious Issues in Counseling. *Counseling and Values*, 55. Doi: 10.1002/j.2161-007X.2010.tb00018.x.

Christopher, J. C., & Maris, J. A. (2010). Integrating Mindfulness as Self-Care Into Counselling and Psychotherapy Training. *Counselling and Psychology Research*, 10(2), 114–125. Doi: 10.1080/14733141003750285.

Compson, J. (2014). Mediation, Trauma and Suffering in Silence: Raising Questions about How Meditation is Taught and Practiced in Western Contexts in the Light of a Contemporary Trauma Resiliency Model. *Contemporary Buddhism*, 15(2), 274–297.

Council for Accreditation of Counseling and Related Educational Programs. (2015). *2016 CACREP Standards*. http://www.cacrep.org/wp-content/uploads/2018/05/2016-Standards-with-Glossary-5.3.2018.pdf.

Epstein, S. (1994). Integration of the Cognitive and the Psychodynamic Unconscious. *American Psychologist*, 49, 709–724.

Flores, K. (2017, April 13). *Keynote Address at the Annual University of Wisconsin LGBTQ+ Ally March [Keynote Speaker]*. Annual University of Wisconsin Oshkosh LGBTQ+ Ally March, Oshkosh, WI, United States.

Grabbe, L., & Miller-Karas, E. (2018). The Trauma Resiliency Model: A "Bottom-Up" Intervention for Trauma Psychotherapy. *Journal of the American Psychiatric Nurses Association*, 24(1), 76–84.

Griffith, B. A., & Frieden, G. (2000). Facilitating Reflective Thinking in Counselor Education. *Counselor Education and Supervision*, 40, 82–93.

Griffith, R. L., Steelman, L. A., Wildman, J. L., LeNoble, C. A., & Zhou, Z. E. (2017). Guided Mindfulness: A Self-Regulatory Approach to Experiential Learning of Complex Skills. *Theoretical Issues in Ergonomics Science*, 18(2), 147–166.

Harper, A., Finerty, P., Martinez, M., Brace, A., Crethar, H. C., Loos, B., Harper, B., Graham, S., Singh, A., Kocet, M., Travis, L., Travis, L., Lambert, S., Burnes, T., Dickey, L. M., & Hammer, T. (2013). ALGBTIC LGBQQIA Competencies Taskforce. Association for Lesbian, Gay, Bisexual, and Transgender Issues in Counseling Competencies for Counseling with Lesbian, Gay, Bisexual, Queer, Questioning, Intersex, and Ally Individuals. *Journal of LGBT Issues in Counseling*, 7(1), 2–43.

Hyland, T. (2015). On the Contemporary Applications of Mindfulness: Some Implications for Education. *Journal of Philosophy of Education*, 49(2), 170–186.

Ivers, N. N., Johnson, D. A., Clarke, P. B., Newsome, D. W., & Berry, R. A. (2016). The Relationship Between Mindfulness and Multicultural Counseling Competence. *Journal of Counseling & Development*, 94(1), 72–82.

Jenkins, R. (2015). The 7 Fundamental Conditions of Learning: Our Quest is not So Much to Figure Out How to Teach Best as to Figure Out How Students Learn Best. *Chronicle of Higher Education*. https://www.chronicle.com/article/the-7-fundamental-conditions-of-learning/?bc_nonce=57h1he90ju5wd6e96ezh68&cid=reg_wall_signup.

Kagnici, D. Y. (2014). Reflections of a Multicultural Counseling Course: A Qualitative Study with Counseling Students and Counselors. *Educational Sciences: Theory and Practice*, 14(1), 53–62.

Lenes, E., Swank, J. M., Hart, K. A., Machado, M. M., Darilus, S., Ardelt, M., Smith, A. S., Rockwood Lane, M., & Puig, A. (2020). Color-Conscious Multicultural Mindfulness Training in the Counseling Field. *Journal of Counseling & Development*, 98(2), 147–158.

Magee, R. V. (2019). *The Inner Work of Racial Justice: Healing Ourselves and Transforming Our Communities Through Mindfulness*. Tarcher-Perigee.

Matthes, E. H. (2016). Cultural Appropriation Without Cultural Essentialism? *Social Theory and Practice*, 42(2), 343–366.

Pipher, M. (2007). *Writing to Change the World*. Riverhead Books.

Ratts, M. J., Singh, A. A., Nassar-McMillan, S., Butler, K. S., & McCullough, J. R. (2015). *Multicultural and Social Justice Counseling Competencies*. Retrieved November 14, 2020, from https://www.counseling.org/docs/default-source/competencies/multicultural-and-social-justice-counseling-competencies.pdf?sfvrsn=20.

Reilly, B. (2016). Mindfulness Infusion Through CACREP Standards. *Journal of Creativity in Mental Health*, 11, 213–224.

Roach, L. F., & Young, M. E. (2007). Do Counselor Education Programs Promote Wellness in Their Students? *Counselor Education and Supervision*, 47, 29–45.

Rose, S. A., Sheffield, D., & Harling, M. (2018). The Integration of the Workable Range Model into a Mindfulness-Based Stress Reduction Course: A Practice-Based Case Study. *Mindfulness*, 9, 430–440.

Schwind, J., McCay, E., Beanlands, H., Schindel, M. L., Martin, J., & Binder, M. (2017). Mindfulness Practice as a Teaching-Learning Strategy in Higher Education: A Qualitative Exploratory Pilot Study. *Nurse Education Today*, 50, 92–96.

Stauffer, D. E., & Pehrsson, M. (2012). Mindfulness Competencies for Counselors and Psychotherapists. *Journal of Mental Counseling*, 34(3), 227–239.

Tobin, D. J., Willow, R. A., Bastow, E. K., & Ratkowski, E. M. (2009). Reflective Learning within a Counselor Education Curriculum. *Journal of Counselor Preparation and Supervision*, 1(1), (1–9). Retrieved on October 31, 2020, from https://repository.wcsu.edu/cgi/viewcontent.cgi?article=1043&context=jcps.

Tomlinson-Clarke, S., & Clarke, D. (2010). Culturally Focused Community-Centered Service Learning: An International Cultural Immersion Experience. *Multicultural Counseling and Development*, 38, 166–175.

Treleaven, D. A. (2018). *Trauma-Sensitive Mindfulness: Practices for Safe and Transformative Healing*. W. W. Norton & Co. Kindle Edition.

Tyler, J. M., & Guth, L. J. (1999). Using Media to Create Experiential Learning in Multicultural and Diversity Issues. *Journal of Multicultural Counseling and Development*, 27(3), 153–169.

Villalba, J. A., & Redmond, R. E. (2008). Crash: Using Popular Film as an Experiential Learning Activity in a Multicultural Counseling Course. *Counselor Education and Supervision*, 47, 264–276.

Wagner, A. E., & Shahjahan, R. A. (2015). Centering Embodied Learning in Anti-Oppressive Pedagogy. *Teaching in Higher Education*, 20(3), 244–254.

Ziomek-Daigle, J. (2017). Using Reflective Practices to Articulate Student Learning in Counselor Education. *Journal of Creativity in Mental Health*, 12(2), 262–270. Retrieved October 31, 2020, from https://doi.org/10.1080/15401383.2016.1187581.

PART IV
Contemplative Practices for Community and Institutional Change

12
REFLECTIONS ON DEVELOPING A CAMPUS-WIDE WORKSHOP SERIES ON CONTEMPLATIVE PRACTICE AND SOCIAL JUSTICE

Jennifer Daubenmier, Christopher J. Koenig, Maiya Evans, Lisa Moore, and Michele J. Eliason

Contemplative practices have been increasingly used in higher education to enhance student well-being and academic success (Chiodelli et al., 2020; Ergas, 2019; Zajonc, 2016). More recently, educators, activists, and researchers are exploring how contemplative practices and perspectives may support social justice on and outside college campuses (e.g., Basu et al., 2019; Magee, 2017). In light of the aftermath of the video recording of the Minneapolis police killing of George Floyd, an African American man, and the widespread protests that erupted against police brutality, we feel this work is particularly relevant at this time. Systemic racism and white privilege are being discussed nationally, along with efforts to revisit our racist history and implement policies, practices, and symbols aligned with racial justice. The #BlackLivesMatter movement has been embraced by large numbers of white Americans who are heightening awareness of white privilege, as evidenced by the *New York Times* Bestseller List comprised predominantly of books on race and white privilege in the United States during the weeks of the protests (McEvoy, 2020). Universities have a vital role to play in maintaining this momentum towards social justice by creating opportunities for students, faculty, staff, and administrators to reflect on systemic racism and white privilege, as well as other forms of oppression and privileges, and increase personal and collective commitment towards more equitable and inclusive practices and policies. Contemplative practices have an important contribution to make towards these efforts. In this chapter, we share the development, execution, evaluation, and reflections of a campus-wide workshop series held at San Francisco State University (SFSU). The series promoted experiential engagement and discussion on the relationship between contemplative practice and social justice to improve campus climate, enhance well-being of campus members, and promote student success.

DOI: 10.4324/9781003201854-16

Background

SFSU is one of the most racially and ethnically diverse student bodies in the United States (US News & World Report, 2019). Our university has a long history of commitment to social justice and opposition to systemic oppression and marginalization, including student protests in 1968–1969 which led to the creation of the first College of Ethnic Studies in the United States. More recently, Alicia Garza, MA, a graduate student in the College of Ethnic Studies in 2013, first inspired the phrase "Black Lives Matter" as a response to the acquittal of George Zimmerman for the shooting death of Trayvon Martin and, along with fellow activists, gave birth to a new civil rights movement (Day, 2015). University commitment to social justice and the college has wavered over time, however, prompting rallies, students camping out on campus, petitions demanding support for ethnic studies, and four students undergoing a 10-day hunger strike in 2016 to pressure the university to reinvest in its social justice mission and support the College of Ethnic Studies (Herrera, 2016).

After the election of President Donald Trump in November 2016, racial tensions and fears across the country increased (Newman et al., 2020; Williamson & Gelfand, 2019). Many campus communities were affected by these events. In the months following the election, 25% of students at one university reported clinically significant levels of stress that could lead to a diagnosis of post-traumatic stress disorder (Hagan et al., 2018). Scores were higher among women and students of color. Given our university's diversity and commitment to social justice, our campus was also deeply affected. Faculty struggled with how to address post-election concerns, climate, and trauma in classrooms.

To address the collective impact of these issues, SFSU initiated a campus-wide call for proposals to sponsor faculty-led workshops, entitled "How to Be a University in a World of Conflict," in order to "foster conversation and strengthen our capacity for mutual understanding, community, and engagement" (San Francisco State University, 2017). Recipients were required to lead at least four workshops in one semester. Proposals were renewable for a second semester with similar requirements.

The first two authors of this chapter, Jennifer Daubenmier and Christopher J. Koenig, had recently presented a poster at the ninth annual Association for Contemplative Mind in Higher Education conference, "Radicalizing Contemplative Education: Compassion, Intersectionality, and Justice in Challenging Times" (Association of Contemplative Mind in Higher Education, October 2017). Meeting a network of colleagues interested in similar ideas gave us confidence to extend conversations at the conference to our institution. We proposed a workshop series entitled "Breathing In, Speaking Up: Contemplative Practice and Social Justice." The overall goal was to explore how contemplative practices and perspectives could contribute to social justice while improving campus climate, well-being of campus members, and student success.

Once the proposal was funded, we formulated a conceptual framework for our workshops. We wanted participants to have experiences with contemplative practice and discussion of contemplative perspectives from contemporary and wisdom traditions. We also wanted to balance workshops with selected short readings and videos with interactive dyadic, small-group, and large-group activities.

Theoretical and Contemplative Influences

We drew on Berila's (2016) *Integrating Mindfulness into Anti-Oppression Pedagogy: Social Justice in Higher Education* as a guiding framework. We began with the premise that external tensions and conflict are influenced by pre-existing values, perceptions, and beliefs resulting from social identities with respect to race, ethnicity, class, gender, sexuality, religion, migration history, immigration status, (dis)ability status, other social categories, as well as family of origin relational dynamics. We wanted the workshops to increase awareness of how we all are socialized into ways of thinking, feeling, and acting that can perpetuate structural systems of oppression. Awareness and transformation of inner and outer conflict is challenging, as it requires vulnerability, patience, and dedication. However, we believe each person has the potential to transform perceptions of self and other and cultivate a greater capacity to respond to conflict in ways that maintain social connection and promote insight for growth.

Our workshops also drew on wisdom traditions that facilitate transformation towards greater self-awareness, interconnection, and social responsibility. His Holiness the Dalai Lama and others have noted that schools and universities predominantly train students to develop skills to enter the workforce, but social-emotional intelligence and ethics for living in a diverse, interconnected world are not routinely taught (Dalai Lama, 2017; Steel, 2014). This oversight poses a challenge in training future generations of citizens who can respond to conflicts peacefully and equitably and not be driven solely by self-interest. In response to these trends, the Dalai Lama called for the creation of universal secular ethics that can be embraced across religions, nationality, and systems of values and beliefs. The goal is to "educate the heart" through reasoning and contemplative skills that cultivate love, compassion, justice, forgiveness, mindfulness, and tolerance in our educational systems in order to create more peaceful and just societies (Dalai Lama, 2001, 2012).

We integrated principles of these secular ethics informed by Buddhist perspectives with Berila's (2016) framework to guide our theoretical approach. Each workshop highlighted one or more of these elements to support dialogues and discussions. We outline these perspectives in a sequential, cohesive manner in Table 12.1.

TABLE 12.1 Guiding Theoretical Principles

1. *Recognition of Basic Dignity.* One function of contemplative practice is to recall, in a felt, embodied manner, our inherent worth, wholeness, and dignity as human beings, not dependent on social standing, performance, achievement, or other conditions. This respect for life is inherent in the living, breathing, knowing person, and each individual has the same dignity as any other individual. Social justice definitions often recognize a fundamental dignity of all human beings (Adams et al., 2007; Rawls, 1971).
2. *Common Humanity.* We all desire similar assurances in life, including to be safe from harm, to have access to basic life necessities, to be well-regarded by others, and to have freedom for self-determination. Just as all human beings desire health and happiness, we all share experiences of sadness, anger, loneliness, and fear, although particular narratives and contexts may differ.
3. *Interdependence.* Each individual is a product of biological, family, community, cultural, national, and environmental factors. Our thoughts, identities, feelings, values, sense of self, and motivation are shaped by these contextual factors. In addition, everyone's life is a product of innumerable actions of others, close and far, that sustain the life of any one individual. Awareness of the interconnection of all life can lead to profound gratitude and appreciation for others.
4. *Awareness of Structural Systems of Oppression.* We are born into social and institutional systems, often with a legacy of oppression, which disproportionately empower and privilege some social groups over others, which thus contributes to inequitable distribution of resources and higher rates of trauma, chronic stress, and lack of self-worth in some group members. We further recognize the interdependence of power and privilege, such that for some groups to enjoy privilege, others need to be disenfranchised. As discussed by Berila (2016), privilege refers to unearned benefits that confer societal acceptance and ease of life for some group members but are denied to other groups, which can result in social marginalization. Societal norms are in favor of White presenting identities, heterosexuals, and men, for example, and those who don't fall into these categories are considered "other" and are vulnerable to discrimination, invisibility, and less access to societal resources (Rothenberg, 2004).
5. *Cultivation of Attention and Self-Care.* Through contemplative practices, such as meditation, movement, and other culturally relevant practices, we can cultivate increased awareness, relaxation, self-compassion, and self-care to release trauma, manage stress, and begin to heal body, mind, and spirit.
6. *Awareness of Internalized Oppression.* We can also cultivate awareness of our social conditioning and recognize it as an internalization of external processes rather than an essential aspect of ourselves. With increased self-awareness, we see patterns, not to blame or judge ourselves, but with curiosity and self-compassion, and to discover the freedom to let go of harmful, dysfunctional, and oppressive beliefs and create new identities, meanings, and actions.
7. *Deep Listening.* With greater calmness and clarity, we can be more present to others. Being heard is healing. Not being heard or seen is alienating, debilitating, painful, and ruptures relationship. Deep listening can increase understanding, compassion, forgiveness, and tolerance. To resolve conflicts, we need to hear and understand each other to understand the whole of which we are a part. Jon Kabat-Zinn said, "to not know what you don't know can be harmful to others" (2018, November 11). This may be particularly relevant for members of dominant groups who may have little understanding of experiences and perspectives from members of marginalized groups. Furthermore, bringing awareness to our own potentially uncomfortable reactions as we listen to others is also a part of deep listening.

8. *Compassion.* After recognizing human dignity, common humanity, the interdependent nature of life, and developing attention, connection, and concern for others, the motivation to alleviate suffering of others is a natural extension. Compassion can be understood as having three components: the awareness of another's suffering or need, the emotional resonance or empathetic response to their suffering, and an intention or motivation to alleviate that suffering (Jinpa, 2015).
9. *Social and Civic Responsibility.* In order to promote social justice, institutional and governmental policies that lead to discrimination and inequities need to be replaced with equitable ones. Individuals and communities must engage in social and political action to change these policies. Engaging in social action and being of service can also enhance one's own health and well-being through meaning, purpose, and satisfaction, and ultimately, the recognition that serving others serves oneself (Jinpa, 2015).

Workshop Format and Content

Campus-wide announcements were made by the Provost's Office, and we additionally recruited participants through our personal networks. We were given a budget of $1000 per semester to cover workshop costs, the majority of which was spent on catering. We held eight, 1.5-hour midday workshops throughout the year and provided lunch for participants with vegetarian and non-vegetarian options. The SFSU Center for Equity and Excellence in Teaching & Learning (CEETL) gave us space to run workshops. The midday time and central location of the workshops facilitated participation across campus. Each session included 9 to 17 participants, including facilitators.

The Fall 2017 workshop sessions were co-facilitated by the first two authors (JD, CJK), and focused on definitional issues of contemplative practice, social justice, their application, and relevance to current events. Participants were faculty, staff, students, and administrators. In the Spring 2018 semester, workshops were co-facilitated with invited colleagues to increase the diversity of perspectives related to contemplative practice and social justice and to engage in conversations we might otherwise not have with our colleagues. Colleagues were offered a modest honorarium.

While each workshop had its own structure, in general, workshops began with self-introductions and an invitation to eat lunch. After 15 minutes, facilitators brought everyone together for a brief meditation and introduced the day's topic. Sessions typically ended with a whole-group discussion. A summary of each workshop's topic and activities follows.

Fall 2017 Semester

Workshop 1: Introduction to contemplative practice and social justice. We began with personal introductions in which people indicated their interest in the topic and what they hoped to learn. The introductions took the majority of time for the first session, as participants had much they wanted to share. We then discussed their understandings of contemplative practice and provided a handout of the Tree of Contemplative Practices (See Figure 1.1 (p. 6) in this volume) to discuss a broad range of practices that can be included (Bergman & Duerr, 2015). One facilitator led a short, guided, sitting mindfulness meditation on body and breath awareness based on Mindfulness-Based Stress Reduction, which lasted five minutes, and ended the session with a bell. Interested participants were encouraged to speak with facilitators about establishing a meditation practice outside of the workshops.

Workshop 2: What is "social justice"? In order to provide continuity to the group discussion from the previous week, we summarized themes raised by participants from workshop 1 in terms of definitions of contemplative practice. We then discussed what social justice meant to individuals in the group and provided definitions collated from social justice organizations. Next, we discussed how we as individuals internalize systems of injustice and adopt beliefs and stereotypes against social groups of which we may be members. We presented a brief video of Beth Berila discussing the "imposter syndrome" (Berila, 2017) as a form of internalized oppression and discussed reactions and our own experiences of the imposter syndrome through the lenses of race, gender, and other identities in a large group.

Workshop 3: How can we integrate contemplative practice and social justice? This workshop showed a short video clip of a conversation between Jon Kabat-Zinn and Angela Davis, discussing how mindfulness and social justice can work together (this video is no longer freely available; however, we recommend two similar videos to consider in its place: Magee et al., 2020; Williams & Kabat-Zinn, 2020). After discussion, we presented a short video by Thich Nhat Hanh on deep listening (Hanh, 2012). We then led a guided meditation to recall an event that involved personal experience with an unresolved social injustice and how the situation could be perceived from a wisdom perspective. In pairs, individuals took turns practicing deep listening as their partner discussed the event and how to resolve or gain insight from it. This exercise took 15 minutes, after which participants shared insights in a larger-group discussion.

Workshop 4: Relating contemplative practice and social justice to current events. We applied the concepts of deep listening to current issues of sexual harassment and racial/ethnic tensions. We used texts focusing on women's stories of sexual harassment and assault that ultimately resulted in the #MeToo movement and people of African descent describing the pain of not being heard (De Robertis, 2017; Eddo-Lodge, 2017). Small groups discussed these issues and shared comments with the full group. We then led a guided meditation on "next steps," focusing on how participants could integrate workshop ideas into their lives and then gave participants the opportunity to write down their next steps and share in the large group. Finally, we gave each participant Thich Nhat Hanh's (1975)

Miracle of Mindfulness to inspire further contemplative practice and, ultimately, service to others, which was funded by the modest workshop stipend.

Spring Semester 2018

Workshop 5: Embodied learning to increase awareness of social-cultural issues. This workshop, led by Maiya Evans, introduced embodied learning activities that build community while addressing social issues. Participants first engaged with an interactive activity to build connection by organizing themselves in chronological birthday order without talking. Participants then explored power dynamics by mimicking movements of a partner in silence. Next, participants explored cultural differences in a simulation game by creating separate fictitious tribes which were ultimately combined to create a third culture combining elements of each tribe. Finally, participants paired up to practice compassion in a silent activity where the pairs contemplated statements of compassion while looking into their partner's eyes. Short discussions followed each activity to address issues of social identity, power dynamics across social groups, and compassion.

Workshop 6: Acknowledging universities as places of evaluation, judgment, and fear. This workshop was led by Lisa Moore. After an opening meditation and introductions, the facilitator discussed the importance and value of acknowledging fear in the classroom among faculty and students and encouraged the practice of fearlessness. When afraid, it is difficult, if not impossible, to be creative, open learners. It is also difficult to meet others and oneself with compassion. Working with justice and diversity requires the capacity to sit with one's fears and hear from people whose vulnerabilities are often not readily visible. Participants were paired with one another in mixed faculty, staff, and student dyads to practice deep listening as each partner shared their fears about the university or larger community for five minutes each and then talked together in pairs for five minutes, for 15 minutes total. Reactions and insights were shared in a large-group discussion for the rest of the session.

Workshop 7: Embodiment as awareness, privilege, and intersection. This workshop, led by Christopher J. Koenig, invited participants to increase awareness of themselves as embodied beings and to explore the relationships between socialization and intersectionality. We practiced awareness of how these processes are experienced and come to inscribe meaning to the body. Exercises included a yogic practice of slowly raising one's arms overhead with a focus on full-body breathing, a five-minute standing meditation, and a ten-minute walking meditation. Interactive exercises included standing in close proximity to another person face-to-face in pairs and trios. We conducted this exercise with eyes open and closed, silently and while talking, to explore how another person's presence can affect one's own embodiment, sense of self, and awareness of privilege and (dis)ability. There was facilitated discussion after each exercise.

Workshop 8: Mindfulness of eating and its social-cultural influences. This workshop, led by Michele J. Eliason, introduced mindful eating and described a research project using Intuitive Eating, a form of mindfulness drawn from the "Health at Every Size" model (Bacon, 2010) and adapted for older sexual minority women. We discussed resistance to the word *mindfulness* among members of nondominant groups. Participants were then guided through a mindful eating exercise with the lunch that was provided, and identified one's own words for physical, psychological, and emotional hunger cues, showing how individuals described their own hunger. In the last half of the workshop, each participant shared how family, social, and cultural background shaped attitudes towards and experiences of eating and food.

Participant Feedback and Evaluation

The institutional support contributed a small budget for meals, honoraria, and books for participants and invited facilitators. While the community of participants may have appreciated these things, interest in contemplative practice and social justice drove participation. On the last workshop of each semester, we administered a survey asking participants a series of fixed response and open-ended questions. We submitted our project to the SFSU Institutional Review Board (IRB) as program evaluation (Protocol #2020–116). It was evaluated as exempt because program evaluation is not considered research, as its aim is not to produce generalizable findings but rather to evaluate the processes, procedures, and products of a program for the purpose of quality improvement and, in our case, to disseminate the lessons we learned about implementing a contemplative practice and social justice program in our institution to help others who may want to adapt these lessons to a new setting. Overall, 20 participants completed the surveys as an overwhelmingly positive experience, with the majority of participants saying the meditations, discussions, and topics were "extremely helpful." We summarized the open-ended comments into three main themes.

First, participants described how workshops increased their understanding of contemplative practice as an important element of self-care that contributes to their quality of life and work. For example, one participant stated that workshops helped them to "slow down and reflect," while another wrote that it helped "to pause during a busy week." Second, participants increasingly became aware of the impact of contemplative practice in their everyday lives. One participant wrote, "I have learned breathing techniques and other mindfulness practices that I can apply at my leisure." Two participants reflected on the importance of mindfulness during work. One wrote, "I will bring this mindfulness with me when I start working. It'll enable me to separate events at work from personal life. And to try not to take things personally." Third, participants described appreciation of a greater sense of community. For example, a participant wrote that as a result of workshops, "I had the opportunity to connect with faculty, students, and staff from different departments, which is extremely helpful."

Participants were diverse in terms of disciplines, colleges, and campus programs and included faculty, staff, administrators, and students. However, participants were primarily white, particularly in the first semester. Facilitators took the opportunity to address issues of white privilege and fragility during discussion in the context of deep listening, particularly in the fourth workshop. However, in the future, we acknowledge the need to explore how to attract more racially/ethnically diverse participants who better reflect the student body and perhaps more clearly address issues of structural oppression at each workshop.

Interestingly, workshops led to several campus and individual-level innovations. For example, one participant who was the director of a campus tutoring center started a meditation group for student tutors with support of the Dean of Undergraduate Education and Academic Planning. Another campus director reported being more explicit about the importance of mental health and wellness in meetings with students and staff. One faculty enrolled in a self-compassion training course for professional development and shared resources with students. In summary, our workshops created an opportunity for interested campus members to come together, but a more long-term, ongoing workshop series would be needed to establish a community of stakeholders who could deepen their understanding of how contemplative and social justice practices can be integrated in order to more fully permeate campus climate, resources, and policies and thereby enhance student success and well-being of the campus community.

Reflections and Recommendations

At the end of the workshop series, the authorship team took an opportunity to reflect individually and collectively on how we were impacted over the course of the workshop series and what we learned. This was our first attempt of coming together as a diverse group of educators to explore how to integrate social justice with contemplative practice. Therefore, we further reflected on our process and how we could improve the workshop series if we were to do it again and provide recommendations to those who may wish to consider implementing similar workshops. Finally, in the last section, based on our observations, we provide a developmental learning model that may be helpful to consider when thinking about how educators can learn to incorporate contemplative practice and social justice pedagogy and perspectives into their classrooms.

The university call for proposals was an opportunity for us to explore the connections and synergy between contemplative practice and social justice in an academic context. After it was funded, the first two authors developed an outline of curriculum and format for the sessions. We did not have a clear roadmap. We wanted to explore ideas organically and envisioned rich discussions that we would facilitate without necessarily providing answers. We began with discussions about definitions of contemplative practice and social justice. After the first workshop, we noticed many participants had genuine interest in these issues but did not necessarily have experience with contemplative practice. Some of us felt a certain self-consciousness discussing meditation on campus, as if people were coming out of the closet from isolated locations to discuss their interests in an open forum. We felt the courage each person had to come to the group and knew we had to establish trust for the group to be successful, to be vulnerable in a safe place among diverse students, faculty, staff, and administrators. We felt the importance of starting each session with a meditation, to shift the norms of typical academic interactions to come together as fellow human beings first and foremost beyond our identities in the academy.

The first two authors were also aware that we were two white, relatively privileged co-facilitators discussing social justice in a diverse group setting with limited training. We wanted to open the facilitation role to other colleagues with similar interests to increase the diversity of perspectives and create greater community among colleagues. It was great fun to reach out to colleagues and invite them to share their interests and expertise in this area. Through their involvement, we learned new ideas and methods for using contemplative practices to engage students in discussions of social justice in the classroom. The overall experience gave us more confidence in establishing trust and talking about challenging issues of oppression, privilege, and social justice in a diverse group setting. Moreover, the rich experiences and insights of the students driven by their diversity opened us up to seeing our students in the classroom as co-creators of knowledge.

Lessons Learned

In this section, we share recommendations and suggestions based on our lessons learned for those who may wish to consider organizing similar workshops on their campuses.

1. Our series met for eight 1.5-hour workshops across two semesters. We found this time frame to be minimally sufficient to introduce and discuss key topics and provide participants with new contemplative skills to incorporate into their lives and respective academic contexts. We suggest either more frequent meetings over a longer period of time or multi-hour workshops to allow for greater immersion, culture building, and language crafting.
2. Leadership and facilitator diversity is important. We felt a shift in participation once we diversified our facilitators to include people of color who had experience with contemplative practice and knowledge about social justice. In particular, we noticed that participants of color felt more at ease, confident, and engaged. Facilitators should both look like the population who attends the workshop and help expand the boundaries of what is typically

thought of as the norm. We believe a commitment at the outset from diverse members of the campus to serve on the core committee is important to ensure greater inclusivity of perspectives during planning, outreach, and implementation stages.

3. We recommend that facilitators in positions of privilege engage in prior reflection of their own privilege to feel comfortable acknowledging it in a diverse group setting. This self-awareness can help create a safer space for those from oppressed groups to share and to help everyone recognize how unacknowledged privilege can harm. Facilitators in positions of privilege may also be challenged in unexpected ways by members of oppressed groups, thus, they should be willing to be humbled, to listen, and to be open to feedback. When such instances arise, these experiences can serve as powerful examples for how participants in positions of privilege could potentially respond to such situations in the future.

4. We made some systematic efforts at outreach for potential participants and determined time availabilities with an initial cohort of interested participants. However, outreach among students, faculty, staff, and administrative leadership takes time to build. We suggest finding allies on campus who can assist with recruitment and to allow plenty of time for this crucial step to ensure diverse, inclusive participation.

5. Set the goals of the group modestly. Start with the assumption that attendees may have little to no preparation for the topics that will be discussed. This will maximize inclusion and help foster ongoing exploration for those with more preparation. If participants come with more experience, conversation can become more nuanced, but it may be helpful to prepare each session to accommodate the least experienced person in the room.

6. Decide a contemplative focus for the group and be open to including your personal contemplative interests (and passions). All the facilitators in our group were dedicated to some form of contemplative practice, including both Theravada and Vajrayana Buddhism, hatha yoga, and mindfulness meditation. We chose mindfulness as a contemplative focus; however, we offered a range of practices. Some of us experienced a tension between offering contemplative practices that were assessable, which were potentially more generic, and practices that were rooted in particular religious and contemplative traditions, which require more context or adaptation to practice in a secular context. While our series was built directly from our personal experiences with contemplative practice, it was the first time some of us tried leading a group of diverse participants in these practices.

7. Include time for contemplative practice to give participants the actual experience of practices they might use outside of sessions. Participants may come with a range of experience in contemplative practice, from absolute beginner to regular practitioner. One goal of our sessions was to introduce contemplative practices that (a) we could conduct within a designated 10- to 15-minute

time frame, and (b) participants could use outside group sessions. In other words, we wanted to introduce contemplative practices that participants could take and adapt for their own use.

8. Be prepared with a safety plan and psychological support for participants. Participants can bring rich life experiences to discussions on contemplative practice and social justice. At the same time, trauma, food and housing insecurity, financial difficulties, systemic oppression, power, and privilege can potentially trigger painful emotional reactions during contemplative practice exercises. Facilitators should be sensitive to these issues and inform participants that these events can occur and give participants the flexibility to disengage with the practice at any time. Be prepared to provide resources and referrals for psychological support as necessary.

9. Be sensitive to current events and incorporate them into workshops as meaningful examples of application of the principles. Our workshop #4 on current events was particularly meaningful. The week we were planning that session, we serendipitously came across stories of women being sexually harassed as part of the #MeToo movement, and a writer of African descent describing the most painful aspect of social oppression, *not being heard or understood*. This helped participants to see a tangible connection between contemplative practice and social justice in the real world: we need to create opportunities and develop skills to hear and acknowledge one another's pain, especially in relation to privilege and oppression, as an important, yet easily overlooked step in creating social change.

10. Be prepared to have uncomfortable conversations. A large part of social justice work is having uncomfortable dialogue, especially in a diverse group in which individuals differ in positions of privilege and oppression. The richness of having a diverse group is that individuals can hear perspectives from those who differ from them in race/ethnicity, gender, class, and other social identities. However, at the same time, individuals may be exposed to their "blind spots," or not know how their perspectives could be offensive or harmful to others. People from marginalized groups may be especially affected when this occurs. Facilitators should be prepared to step in to acknowledge and address potential harm while also acknowledging that such conversations are valuable for expanding our knowledge about experiences of people who are different from us.

11. Use workshops as an opportunity for reflection and growth in your role as an educator. As the workshops were open to students as well as faculty, staff, and administrators, typical power hierarchies between students and faculty were blurred, allowing faculty and students to participate more equally as co-creators of knowledge. Thus, each workshop raised critical questions about positionality and power that were generalizable to classroom pedagogy. For example, one facilitator asked: How can I walk the razor's edge of tempering my ascribed privilege while being responsible for the learning

of students who differ from me in age, ethnicity, race, and other social identities? Another facilitator was challenged to be more thoughtful about acknowledging students' real-world experiences when practicing contemplative methods. Students offered key insights with regard to their everyday struggles as students and their life experiences. Oftentimes as educators, we focus so closely on class material that we are not always attuned to the needs and experiences of the students.

12. Be open to personal and professional integration and institutional transformation. Collectively, our workshops helped to move us out of our comfort zone as educators by trying new techniques to create meaningful learning experiences without holding too tightly to our own expectations about the learning process. Many of us valued the experience of bringing our personal contemplative practice into an academic context. One facilitator noted: "It was lovely and liberating to bring the work I have done elsewhere into the place where I spend the most time and have witnessed quite a lot of pain." The experience of bringing our contemplative work "out of the closet" gave us more confidence. Furthermore, it allowed us to see how contemplative practices can be used as tools to better understand meta-concerns related to social justice in academia. For example, a common disjunct between professed ideals and actual practice of social justice in academia can be understood intellectually by gathering and analyzing data. Yet, this tension can be eased and transformed by contemplative practices that admit confusion and ambiguity and that do not let us retreat into rigid structures and scripts. Overall, we felt we were bringing a transformative process to academia, which is necessary in order to meet the challenges of our world and our time.

Developmental Learning Model of Contemplative Practice and Social Justice for Educators

Our yearlong workshop series at SFSU addressing the intersection of contemplative practice and social justice was well-received and highly attended. However, as our reflections show, there is much more work yet to be done.

First, although most instructors at our institution consider themselves to be aligned with social justice issues, very few have training in how to teach within a social justice framework. While an instructor might introduce controversial topics via readings, films, or discussions, most have no systematic way of thinking about their pedagogy when teaching social justice content. What is true with regards to social justice is doubly so concerning contemplative practice. While several participants in our workshop series had personal experience with contemplative practices, few had any experience bringing them into the classroom or other campus setting. Both contemplative practice and social justice are complex topics that may need to be considered—and practiced—separately before they can be integrated. Our workshops were designed to increase awareness and demonstrate some practices that could be used in the classroom, but for logistical reasons, we did not have time for participants to actually practice these activities in their own settings and provide reflection and feedback. To fully integrate these topics, participants could likely use scaffolding in their awareness and implementation of both social justice and contemplative practice pedagogy. For example, many participants noted that they were students of a contemplative practice, such as yoga or meditation, but may not have considered that they could teach some forms of these practices in their classrooms. They may need support to explore which practices they feel confident to share with students, starting with very simple activities. Similarly, social justice pedagogy builds from simple changes in a class to more transformative practices. Both might be introduced in increments.

Second, participants were eager to engage in discussions about contemplative practice, yet most lacked confidence about how to incorporate contemplation into their individual roles and identities within the institution. Teaching faculty were unsure how to incorporate contemplation into classrooms. Staff, administrators, and leadership were eager to embrace contemplative experience but wanted ideas for how to apply these activities in their organizational units. Students were eager to explore ideas and experience different contemplative approaches to help manage anxiety and stress and to bolster well-being, but they also raised questions about how to apply contemplative tools in different areas of their lives. Everyone seemed to want a community to explore contemplative practice and social justice, and our workshops helped to create a temporary community at the university to hold this space.

Reflecting on the final evaluation comments and discussion in the workshops over the year leads us to the conclusion that participants first needed to learn about and experience contemplative practices before they could apply them to social justice education. In other words, we suggest that integrating contemplative practice and social justice may occur as a series of *developmental stages* (see Kegan, 1982).

1. The first stage may be to talk about contemplative practice (or social justice, or both) in academia and learn to feel comfortable "coming out of the closet" as a contemplative practitioner. For example, as a result of an individual's experience with a contemplative practice, they may first reflect on the role of contemplative practices in their own lives. This reflection may lead to ideas about how these tools might be applied to their teaching, workplace, and everyday lives.
2. A second stage may be to learn basic skills for how to introduce contemplative practice in the classroom as a social justice issue. Imposter syndrome, stress and anxiety, and systemic inequality, including racism, homophobia, and misogyny, can all be addressed with both contemplation and social justice practices. That is, social justice topics may raise emotional responses (painful memories, anger, sadness, frustration, guilt, blame, hopelessness) that can interfere with learning; contemplative practices can be used to help students move through these emotional states and not shut down in the

classroom. This stage may include several pilot tests with small exercises that take little time to implement. After each session, the individual should take time to reflect on how the practices did or did not work and why. This could serve as the basis to develop a framework for evaluating their own reflective teaching practice.
3. A third stage may be to begin to integrate contemplative practice and social justice more systematically throughout a curriculum. This may involve imbedding contemplative practices throughout the semester, or even throughout a program so that they become a natural part of the learning process for faculty and students.

Resistance is likely to pop up at every stage. Historically, the mind-body-spirit split in Western culture has led to a belief that academic institutions should focus only on cognitive strategies for learning, so contemplative practices are relegated to emotional, spiritual, or religious activities that are not considered as pedagogy. This belief needs to be explored and dismantled so that academic institutions learn to value contemplative practices for the ways that they complement and enhance other forms of learning. While our workshops created an opportunity for diverse stakeholders to come together to discuss these issues, a longer-term, ongoing series would be needed to develop and deepen our understanding of the connections between contemplative practice and social justice and support faculty as they explore implementing new pedagogies in their classes.

Studying the processes of teaching within a contemplative framework is relatively new, but Owen-Smith's (2018) *The Contemplative Mind in the Scholarship of Teaching and Learning* offers frameworks for teaching and research. She suggests that contemplation was originally at the heart of education, but the contemplation piece was lost in the last century as educational practices became more pragmatic, technological, and skills-based. The resurgence of interest in contemplative practices stands to improve the quality of education in general and provide students with knowledge and skills that extend beyond the intellectual/cognitive realm that will serve them well in life. Research also indicates that contemplation practices such as mindfulness meditation may improve well-being and academic performance of undergraduate students (e.g., Calma-Birling & Gurung, 2017; Canby et al., 2015; Greeson et al., 2014). Providing students with contemplative practice is both a life skill and a social justice issue vital to all beings living in the early 21st century. Our hope is that others can learn from our experience and be inspired to offer related programs in their own universities to create a more reflective, compassionate, and just world.

Acknowledgments

We would like to thank all of our participants, and Adam Burke, PhD, MPH, Lac, and Stephanie Windle, DNP, RN, for their early support of our initiative. We would also like to thank funders of the Year of Conversation workshop series at

San Francisco State University, including the Office of the President led by Leslie E. Wong, the Office of the Provost led by Jennifer Summit, and the Academic Senate Office chaired by Nancy Gerber, for supporting our workshop series.

References

Adams, M., Bell, L. A., & Griffin, P. (Eds.). (2007). *Teaching for Diversity and Social Justice* (pp. 1–14). Routledge/Taylor & Francis Group.

Association for Contemplative Mind in Higher Education. (2017, October). *Radicalizing Contemplative Education: Compassion, Intersectionality, and Justice in Challenging Times*. Retrieved February 28, 2019, from https://2017.acmheconference.org/.

Bacon, L. (2010). *Health at Every Size. The Surprising Truth About Your Weight*. Benbella Books, Inc.

Basu, R., Ahlers, J., Thomas, J., Thomas, M., & Weigt, J. (2019). Working Toward Beloved Community: Contemplative Practice and Social Justice in One Public University. *The Journal of Contemplative Inquiry*, 6(1), 231–225.

Bergman, C., & Duerr, M. (2015, February 28). *The Tree of Contemplative Practices*. https://onbeing.org/blog/the-tree-of-contemplative-practices/.

Berila, B. (2016). *Integrating Mindfulness into Anti-Oppression Pedagogy: Social Justice in Higher Education*. New York: Routledge.

Berila, B. (2017, April 3). *Imposter Syndrome*. http://www.bethberila.com/whats-new/2017/4/3/imposter-syndrome.

Calma-Birling, D., & Gurung, R. A. (2017). Does a Brief Mindfulness Intervention Impact Quiz Performance? *Psychology Learning and Teaching*, 16, 323–335. https://doi.org/10.1177/1475725717712785.

Canby, N. K., Cameron, I. M., Calhoun, A. T., et al. (2015). A Brief Mindfulness Intervention for Healthy College Students and Its Effects on Psychological Distress, Self-Control, Meta-Mood, and Subjective Vitality. *Mindfulness*, 6, 1071. https://doi.org/10.1007/s12671-014-0356-5.

Chiodelli, R., Nesi de Mello, L. T., Neves de Jesus, S., Beneton, E. R., Russel, T., & Andretta, I. (2020). Mindfulness-Based Interventions in Undergraduate Students: A Systematic Review. *Journal of American College Health*. Doi: 10.1080/07448481.2020.1767109.

Dalai Lama [Tenzin Gyatso]. (2001). *Ethics for a New Millennium*. Riverside Books.

Dalai Lama [Tenzin Gyatso]. (2012). *Beyond Religion: Ethics for a Whole World*. Houghton Mifflin Harcourt Publishing Company.

Dalai Lama [Tenzin Gyatso]. (2017, November 14). *His Holiness the Dalai Lama Calls for an Education of the Heart*. https://tibet.net/2017/11/his-holiness-the-dalai-lama-calls-for-an-education-of-the-heart/.

Day, E. (2015, October 15). #BlackLivesMatter: The Birth of a New Civil Rights Movement. *The Guardian*. https://www.theguardian.com/world/2015/jul/19/blacklivesmatter-birth-civil-rights-movement.

De Robertis, C. (2017, December 6). Why We Must Listen to Women. *East Bay Express*.

Eddo-Lodge, R. (2017). *Why I Am No Longer Talking to White People About Race*. Bloomsbury Publishing.

Ergas, O. (2019). A Contemplative Turn in Education: Charting a Curricular-Pedagogical Countermovement. *Pedagogy, Culture & Society*, 27(2), 251–270.

Greeson, J., Juberg, M. K., Maytan, M., James, K., & Rogers, H. (2014). A Randomized Controlled Trial of Koru: A Mindfulness Program for College Students and

Other Emerging Adults. *Journal of American College Health*, 62(4), 222–233. Doi: 10.1080/07448481.2014.887571.

Hagan, M. J., Sladek, M. R., Luecken, L. J., & Doane, L. D. (2018). Event-Related Clinical Distress in College Students: Responses to the 2016 U.S. Presidential Election. *Journal of American College Health*. Doi: 10.1080/07448481.2018.1515763.

Hanh, T. N. (1975). *Miracle of Mindfulness*. Beacon Press.

Hanh, T. N. (2012, May 6). *Thich Nhat Hanh on Compassionate Listening*. http://www.oprah.com/own-super-soul-sunday/thich-nhat-hanh-on-compassionate-listening-video.

Herrera, J. (2016, May 22). *10-Day Hunger Strike = Victory for SFSU Students*. https://www.usatoday.com/story/college/2016/05/22/10-day-hunger-strike-victory-for-sfsu-students/37417869/.

Jinpa, T. (2015). *A Fearless Heart: How the Courage to be Compassionate Can Transform Our Lives*. Hudson Street Press.

Kabat-Zinn, J. (2018, November 11). *Where Is This All Going, and What's Love—and Insight, Embodied Wisdom, and Community—Got to Do with It?* Keynote address presented at International Symposium for Contemplative Research 2018 in Phoenix, AZ.

Kegan, R. (1982). *The Evolving Self*. Harvard University Press.

Magee, R. (2017). One Field, Different Doors in: Contemplative Higher Education, Transformative Education, and Education for Social Justice. *Initiative for Contemplative Equity and Action Journal*, 1, 119–127.

Magee, R. V., Kabat-Zinn, J., & Cooper, A. [Wisdom 2.0]. (2020, May 28). *A Mindful Approach to Race and Social Justice | Rhonda Magee, Jon Kabat-Zinn, Anderson Cooper* [Video]. https://www.youtube.com/watch?v=1DPw09eTa7o.

McEvoy, J. (2020, June 11). *Books about Racism Dominates Best-Seller Lists Amidst Protests*. https://www.forbes.com/sites/jemimamcevoy/2020/06/11/black-lives-matter-dominates-best-seller-lists-amid-protests/#30df7d3d4b67.

Mind and Life Institute. (November, 2018). *International Symposium for Contemplative Research 2018*. Phoenix, A. https://iscr2018.org/.

Newman, B., Merolla, J., Shah, S., Lemi, D., Collingwood, L., & Ramakrishnan, S. (2020). The Trump Effect: An Experimental Investigation of the Emboldening Effect of Racially Inflammatory Elite Communication. *British Journal of Political Science*, 1–22. Doi: 10.1017/S0007123419000590.

Owen-Smith, P. (2018). *The Contemplative Mind in the Scholarship of Teaching and Learning*. Indiana University Press.

Rawls, J. (1971). *A Theory of Justice*. Belknap Press: An Imprint of Harvard University Press.

Rothenberg, P. S. (2004). *White Privilege: Essential Readings on the Other Side of Racism* (2nd ed.). Worth.

San Francisco State University. (2017, August 21). *How to Be a University in a World of Conflict* [Call for Proposals]. https://campusmemo.sfsu.edu/content/august-212017.

Steel, S. (2014). *The Pursuit of Wisdom and Happiness in Education: Historical Sources and Contemplative Practices*. State University of New York Press.

US News & World Report. (2019). *Campus Ethnic Diversity*: National Universities. https://www.usnews.com/best-colleges/rankings/national-universities/campus-ethnic-diversity.

Watts, R. J., Diemer, M. A., & Voight, A. M. (2011). Critical Consciousness: Current Status and Future directions. *New Directions for Child and Adolescent Development*, 2011(134), 43–57.

Williams, Rev. A. K., & Kabat-Zinn, J. (2020, April 16). *Love and awakening in a global Pandemic* [Video file]. https://www.eomega.org/videos/love-awakening-in-a-global-pandemic.

Williamson, V., & Gelfand, I. (2019, August 13). *Trump and racism: What do the data say?* https://www.brookings.edu/blog/fixgov/2019/08/14/trump-and-racism-what-do-the-data-say/.

Zajonc, A. (2016). Contemplation in education. In *Handbook of Mindfulness in Education* (pp. 17–28). Springer.

13
USING NEUROSCIENCE AND MINDFULNESS TO FORM NEW HABITS OF MIND AROUND RACE

Renee Owen and Danaé Jones Aicher

We are a pair of professional women, one of us African American (Danaé), and one of us Euro-American (Renee). We teach classes that transform implicit biases in the workforce. We help our students see racial bias and injustice from a completely new perspective, and commit to taking steps to making their workplaces more inclusive. But our real work, as we see it, is to take adult learners on a journey of transformative learning.

We find that teaching in a mixed-race team works well for the sensitive topic of racial bias. Studies show that exposing white people to an African American teacher helps to build a positive bias toward Black people (Eberhardt, 2019; Fiske, 2002). Danaé portrays a professional voice of experience from the Black perspective. She also provides some emotional safety for students of color in the class, while helping to defray the potential for students of color in the class having to bear the burden of teaching the white students in the class (DiAngelo, 2018). Renee offers emotional support for the white folks in the room. She has empathy for what white students are going through when they begin to experience some of the same fragile emotions she experienced when confronted with her role in a racist society—what DiAngelo calls *white fragility* (2018).

We teach in a small city in the Appalachian Mountains. The local businesses we have worked with span a range of small nonprofit organizations, public and private schools, and small to midsize for-profit establishments. Typically, fewer than 10% of the employees identify as BIPOC. Our workshops last from under four hours to daylong sessions. Since our students are generally about 90% white, our primary strategy explores changing the perspectives and habits of mind for white people around race, while also increasing identity-awareness and antiracist agency for people of color. We do not approach racism as an individual act of intentional aggression or malice, but rather define racism as a societal condition that almost everyone enacts on a daily basis, typically outside of awareness (DiAngelo, 2018; Eberhardt, 2019; Magee, 2019). As such, our classes often include a historical analysis of the ways racist ideas have been deeply embedded into our laws, our national policies and practices, and our culture, resulting in a racialized experience for us all—a fact most white people aren't necessarily aware of.

Transformative Learning

Teaching with the goal of changing people's perspectives and habits of mind is a complex task. We draw heavily from the theoretical lens of transformative learning theory, as defined by Mezirow:

> Transformative learning is learning that transforms problematic frames of reference—sets of fixed assumptions and expectations (habits of mind, meaning perspectives, mindsets)—to make them more inclusive, discriminating, open, reflective, and emotionally able to change. Such frames of reference are better than others because they are more likely to generate beliefs and opinions that will prove more true or justified to guide action.
> (Mezirow, 2003, pp. 58–59)

Viewing racism through Mezirow's lens of transformative learning, we are trying to transform the way people see, think, and act in regard to race. Teaching from a transformative learning perspective is completely different from teaching content knowledge. We are not teaching *about* racism; we are helping students undergo a transformation.

Our first intention in implicit bias classes is to help students see racism that was invisible to them—what some might call a blind spot, or what Mezirow refers to as seeing problematic "habits of mind." We are asking students to examine unconscious assumptions about race that were previously outside of their awareness. Students learn that the way they previously thought about the world may not be righteous or true. Mezirow (1991) calls this a "disorienting dilemma," when a learner is faced with their identity being challenged, or when a long-held belief or assumption about oneself or the world is suddenly challenged. A disorienting dilemma can be a terrifying experience. When white students who previously saw themselves as "good people" who are not racist are then provided with information and experiences revealing the ways they have contributed to harmful racist outcomes for people of color, they are faced with intense emotions (DiAngelo, 2018; Eberhardt, 2019). We have compassion for how destabilizing this experience is for white students.

Students of color are often having a different experience, and those different experiences also depend on and are informed by how they identify racially, because their racialized experiences are different. We have learned that Black students and some Latinx students can feel affirmed by the learning experience, which, in and of itself, can be transformational given a lifetime of learning experiences causing cultural erasure, at best.

Our second goal is to help students to change their mental habits. We help them to be "emotionally able to change," as Mezirow describes the transformative learning process, so they can become more inclusive (Mezirow, 2003, pp. 58–59). Our ultimate goal is for students to be armed with the intention and ability to permanently change the way they act, "taking on a new role" (Mezirow, 2003, pp. 58–59). Transformed students are able to reintegrate back into their life with their new role, a changed identity, and new meaning perspectives. By taking students on this transformative journey, our intention is not only to change how they think, but also how they act, which requires a paradigm shift in how they view the world. Transformative learning creates "significant and irreversible changes in the way a person experiences, conceptualizes, and interacts with the world" (Hoggan & Browning, 2019, p. 30).

Mindfulness and Neuroscience as Transformative Tools

We employ practices from mindfulness and knowledge from neuroscience to aid in the transformative processes in our implicit bias classes. Mindfulness practices during class can help students calm their nervous systems and open their minds to the possibility of seeing through new eyes. Sharing the neuroscience with students is one strategy for helping students become more aware of how their minds work and thus better able to reflect on their potential biases, creating a willingness to change. Figure 13.1 demonstrates the use of mindfulness, paired with neuroscientific knowledge, in our racial bias trainings to create the conditions for transformative learning.

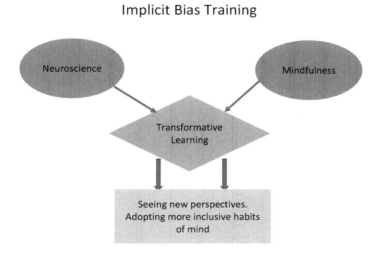

FIGURE 13.1   Method for implicit bias training

Transformative learning in regard to race is emotionally, socially, and neurologically challenging. As teachers of racial equity classes, we need to acknowledge it is difficult to "lean into discomfort," but mindfulness facilitates this process.

In the sections that follow, we share a few features of our implicit bias classes, describing some of the neuroscience and mindfulness activities offered to students, and explaining how these features facilitate transformative learning around race. This is by no means a "playbook" for an entire class. Instead, we offer concepts and activities we insert into class content, which experienced facilitators may integrate into their own instruction.

A Safe Beginning

To create conditions for transformative learning, students need a comfortable, supportive class climate, where it feels safe to be vulnerable and take risks. Therefore, we begin with a low-risk introductory activity. After giving a somewhat humorous introduction of ourselves, which helps to loosen folks up, we provide research from Doris Chang (personal communication, n.d.) around the five ways people typically react to "diversity classes": freeze, antagonize, avoid, overcompensate, and engage (Trawalter et al., 2009). Renee shares a couple of personal stories of when she was in diversity classes, and she started to freeze when racial conflict arose and the conversation became agitated or tense. Sometimes, she offers stories of how she would overcompensate by trying to show the teacher, or people of color, how "woke" she already was with her knowledge about equity.

By sharing personal stories, we send a message to students that they are not alone. They share a common humanity with other people who experience similar emotions and phenomena. As Siegel (2010) says, if we "can name it we can tame it." So, by naming the fear that people may start to feel during a discussion around race, we are better able to explain to our students why we will employ mindfulness during class to help them notice these feelings and work through them. We explain that all these emotional reactions are completely natural and common, and as facilitators, we are not here to judge. With this, we can feel the tension dropping and people opening up.

The "Where Are You From" Activity

When the class opens, Danaé asks everyone to introduce themselves by sharing their name, something about their role in the organization, and where they grew up. We model this, and as people share this information, we ask them to explain if their location(s) for growing up would be described as urban, rural, suburban, and so on. The information they share is preparation for the first group activity, called "Where Are You From," which engages students in a reflective discussion.

The activity is simple. In groups of four or five, we ask students to share what people often assume about them simply based on learning where they grew up. Each group has about five minutes, or one minute per person, to do this. Then we reassemble as a whole class and ask for people to share examples that came up in their group. Before talking about race, this is a nonthreatening activity that helps students to see that everyone, including each of them, has biases. Since we are located in the South, there are often jokes about Floridians from flat land who have a reputation for being poor drivers in the mountains, Californians who are assumed to be New Agers, or people from the Northeast who are seen as aggressive, and so on. By confessing to these fairly benign, sometimes humorous biases, students can open their minds toward seeing their own assumptions, before admitting they have racial biases. This opens the ego, and therefore the mental doorway, to transformative learning (Heron, 1992). Additionally, this activity gives students an opportunity to openly share biases they notice people have about them, which helps eliminate some of the white fragility that commonly pops up in discussions of race. White people often want to talk about how people are prejudiced *toward them*, so we get that out of the way at the beginning (Hardiman & Keehn, 2012). This activity is helpful for people of all backgrounds to feel seen and to talk about biases with more compassion, thereby preparing the ground for addressing the topic of race.

Soon after this activity, Danaé provides a definition of implicit, or unconscious, bias, and we give a brief review of research on the neurological and psychological aspects of human bias, backed by examples from empirical studies. We use personal stories people told from the "Where Are You From" activity to demonstrate some key points that make the academic research relevant to our students.

Learning About the Science of Human Bias

It all starts with the brain, and how we are neurologically and psychologically wired as human beings. Using slides, we provide an overview of the science of bias in three sections: the primal brain, the short-cut brain, and the tribal brain.

Fast Brain and Slow Brain

Our brains developed over a period of millennia. Showing a simple diagram of a brain, we point to the oldest part of the brain, the "reptilian brain," that controls most of our bodily functions—the autonomic nervous system that keeps our heart pumping, keeps our lungs breathing, and keeps us alive (Siegel, 2010). The reptilian brain is wired to keep us alive in another way too: it is constantly scanning for danger, alerting the rest of our brain and body when we need to react to a threat (Choudhury, 2015). The next layer of our brain is the limbic system, which is the seat of our emotions, and works closely with the reptilian brain. Memories that are linked with fear, for example, create emotions that signal our body to react with fear before we have a chance to intervene. Perhaps to safeguard our very survival, this "old" part of our brain—the reptilian and limbic system—is also the fastest part of our brain.

The slower part of our brain is the neo-cortex, the outer layer of the brain, and also the newest part of our brain to develop. When we talk about our brain, or we talk about "thinking," the neo-cortex is the part of our brain we are identifying. This is where rational thought takes place, where language develops, and where we can make wise, patient decisions. The neo-cortex is slow but more accurate, whereas the fast brain is impulsive and extremely error prone (Siegel, 2010). The fast part of our brain is dominant in making us more emotional beings, who primarily react out of hopes, fears, memories, emotions, images, and other largely unconscious and subconscious activities. Although our primal brain kept our species alive for millennia, the fast brain's mechanisms for keeping us safe aren't so helpful for today's industrialized society, where wild animals are not our top threats to survival; yet, our fast brain is on high alert all the time, scanning for danger and primed to react, as if we still lived like our distant, primal ancestors (Choudhury, 2015). Unfortunately, in a racist, sexist, and homophobic society, the fast brain can be lifesaving for those most often targeted in hate crimes.

The Short-Cut Brain

These two parts of our brain—the fast brain and the slow brain (or old brain and new brain)—work together to help us function efficiently. The brain uses about 20% of our total bodily energy, so it needs to conserve energy. Our brain makes a short-cut out of everything like walking, driving, writing, reading, and countless other activities and thoughts. We would be completely overwhelmed if we had to think about each aspect of these activities every time we performed them.

The brain also takes short-cuts to save energy by making judgments quickly, and this can lead to bias. Our brain places everything into categories based on previous knowledge and experiences (Eberhardt, 2019) and makes associations. Here, we can give examples from what we shared in the "Where Are You From" activity because this is how stereotyping happens—it's something the human brain does completely outside of conscious awareness. In this sense, biases are the result of our brain making short-cuts (Eberhardt, 2019). To demonstrate the fast brain/slow brain concept, we engage students in a few cognitive perception and optical illusion exercises (i.e. Seth, 2017; MyLovelyReptile, 2010). Showing optical illusions helps students recognize that we are not our brain. Our brain thinks it is the perceiver and knower of reality, but it isn't. As Seth (2017) says, "It's dark in there"; our brain cannot actually see, or hear, or touch. It is trying to come to conclusions about reality based on nothing more than chemical and electrical signals it is receiving. We can't trust it to show us what is real.

The Tribal Brain

Humans are tribal in nature, influencing another critical aspect of how our primal brain responds to our environment. We developed as social beings out of fear and survival: we needed our tribe to stay safe. Being exiled from the band or losing our tribe was the virtual equivalent of death (Owen, 2019). The modern-day impact of our tribal nature is twofold. First, we are pumped with fear if we think we don't belong in any situation. Our old brain frantically fires and screams, "Danger!" to the rest of our brain and body. In class, we ask students if they had any experiences in middle school where they were socially excluded or unpopular, which usually brings murmurs of memories. We now know when we are experiencing intense fear, to our brain it is the equivalent of physical pain, and when we are socially excluded, our old brain is telling us we are about to die! Therefore, we are always looking for people like us and trying to be continually accepted.

The flipside of our tribal nature is that our brain is also constantly scanning for enemies, or anything unfamiliar. When we meet someone new, our brain is trying to keep us safe by instantly deciding if this person is in our same group or an out-group (Eberhardt, 2019). As instructors, we sometimes point out to the class that the moment they saw that we were their instructors (typically before class starts), their subconscious brains began trying to determine if each of us was cool or not, nice or mean, rich or poor—essentially, whether we are friend or foe. Unfortunately, whether an unfamiliar person looks like us or not is a large part of our fast brain's determining factors (Arizona State University, 2005).

While we don't overwhelm our students with too much research data, it is important for instructors to be familiar with the studies that support this in-group/out-group bias concept. It is also important to recognize the ways in which race adds an extra layer of complexity to bias, because everyone is racialized. Danaé regularly points to the ways our national narrative around race further informs our bias, for both white students who believe they are not "racist," and for students of color who also grew up raised on the same narratives.

The foundation for some of the research on racial bias is the now-famous Harvard Implicit Association Test, or the IAT (Eberhardt, 2019; Choudhury, 2015). The test measures the response time of participants associating images with bad or good. The IAT has undergone iterations and improvements since its inception in 1995, but it continues to accurately assess the implicit racial bias of research participants, regardless of their stated or explicit racial values or biases (Dasgupta et al., 2000). Instead of overwhelming students with research on implicit bias with each class, we share a study to demonstrate the neuroscientific empirical evidence of racial bias (Gutsell & Inzlicht, 2010). The participants (all white) in this study were brought into an empty room with only a video screen, where they were connected to an electroencephalogram (EEG) machine. The screen would show videos of people with different races drinking water. Researchers found that the motor cortex of the research participants displayed mental activity that appeared as if they were, themselves, actively drinking the glass of water when they watched other white people on the screen. Mirror neurons are responsible for this phenomenon, where humans appear to mentally mimic other humans' behavior—a response that is attributed to the human capacity for empathy. However, while watching people of other races drink water, the EEG measurements did not pick up on the same level of motor cortex activity. According to the research, for some "their brains actually registered as little activity as when they watched a blank screen" (University of Toronto, 2010). This study seems to indicate that humans may feel less empathy for people of another race (Choudhury, 2015).

Activating and Utilizing "Disorienting Dilemmas"

After learning about the neuroscience of bias, and particularly the "drinking water study," many students in class begin experiencing what Mezirow (2012) calls a "disorienting dilemma," the first step of transformative learning. Most people—about 80%—think of themselves as unbiased people around race (Fiske, 2002). It is common for white people to have been socialized to be color blind, believing it is wrong to see race. Yet, in class they are being confronted with evidence that being color blind is neuroscientifically impossible, and how they have thought about race and bias was likely all wrong (Banaji & Greenwald, 2016).

At this juncture in the class, most students are grappling with the idea that they are biased, when they were taught all their life that biased people are racist. Their identity as a good person who is not racist is being disturbed (Choudhury, 2015; DiAngelo, 2018). This is also one of the times during the training when we find the antagonistic reaction showing up, primarily from white students, who are searching for a way to discredit the study. Students of color are typically quiet through this portion. Some express gratitude for confirming a lived experience. For some students there is general discomfort pointing to race so explicitly in predominantly white spaces. According to transformative learning theory, the students now need open dialogue so they can reflect on their thoughts and emotions if they are to move through the distressing "disorienting dilemma" they are experiencing, and toward transforming their perspectives.

One critical note: It's important that students don't think that racial bias is inevitable. Choudhury (2015) compares racial bias to a computer, saying that bias is our computer hardware—simply the brains and psyches we are given. We are going to have biases, but which *type* of biases we have is our software. Society and our upbringing have programmed us to have certain biases (Eberhardt, 2019).

The class next moves through several small-group and whole-group activities and discussions that provide opportunity to reflect on what students have just learned, and to further help them see the negative consequences of bias on a large, systemic scale for people of color and for society at large. We look at how micro-aggression is typically an unintentional slight that demonstrates a sense of superiority for the aggressor and ends up creating a sense of someone being categorized, or "othered," and repeatedly experiencing a subtly hostile atmosphere (Fiske, 2002; Sue et al., 2007). Eventually, we grapple with the term *white privilege*, and by the end of class we hope we have helped students view white privilege as something white people can use to interrupt racism.

Introducing Mindfulness Activities

It is important for the facilitators to provide students with the rationale for using mindfulness. During class introductions, we prepare students by letting them know we will be using some mindfulness techniques. When presenting neuroscientific evidence around bias and the ability for the brain to change, we mention that mindfulness has been shown to increase brain plasticity. The mindfulness activities are used to help create an open mind that is accepting of the present—including their biases and contributions to a racist society—with self-compassion and with greater empathy for others.

While students are experiencing a disorienting dilemma around how their brains are wired for bias, they also learn that brains are capable of changing (Eberhardt, 2019). Mindfulness helps "rewire" the brain to build one's capacity to be aware enough to interrupt racial biases (Hafenbrack et al., 2014; Hopthrow et al., 2017; Siegel, 2010) and reduce reliance on automatic associations (Lueke & Gibson, 2015). Mindfulness serves another, perhaps altogether different, function for students of color, whose nervous systems are also activated by a different sense of danger—the danger of white people being placed in such a vulnerable position coming face-to-face with racial bias, and the urgency for people of color to be able to think quickly and calmly, and to act for self-protection.

Before beginning mindfulness activities, we give students a definition of mindfulness as simply a method of being more aware in the present moment, without judgment (Kabat-Zinn, 2005). Mindfulness is an important tool for helping us become more aware of our unconscious bias (Berila, 2014) and may help students experience less reactivity during disturbing class content.

Mindfulness Activity: Simply Breathe

After introducing students to the neuroscience of bias in our subconscious mind, we find it useful to introduce a simple mindfulness activity that focuses on the breath. Renee helps students use their breath as an anchor and explains that they are simply noticing their breath, without any judgment, and there is no need to change their breathing in any way. She points out that we do not regularly notice our breathing, and this activity helps us become more aware of ourselves and what our brain and body are continually doing outside our awareness. Since our biases are usually outside of our awareness, we are building our ability to notice what's going on behind our conscious mind, simply by noticing our breathing. After a brief breath-awareness, we ask participants if they have noticed anything different. Typical comments are things such as "feeling calm," "more open," "peaceful," "noticing sounds," "feeling more connected."

As part of the after-activity reflection, we like to point out that our fast brain, which constantly makes biased judgments outside of our awareness, takes over when we are stressed, especially if we are multitasking (Eberhardt, 2019). While most people literally cannot move any slower during their hectic jobs, we point out that it is important to understand mindfulness as a way to exercise the mind and prepare it to be more aware under stressful and fast-paced circumstances.

Mindfulness Activity: Watch Your Thoughts

The breathing activity helps students acclimate to doing mindfulness together. Using the same techniques, Renee later drops them into a mindfulness state and asks them to watch their thoughts, or their "mental activities," which also includes emotions (Siegel, 2010). They are asked not to change anything or to judge, but to simply observe their mental activities. At some point Renee typically says, "By now your mind may have wandered, and you are lost in your thoughts, rather than watching them. Gently bring your attention back to your mental activities." Upon returning their attention to the room, we remind students that by watching their thoughts, similar to the breathing activity, they are exercising their capacity to be more aware of their subconscious mental activities. Research indicates a strong correlation between mindfulness and bias-reduction (i.e., Hafenbrack et al., 2014; Hopthrow et al., 2017). By being in the present, and not wandering into the past or future, we are more mindful of current reality, and less likely to project our biases from the past onto individuals in the present.

Mindfulness Activities of Compassion and Kindness

Danaé, a historian, provides a chronological history of race and institutional, structural racism in the United States, from housing and banking to health care, education, and the justice system, that adds up to a giant, overarching system of oppression. She shares a long list of the negative outcomes for people of color, which students are now better able to recognize as an aspect of interconnected systems, where their previous biases may have blamed the victims, or assumed that the difference in status between white people and people of color is simply a given (Magee, 2019).

Mindfulness Activity: Self-Compassion

By the end of this content, students of any race can often be feeling overwhelmed with emotion—fear, anger, or even rage. This is a good time to introduce a self-compassion exercise, material we adapted from Neff (n.d.). We explain to students that they may be experiencing some intense emotions, and that the first step of the self-compassion mindfulness activity is to simply acknowledge those emotions nonjudgmentally. Renee says to the class,

> You can choose to simply put one hand or both hands on your heart, which sends a message to yourself that you acknowledge and accept the emotions you are experiencing. The next step is an action of compassion toward yourself, which is to say silently to yourself, "All humans experience this emotion. I am only human."

She explains that these actions establish a sense of common humanity, which soothes the fight-or-flight defenses of the brain. Renee continues, "The third step is to offer yourself a gift, something you need in this moment. It may be strength; it may be forgiveness; it may be peace."

The self-compassion activity has many purposes. Most immediately, the activity helps students work through intense emotions, so they can be ready to return to the room. Huntsinger et al. (2014) found that mindful self-compassion can have a positive effect on race relations. In the context of transformative learning theory, an essential step in the transformative process is recognizing that one's "discontent and the process of transformation are shared" (Mezirow, 2012, p. 86) with the experiences of others. For students of color, the activity helps build a place of safety—a reminder of solidarity. For white students, it can help them recognize they aren't "bad people," but that all of humanity, in some way, shares their shame. Recognizing emotions as a shared human experience helps white students advance through the transformative journey, rather than retreating into defensiveness or fragility. Ultimately, the self-compassion exercise helps build resilience.

Mindfulness Activity: Loving-Kindness Meditation

Some of the later steps in Mezirow's (2012) transformative learning theory are for learners to begin the "exploration of options for new roles, relationships, and actions," and to "build competence and self-confidence in [those] new roles" (p. 86). Ideally, our goal as facilitators is for students to build their capacity to take on the role of being actively antiracist in their workplaces. To help students envision themselves in a new role and to embody compassion toward others, we engage students in a "loving-kindness" meditation, also known as "metta mindfulness." Metta mindfulness can help meditators experience a sense of connectedness with all living beings (Magee, 2019), and more than one study has demonstrated a correlation between metta meditation and a reduction in racial bias (Block-Lerner et al., 2007; Hopthrow et al., 2017; Huntsinger et al., 2014; Kang et al., 2013).

In a typical loving-kindness meditation, the facilitator asks the meditator to begin by offering well wishes to themselves and to repeat the offering with various people in mind, beginning with a loved one, then a neutral person, and eventually a difficult person, then all living beings (Chödrön, 2001). For a racial equity class, we ask students to envision someone very different from themselves, such as someone of a different race.

The metta meditation can be thought of as a touchstone, or finale for the class that isn't simply about how people treat one another at work, but also about helping humans increase our capacity for compassion and justice by recognizing our inherent interconnectivity—something mystics from various wisdom traditions recognize. Thich Nhat Hanh (1999) calls this recognition "interbeing," and His Holiness the Dalai Lama (1999) frequently speaks of the common human desire to reduce suffering and increase happiness. The beauty of metta is that when humans recognize our suffering as shared with all of humanity, it prompts us to act more compassionately toward others, helping to alleviate suffering, and giving rise to joy. Mezirow (2012) states, "What we have in common are human connectedness, the desire to understand, and spiritual incompleteness" (p. 76). He saw transformative learning as a path of liberation that can only come about through what he called mindful learning, defined as "the continuous creation of new categories, openness to new information, and an implicit awareness of more than one perspective" (p. 76.)

Conclusion

Mindfulness is useful for helping students recognize habits of mind, open their minds to new perspectives, and enact more inclusive ways of being—key features of transformative learning. For white students who might otherwise seize upon reactions and tactics of white fragility, such as defensiveness, blaming, or crying, combining transformative learning and mindfulness helps students cultivate self-acceptance and self-compassion for their own biased fallibility, so they can begin to move forward in changing their perspective and roles. Students learn to "respond rather than to react" to their racial sensitivity (Magee, 2019, p. 99).

In any situation where an instructor is implementing mindfulness techniques, the approach can be successful only if the instructors are doing their own "work" and taking on their own mindfulness practice. Moreover, it is crucial for instructors to be consistently engaged in doing their own work around race and equity; otherwise, even our mindfulness practices may center whiteness and fail to enable students to shift their views.

We can only teach what we can model.

References

Arizona State University. (2005, May 25). Prejudice is Hard-Wired into the Human Brain, Says ASU Study. *ScienceDaily*.

Banaji, M. R., & Greenwald, A. (2016). *Blindspot: Hidden Biases of Good People*. Bantam Books.

Berila, B. (2014). Contemplating the Effects of Oppression: Integrating Mindfulness into Diversity Classrooms. *The Journal of Contemplative Inquiry*, 1(1), 55–68.

Block-Lerner, J., Adair, C., Plumb, J. C., Rhatigan, D. L., & Orsillo, S. M. (2007). The Case for Mindfulness-Based Approaches in the Cultivation of Empathy: Does Nonjudgmental, Present Moment Awareness Increase Capacity for Perspective Taking and Empathic Concern? *Journal of Marital and Family Therapy*, 33(4), 501–516.

Chödrön, P. (2001). *Tonglen: The Path of Transformation*. Vajradhatu.

Choudhury, S. (2015). *Deep Diversity: Overcoming us vs. Them*. Between the Lines.

Dalai Lama. (1999). *Ethics for a New Millennium*. Riverhead Books.

Dasgupta, N., McGhee, D. E., Greenwald, A. G., & Banaji, M. R. (2000). Automatic Preference for White Americans: Eliminating the Familiarity Explanation. *Journal of Experimental Social Psychology*, 56, 5–18.

DiAngelo, R. (2018). *White Fragility: Why It's so Hard for White People to Talk about Racism*. Beacon Press.

Eberhardt, J. (2019). *Biased: Uncovering the Hidden Prejudice That Shapes What We See, Think, and Do*. Viking Press.

Fiske, S. (2002). What We Know Now about Bias and Intergroup Conflict, the Problem of the Century. *American Psychological Society*, 11(4), 123–128.

Gutsell, J., & Inzlicht, M. (2010). Empathy Constrained: Prejudice Predicts Reduced Mental Simulation of Actions During Observation of Outgroups. *Journal of Experimental Social Psychology*, 46(5), 841–845.

Hafenbrack, A. C., Kinias, Z., & Barsade, S. G. (2014). Debiasing the Mind Through Meditation: Mindfulness and the Sunk-Cost Bias. *Psychological Science*, 25, 369–376.

Hanh, T. N. (1999). *The Miracle of Mindfulness: An Introduction to the Practice of Meditation*. Beacon Press.

Hardiman, R., & Keehn, M. (2012). White Identity Development Revisited: Listening to White Students. In C. Wijeyesinghe & B. Jackson (Eds.), *New Perspectives on Racial Identify Development: Integrating Merging Frameworks*. New York University Press.

Heron, J. (1992). *Feeling and Personhood: Psychology in Another Key*. Sage.

Hoggan, C., & Browning, B. (2019). *Transformational Learning in Community Colleges: Charting a Course for Academic and Personal Success*. Harvard University Press.

Hopthrow, T., Hooper, N., Mahmood, L., Meier, B. P., & Weger, U. (2017). Mindfulness Reduces the Correspondence Bias. *The Quarterly Journal of Experimental Psychology*, 70(3), 351–360.

Huntsinger, M., Livingston, R., & Isbell, L. (2014). Spirituality and Intergroup Harmony: Meditation and Racial Prejudice. *Mindfulness*, 5, 139–144.

Kabat-Zinn, J. (2005). *Wherever You Go, There You Are: Mindfulness Meditation in Everyday Life*. Hyperion.

Kang, Y., Gruber, J., & Gray, J. R. (2013). Mindfulness and De-automatization. *Emotion Review*, 5, 195–201.

Lueke, A., & Gibson, B. (2015). Mindfulness Meditation Reduces Implicit Age and Race Bias: The Role of Reduced Automaticity of Responding. *Social Psychological and Personality Science*, 6(3), 284–291.

Magee, R. V. (2019). *The Inner Work of Racial Justice: Healing Ourselves and Transforming Our Communities through Mindfulness*. TarcherPerigee.

Mezirow, J. (1991). *Transformative Dimensions of Adult Learning*. Jossey-Bass.

Mezirow, J. (2003). Transformative Learning as Discourse. *Journal of Transformative Education*, 1(1), 58–63.
Mezirow, J. (2012). Learning to Think Like an Adult: Core Concepts of Transformation Theory. In E. W. Taylor & P. Cranton (Eds.), *The Handbook of Transformative Learning: Theory, Research, and Practice* (pp. 73–96). Jossey-Bass.
MyLovelyReptile. (2010). Optical Illusion- Lilac Chaser [Video]. *YouTube*. https://www.youtube.com/watch?v=K7bgUPh4sHo.
Neff, K. (n.d.). *Self Compassion Break*. https://self-compassion.org/exercise-2-self-compassion-break/.
Owen, R. (2019). *Learning That Meets Life: The Lived Experience of Teaching with Secular Spiritual Pedagogy* (Doctoral dissertation). Teachers College, Columbia University. https://academiccommons.columbia.edu/doi/10.7916/d8-0421-jx97.
Seth, A. (2017). *Your Brain Hallucinates Your Conscious Reality*. https://www.ted.com/talks/anil_seth_your_brain_hallucinates_your_conscious_reality?utm_campaign=tedspread&utm_medium=referral&utm_source=tedcomshae.
Siegel, D. J. (2010). *Mindsight: The New Science of Personal Transformation*. Bantam.
Sue, D. W., Capodilupo, C. M., Torino, G. C., Bucceri, J. M., Holder, A. M. B., Nadal, K. L., & Esquilin, M. (2007). Racial Microaggressions in Everyday Life: Implications for Clinical Practice. *American Psychologist*, 62(4), 271–286.
Trawalter, S., Richeson, J. A., & Shelton, J. N. (2009). Predicting Behavior During Interracial Interactions: A Stress and Coping Approach. *Personality and Social Psychology Review*, 13(4), 243.
University of Toronto. (2010, April 27). Human Brain Recognizes and Reacts to Race. *ScienceDaily*. www.sciencedaily.com/releases/2010/04/100426113108.htm.

14
CONTEMPLATIVE LEARNING COMMUNITIES

Transforming Universities by Embedding Contemplative Practices in the Academic Life

Bengü Ergüner-Tekinalp

Although research on integrating mindfulness and contemplative practices in higher education is relatively new, scholar-educators are bringing contemplation *back* because it was once an essential element of intellectual life (Barbezat & Bush, 2014). While efforts to integrate contemplative practices have been increasing primarily with isolated individual courses or educators, creating a system that supports, sustains, and operates with mindfulness is needed for transforming an institution's culture. Accordingly, this chapter describes our journey of establishing a Contemplative Practices Learning Community (CPLC). The goal of our learning community is to create a mindful campus, defined as an organization integrating contemplative practices in education, curriculum, co-curriculum, and leadership (Coutant & Caldwell, 2017). While some institutions have been working towards this goal more systematically, obtaining funding, structures, and support, our CPLC is currently an effort of highly committed faculty trying to make a difference.

My contemplative practices journey started with my commitment to Adlerian, humanistic and positive psychology research and the desire to explore ways for individuals to connect nonjudgmentally as equals. After ten years in the academy, I felt a void in my work, feeling less and less connected to myself, my core values, my colleagues, and my students. As I reflected, explored, read, and learned, I started to name what was (perhaps purposely) missing in my training and work as an academic. In a culture and a system that measures our worth with how busy we are, contemplative practices invite us to pause, slow down, notice, be curious, and be in touch with ourselves and those around us. Rather than rushing with busyness, the "Slow Professor" (Berg & Seeber, 2016) invites deliberation and thoughtfulness, cultivating emotional and intellectual resilience to the effects of the corporatization of higher education, and restoring a sense of community and conviviality.

Our academic training, both for research and teaching, has focused on what to do. On the other hand, contemplative practices are a way of being fully connected to ourselves, others, the world, nature, and what we study. The objectivist model of knowing, teaching, and learning has dominated and deformed higher education (Barbezat & Bush, 2014; Rendón, 2009). As a result, we are distant not only from what we study but also from ourselves and others. After I found the name for my yearning, contemplative practices became the common thread that connected my values, research interest, and pedagogy. I felt a significant call to explore this area more deeply.

This chapter aims to contribute to the contemplative scholarship and provide a perspective on the need for systemic change through increased self-awareness, challenging conditioned expectations. It calls for more humane higher education through pausing, self-reflection, deep work, and building a sense of community and belonging.

Establishing a Contemplative Learning Community

I work in a midsize, private, nonprofit, predominantly white university offering undergraduate and graduate programs; I teach in the graduate program. I am a culturally influenced Muslim, and an immigrant with English as a second language. My contemplative practices are guided by the Earth-based spiritual practices of Turkey, my native land. In the summer of 2017, I attended the Annual Summer Session on Contemplative Learning in Higher Education, which was a transformative experience, so I had an overwhelming desire to share my learning with my colleagues. I reached out to the administration and offered a workshop. To my surprise, there were many faculty and staff interested, many of whom had already been meditating. With their support, I started a Contemplative Practices Learning Community (CLPC) that Fall. Rumi says, "Sometimes you hear a voice through the door calling you. . . . This turning toward what you deeply love saves you" (cited in Barks, 2001). I can easily say contemplative practices saved me by giving depth, purpose, and meaning to my work.

Our learning community has been meeting regularly with new members, and over time, the momentum, interest, and excitement grew. I took the role of organizing the meetings, bringing the practices to explore, and sharing resources. Eventually, members started to share their practices and lead our gatherings, which became not only a place for exploring contemplative practices but also a place for sharing our dreams and supporting one another.

Contemplative practices invite us to ask *why* and *how* questions. They are not about what we are offering or doing, but *why* and *how* we are offering—finding this reason, this desire, guides our motivation. Then, as the *why* becomes clear, we can start exploring the *how*.

The *Why* of Contemplative Learning Communities

An academic system that emphasizes overload and overwork must be fruitfully challenged and creatively disrupted if it is to become sustainable for students, faculty, and staff alike. We need to resist the tyranny of "busyness" through exploring and implementing contemplative practices into our collective and connected lives in the higher education context. By using contemplative invitational techniques, we can transform our institutions. While doing so, we should avoid repeating hierarchical relational patterns by honoring diverse voices from faculty, staff, and students, as "working more effectively through our suffering together in the mixed settings of our classrooms builds resiliency, trust" (Magee, 2017). We cannot separate our internal experiences from the external cultural and societal context, which includes changing expectations in academic work, increasing administrative duties, the neoliberal student-as-customer model, unsupported and unrealistic research expectations, along with expectations of 24–7 availability to colleagues and students, and lack of job security (program cuts and non-tenure status) (Berg & Seeber, 2016).

It is no coincidence that college students, faculty, and staff across all sectors of American higher education report higher rates of mental health concerns, relationship problems, burnout, low morale, and job dissatisfaction—experiences that can be attributed to institutional norms operating within the scarcity mindset and a culture that glorifies overwork (Trail, 2019). Stress and chronic overwork are now accepted as ordinary experiences in academia. These emotional states permeate individuals' multiple life domains and leave students, faculty, and staff feeling physically and mentally exhausted, disconnected from each other, their core selves, values, and their original motivations for joining a higher education community. In my university, Drake, we even say among ourselves, "Drake Busy," signifying the unique imperative to busyness and showing what our culture incentivizes.

Divisive social rhetoric and oppressive practices linking higher education with the larger society are all familiar to us. In this context, "contemplative pedagogy can assist in developing the capacity to create spaces where our suffering may be honored and held with compassion, and where all of our particular challenges may be met with capacity and with heart" (Magee, 2017). Deep inner and community work allow for deep equity and justice work as we learn to notice and stay with suffering (Magee, 2019, 2017). An institution that operates as a contemplative organization can help address such mental well-being concerns presented by students, faculty, and staff and support all individuals to flourish, reach their full potential, and be equipped to engage in social justice issues.

The integration of contemplative practices in our institutions can also help to create positive learning environments, bridge course content with students' embodied awareness, enable deep engaged learning, empower our students, create a campus climate that enhances deeper personal and social awareness, encourage critical inquiry, and help provide a transformed experience of higher education where students see their interconnectedness and take responsibility to reach their fullest potential. Contemplative practices bring self-awareness, ongoing reflexivity rather than reactivity, and the capacity to see our social conditioning more clearly and, therefore, become transformative (Magee, 2017). Such transformation will be possible at all levels: intra-personal and interpersonal to classroom and campus, workplace, and the larger society.

Equity work requires emotional, psychological, spiritual, energetic, and material intensity as we are asked to "remain open, present, engaged, and non-reactionary without resorting to false 'politeness' or polarization/demonization of so-called 'others'" (Magee, 2017). Today, we witness global unrest, confusion, violence, increased isolation, environmental crisis, toxic polarization, and individual and societal pain and suffering. Individuals are expected to embrace a broad range of human differences, move beyond plain tolerance and develop awareness in understanding the impact of historical injustices, and act to alleviate social and ecological suffering. Contemplative practices help individuals cross the boundaries of all differences, not only with fellow humans but also with nonhuman species. Responsible institutions must move beyond merely alleviating the symptoms of overwork and social injustices, and transform "business as usual." Creating a system that supports, sustains, and operates with mindfulness can bring real change. To ground that change, the "Slow Professor" (Berg & Seeber, 2016) practices of deliberation and thoughtfulness, integrating contemplation and mindfulness will help. Transforming our institutions cannot happen with individual efforts. We must work collectively, changing the institutions in order to nurture and embed contemplative practices on our campuses.

The *How* of Contemplative Learning Communities

Academic culture operates with the "not enough-ness" principle. Our teaching, research, grants, service are never enough; we never feel enough; we *are* not enough. Such a design of "notgoodenoughness" operates within the scarcity mindset and creates a culture of busyness and overwhelm. With this context in mind, one of the main challenges our learning community faced immediately was finding a common time that would work for everyone. We tried different options; however, other tasks prevented attending meetings consistently no matter what we tried. No matter what micro-level change we did, nothing was helpful. It was clear that the system was designed to produce such a result. Hence, we implemented the "show up when you can, do what you can" attitude.

Creating a culture of prioritizing one's development and learning is needed. Universities can offer consistent professional/personal development days or hours for people to have the freedom and flexibility in their schedules to use for professional and personal growth opportunities without feeling guilty. Naropa University has been implementing a practice of blocking 90 minutes every Wednesday, during which no classes or meetings are scheduled (Duerr et al., 2004). During COVID-19 challenges, my university started implementing monthly "meeting-free" days. Such meeting-free days can be offered weekly at times designated for similar gatherings or personal "breathing moments."

Along with tight scheduling, another challenge I noticed was the spaces we were using for our gatherings. All the rooms we used were either classrooms or meeting rooms with big tables in the middle. Although there is a designated "quiet room" and a chapel, neither one fits our needs. It seemed as if our campus spaces were designed to prevent us from being intimate, cozy, and reflective, for in each of the rooms, a sense of hierarchy and psychological distance was evident. Researchers confirm that the design of space influences the mental perceptions of the users of the space (Colenberg et al., 2021). A contemplative campus must reflect the support of contemplative practices in physical, nonphysical, and financial structures (DuFon & Christian, 2013).

Contemplative practices invite us not only to look inward but also to be in touch with our surroundings. Research in interior design and psychology points out a relationship between our immediate environment and our inner experiences. Lee (2018) explores that even mundane spaces and objects have potent effects on our mood. Our spaces and the color, texture, form, and movement of objects in our spaces impact our emotions. It might be for this reason that we felt most connected, joyful, and at ease during our gatherings at my home, at the art center, or at a local park for walking meditation. Only a limited number of aesthetics of joy (Lee, 2018) are present in our current academic spaces, which rarely induce joy, harmony, a sense of equality, and contentment. There is a need for spaces dedicated to silent reflection in higher education institutions, rooms that convey nonhierarchical gatherings, and outdoor contemplative spaces (Duerr et al., 2004; DuFon & Christian, 2013).

Audit of Policies and Practices

The aforementioned results our systems are producing are not coincidental. The patterns, policies, structures, norms, and habits create and maintain the results (Petty, 2017). To change the system or integrate contemplative practices in our university systems, at least six changes must be implemented in (1) faculty and student organizations, (2) professional development opportunities, (3) annual events, (4) academic and extracurricular courses, (5) a student affairs emphasis, and (6) various levels of administrative authority that support enhanced teaching and learning (DuFon & Christian, 2013). For assessment, an audit of institutional policies and practices can be conducted in teams that consist of administration, faculty, staff, and students. Groups can check written policies for tone, rhetoric, language, and narrative (Cobb, 2017) and answer:

- What practices or beliefs are we holding onto?
- What's not serving us anymore?

- What creates isolation from one another?
- What gets in our way of seeing each other as fellow humans, not as roles and responsibilities (i.e., secretary, student)?

Identifying and reevaluating organizational norms creating overwork as an expectation is the first step in laying the groundwork. We need to take responsibility for the transformation of our institutions. We are the ones who make, interpret, and implement policy; however, if we see the policy as outside of ourselves, we resign our responsibility in creating and maintaining, and benefiting from, such unhealthy work environments (Cobb, 2017).

The COVID-19 pandemic forced us to realize that we can take time off when we are sick, that we are more connected to one another than we are willing to acknowledge, and that we need each other. We became more understanding of our students, more compassionate, and saw them in their context. They became more than students, more than their role in front of our eyes. We practiced patience and understanding of our colleagues' and students' situations, and we stepped up to cover for our colleagues when needed; we had fewer meetings and gave each other permission to struggle; we gave up on expecting/demanding perfection from one another and ourselves; we were genuinely concerned about the well-being of our colleagues. These radical changes that helped our survival were contemplative practices. Now, we can take what this crisis has taught us and use it to make changes to the current system, generating simple but effective steps towards its transformation into a contemplative campus.

Contemplative Administration

Contemplative administration is centered around openness, clarity of intellect, appreciation and gratitude, communication and relationship, effective action, respect, individual strengths and weaknesses, stillness, and bringing our whole self to work (Beer, 2010). Through contemplation, members of the institutions can identify shared core values to guide the work culture. Guided by values, we can identify strategies and processes to center contemplative practices in our academic lives. Individual members can be supported to hone their practices, experiment, share them, and grow from these practices. Through such efforts, a community of contemplative practitioners who are committed to transformational change can be built.

Contemplative Fellows

During the weekly meetings of our learning community, we reflected on the story of *Twig and Nest* (Nepo, 2020). Nepo shares a story of a bird struggling to carry a big stick to build a nest, then giving up and picking one that fits. He invites us to consider the things that are too big to fit, things we are holding onto that cannot complete our nest. As we are trying to integrate contemplative practices and anti-oppressive pedagogy in our work, we may end up trying to carry a stick that is too big. Letting go means engaging in interruptions of those patterns repeatedly, personally, interpersonally, and systematically or institutionally (Sherrell & Simmer-Brown, 2017). When the stick is too big to carry, a systematic process with a shared responsibility to support and sustain the work is possible.

One way to systematize integrating mindfulness is to create a system of shared responsibility via *Contemplative Fellows*. Each academic unit and office can identify persons to serve as the point of contact and leading facilitator, and promoter of contemplative practices. Using the train-the-trainer model, these fellows can receive training and work in their units to provide training, coordinate programming and activities on mindfulness, and support and to facilitate changes in procedures.

Mindful Meetings

As we work towards the big, long-term goal of contemplative integration, small changes in our daily engagement can bring significant change, such as *mindful meetings*. Duerr and colleagues (2004) describe some principles of contemplative meetings at Naropa, such as paying attention to how a room is set up, including natural light, providing refreshments (water and snacks), and setting up a circle of chairs to facilitate eye contact and open communication. Community parameters for conduct should be collaboratively set and can be flexibly revisited and reshaped as needed. A sense of safety is needed so that everyone can bring their whole selves to the meeting.

Meetings are needed for many purposes in higher education and are commonly dreaded. We can, however, engage in meetings more mindfully. In my role as a department co-chair, I explored ways to invite my colleagues for a very brief grounding and increasing our presence. These brief activities can be used as warm-ups:

- Sharing a piece of poetry, quote, or an abstract picture at the start of the meeting helps reflect and focus on the theme.
- Start or end meetings with sharing gratitude.
- Start the meeting with listening to music and reflecting with a word.
- Start with a brief breath awareness.
- Invite members to set a personal intention (i.e., bringing calm, being open) for their presence in the meeting.
- Brief personal check-ins invite our humanness to work.
    o Share an emotional weather report.
    o Describe one's mood with a traffic sign (how are you entering this meeting? red- tense, not present, tired, anxious, yellow, some difficulty but can focus, or green, ready, alert, relaxed) (Crissinger & Vandenbrink, 2020).

- o Rose (something good), bud (something emerging/developing), or thorn (something difficult/challenging) (Aloha Foundation, n.d.).
- o Reflect on feelings—"what do you have in mind, how do you feel about that, and how do you feel about this feeling?"
- o Increase community feeling by "What do you need in general (or to increase focus, to problem solve) in this meeting?," "How can we help/support you?"
- o Humor (i.e., memes on a scale of dogs or cats to rate our feelings).

Instead of rushing with the agenda, we started with a moment to arrive fully, in brief silence, before transitioning to the task at hand. Recognizing stressors due to the global crisis and seeing we were all indeed in this together created connection. There was no resistance, and people appreciated the opportunity to fully "arrive" and be present. These practices were brief and invitational. While some members of the department did not participate initially, they did so eventually, and I received comments like "something is different" and "I feel better about meetings." Mindful meetings brought focus to the meeting, created space for intentional presence to arise, and invited us to connect deeply. In addition to beginnings and endings, we can conduct the meeting process to be more mindful by inviting all our colleagues to mindfully watch the space and time they are taking to contribute to problem-solving. Allowing for all voices, acknowledging multiple perspectives, and being patient with each other will infuse the meeting with mindfulness.

Faculty Development

Contemplative practices are about how we are present and the methods we use; therefore, learning communities should focus both on teaching as well as self and community care. Our CPLC spent one semester on self and community care activities, and this topic became the focus again during the pandemic lockdowns.

Contemplative Teaching

Contemplative teaching invites the teacher's whole self and considers teaching as a practice of designing learning experiences that are worthwhile, challenging, enjoyable, and memorable—experiences through which our students can also bring their whole selves and connect with course materials deeply and intuitively, bridging the traditional separation between knower and known (Barbezat & Bush, 2014). Contemplative teaching invites profound attentiveness to the phenomena under study (Zajonc, 2009), transforming education from alienated cognitions by integrating emotions (Rendón, 2009). Descartes's "I think therefore I am" is no longer privileged; instead, "I feel, therefore I can be free" (Lorde,

2007) is centered (Rendón, 2009). To invite the whole self and nourish deep contemplation, we need to reflect on what is essential in our courses. The 14th-century Persian poet, Hafiz, says "My dear, is it true that your mind is sometimes like a battering ram, running all through the city, shouting so madly inside and out about the 10,000 things that do not matter?" (as cited in Ladinsky, 2003). It is helpful to reflect on and identify the 10,000 things that our minds scream about, finding out what matters and how we can bring what matters to our awareness, allowing it to guide us in designing our courses.

The contemplative teaching philosophy is a "pedagogy of love" (Kaufman & Schipper, 2018) which is caring about both *what* students are learning and *who they are* as human beings (Magee, 2017) and establishing high standards and rigor. However, without compassion as a base and supportive value, rigor can be ego-driven rather than guided by student learning goals (Kaufman & Schipper, 2018; Palmer, 2007). Contemplative teaching thus asks us to be fully present in our courses by reflecting on how we are with ourselves, our students, and our colleagues. If our compassion is missing in any of these areas, our contemplative teaching practice is incomplete.

Our Presence

At the beginning of my contemplative journey, I focused on methods, techniques, and practices: in other words, I was *"doing* the contemplation." As my practice and applications in teaching deepened, I realized this work is more about *being*, embodying, living contemplation; it is the *how*. Our practices lead us to show up in a contemplative way: "The connections made by good teachers are held not in their methods but their hearts—meaning heart in its ancient sense, as the place where intellect and emotion and spirit will converge" (Palmer, 2007). Contemplative teaching means having an impeccable method, yet not relying solely on the tricks and strategies in teaching. Instead, it is teaching with deep connections with one's values, principles, expectations and passion as well as shortcomings, triggers, and pet peeves so that an open, flexible, respectful learning journey can be set. Magee (2017) calls this the "pedagogy of vulnerability," which challenges teachers to render their frames of knowing, feeling, and doing more visible.

Our Role

Contemplative teaching needs a safe environment to explore and strive for learning. It asks us to strip ourselves from our roles and invites us to be human. We are asked to have "the courage to be imperfect" (Lazarsfeld, 1966). These approaches are contrary to the traditional model where the teacher is positioned as the "sage on the stage," the hierarchy of teachers always knowing all and students always learning from the teacher (Palmer, 2007; Magee, 2017). As we strive to be contemplative educators, we will inevitably face an inner conflict as our core values may clash with the standard practices of higher education. For example, many of us believe in progression and continuous growth in learning. Development and transformation through education do not fall neatly into the shape of a semester (Magee, 2017).

The grading process is a prime example of such inner conflict. No faculty enjoys grading; it sets our role as the punisher (if you don't do this, you fail) and students as our adversaries. Students focus on the end goal rather than on their learning. Contemplative teaching is about understanding the process of learning, identifying the barriers in their learning, and helping students to move in the direction of learning and growth. For student learning outcomes, we can include attending to the inner-life competencies, critical consciousness, awareness, and appreciating diverse ways of knowing, moving beyond self-awareness to social change (Rendón, 2017). There are many books in this area of grading and alternative practices (i.e., Blum, 2020). My experience is that it is hard to incorporate alternative un-grading practices independently, in isolation from the larger institutional context. A collective community-wide discussion and the slow process of building a system that allows un-grading will be more effective.

Centering Teaching Values

As designers of learning experiences, we are not teachers (doing the teaching) but facilitators of learning. This attitude requires self-reflection, self-awareness, balance, and mindfulness. Having a solid base guided by our teaching philosophy, values and principles create the foundation (Gannon, 2020).

Practice: Finding our Practices—What Sustains Us

This activity started with discussing the "tree of contemplative practices" (CMind, 2014). We then discussed our own practices, what we find meaningful and what sustains our energy. On a printout of a blank tree (Figure 14.1), we all took turns to write our practices:

- Roots—what nourishes our practice, what we are bringing from our ancestors, personal and social history.
- Trunk—what practices sustain us as people.
- Branches, leaves, and fruits—what practices we can bring to our work and our classroom.

This practice brought valuable insight for faculty as they realized they utilized more contemplative practices than they allowed themselves to know: "Contemplation is a third way of knowing that complements rational and sensory

Contemplative Learning Communities 241

FIGURE 14.1 The Blank Tree of Contemplative Practices

knowing. Rather than addressing what we know or should know, contemplative knowing addresses how we know" (Cobb, 2017). The *how* of our complexities as whole humans comes out as a result of our practice. In the subsequent meeting, our practice group discussed the values emerging out of the Contemplative Tree. Honoring confidentiality for other participants, I list here the values and guiding principles that emerged for me: love and compassion, mindfulness, the courage to be imperfect, relationship-centered teaching, safety, appropriate challenge, and cultural competence. Values guide us when we are preparing our course syllabi, making decisions about readings, setting up our class meetings, responding to students, and making decisions throughout the semester.

Sample Practices From Our Learning Community

In this chapter, I provide a couple of practices as examples for readers to use or adapt in their courses or learning communities.

Short Practices for Beginning Classes or Meetings

Inviting students to mindfulness in the beginning, as transitions from one activity to the next in a class period, or at the end of the class period are simple yet effective times for contemplative practices. Below are some example prompts we explored in our CPLC:

- "Arrive to the room to the present moment. Just arrive . . ." (surprisingly, we know how to do it, no need for tricks and special skills).
- "Fall into your awareness." (Pause and give them a couple of minutes. No other instructions are needed.)
- "Permit yourself to let go of your busy day."
- "Let's spend a few moments to sit quietly, breathe slowly and deeply, and then we can be ready to focus collectively on the subject of our meeting."

Faculty can practice "doorknob meditation" (Epstein, 2017): when entering the classroom, one can pause and pay full attention to the doorknob.

Inviting Intentions

This practice invites students to set goals or intentions to operate less in automatic pilot and be more mindful. The practice can be helpful during the first meetings of the semester. The following is a sample prompt:

> As we start a new semester, I would like us to spend a little bit of time to reflect on our goals and set intentions for this semester (course or today). Setting our intentions and being mindful of our actions and choices are

powerful ways to start. Your intentions might be ambitious, like "I will put my best effort to learn," or they may not be ambitious as the school may not be the highest priority for you at the moment, and that's OK. What is important is that you are aware of your circumstances, and you are intentional. Rather than reacting to life or day-to-day events, you will be moving with awareness and intentionality.

Now let's take a moment to consider your intentions for the course or the semester, how you will arrive here, and be willing and able to open to your goals, drives, and your possibilities of the semester. Take a deep breath, notice your breath, sit still, and take a couple of minutes to think of and reflect on your intentions. You can think about your intentions, write, or doodle.

A similar practice can be introduced at the beginning of a semester or a class period. This is particularly helpful for my graduate students, most of whom work full time and attend classes in the evenings or on weekends. It is typical for them to miss their children's activities or other family events. This practice acknowledges their whole experience as individuals, invites imperfections, and reminds them of their goal of attending graduate school.

I invite you to take a moment to focus on your intention for our class today. There might be a better place to be at this moment, home with loved ones, out with friends, in your solitude with a movie or a book. But you are here for the moment, and I thought we could be intentional, rather than treating this meeting as just another class you have to attend until your dream comes true. Let's treat the class meeting as moments of learning and teaching, being with one another intentionally.

Acting Mindfully

One of the challenges I experienced in the classroom was students' use of technology unrelated to course content (i.e., checking email, social media). Deducting points, not allowing the use of phones, or reminding students didn't work. Being a contemplative teacher, however, first of all, allowed me to stop taking student behavior personally, and letting go of the unhelpful desire to control. A mindful invitation to my students noticing their intentions helped them not to act on automatic pilot (Levy, 2017). After this invitational practice a couple of times, surprisingly, the use of technology for unrelated reasons disappeared.

Take a couple of breaths; notice your breath. just breathe naturally. Notice your body, any tense points. Relax. I invite you to be intentional and make intentional, conscious decisions throughout our meeting today; there will be moments in this class that you might feel disengaged, bored, challenged, or preoccupied with some other things happening outside of class. When this happens, you may have an impulse, such as checking email or social media. I just want you to notice and be aware when this happens. Note whatever the feeling or thought that is emerging. Bored, challenged, to-do list, etc., and make a conscious, intentional decision to check email or whatever you habitually do. Just be intentional.

Faculty can also offer students an opportunity to write down what they are experiencing at the moment, to raise their hand and contribute that experience if that might be helpful to others. This might help if students are confused with the material, needing clarification, or the topic is already covered in other courses.

Emptying the Mind

This Sufi-informed practice is helpful when I need students' full engagement without getting stuck in their preconceived ideas.

> "One of the practices of Sufism is clearing and quieting mental images and distractions. One way to clear these images begins by bringing them to our attention—the field of our conscious awareness. When we clear these images and start fresh, there is an opening for new knowledge. On a more advanced level, it may facilitate critical thinking skills as we may find ourselves to see the 'falsity in what we believe, truth in what we are opposing (Bhattacharya, 2017).'
>
> "Find a comfortable yet alert position, sit straight with your spine straight, take a few breaths. As we continue to breathe in a natural, unencumbered way, take a few moments to call to mind whatever images you hold about the topics we have been and will be exploring. In your mind, make these images as clear as possible; spend a little time to clarify these pictures. Once you have a clear picture, now you have the opportunity and the option of clearing them from your mind. You can put these pictures away, let them dissolve, put them in a jar, empty the jar, and erase them with an eraser. Whatever works. Clear the image. . . ." Now we have an opening for new knowledge.
>
> (Pryor, 2000)

Conclusion

While some institutions introduce contemplative practices through mindfulness or contemplative studies centers, all universities can utilize existing structures to create a contemplative campus. Individuals can work together to integrate contemplative practices into their personal, professional, and academic lives. A contemplative campus is possible by exploring policies and practices that impede or facilitate contemplation, identify values and act accordingly, and establish supportive learning communities. By cultivating contemplative practices, we can transform our campuses to become "more human, more loving, compassionate, and kind, to one's self and all other human beings" (Murphy-Shigematsu, 2018).

Acknowledgments

I want to thank all my colleagues who attended, supported, contributed and shared in our Contemplative Practices Learning Community.

References

Aloha Foundation. (n.d.) *Rose, Thorn, Bud.* https://alohafoundation.org/wp-content/uploads/2020/03/Rose-Thorn-Bud.pdf.
Barbezat, D. P., & Bush, M. (2014). *Contemplative Practices in Higher Education: Powerful Methods to Transform Teaching and Learning.* Jossey-Bass.
Barks, C. (2001). *The Glance: Songs of Soul-Meeting.* Penguin Publishing.
Bhattacharya, K. (2017). *Keynote Speech.* CMIND Summer School. Smith College.
Beer, L. E. (2010). Contemplative Administration: Transforming the Workplace Culture of Higher Education. *Innovations in Higher Education,* 35, 217–231.
Berg, M., & Seeber, B. K. (2016). *The Slow Professor: Challenging the Culture of Speed in the Academy.* University of Toronto Press.
Blum, S. (2020). *Upgrading: Why Rating Students Undermines Learning (and What to Do Instead).* West Virginia University Press.
Cobb, V. L. (2017). The Question about the Question: Transforming Educational Policy from the Inside Out. *ICEA Journal,* 1(1), 95–110.
Colenberg, S., Jylhä, T., & Arkesteijn, M. (2021). The Relationship between Interior Office Space and Employee Health and Wellbeing—a Literature Review. *Building Research & Information,* 49(3), 352–366.
Contemplative Mind in Higher Education. (2014). *Tree of Contemplative Practices.* https://www.contemplativemind.org/practices/tree.
www.contemplativemind.org/communitytoolkit.
Coutant, L., & Caldwell, K. (2017). Mindful Campus: Organizational Structure and Culture. *The Journal of Contemplative Inquiry,* 4(1), 229–250.
Crissinger, A., & Vandenbrink, C. (2020, June 18). Red-Yellow-Green Check-ins [Audio podcast episode]. *Reboot Podcast.* https://www.reboot.io/episode/extras-11-red-yellow-green-check-ins-with-andy-crissinger-chris-vandenbrink/.
Duerr, M., Nortonsmith, G., & Vega-Frey, J. (2004). *Creating the Contemplative Organization: Lessons from the Field.* The Center for Contemplative Mind in Society.
DuFon, M. A., & Christian, J. (2013). The Formation and Development of the Mindful Campus. *New Directions in Teaching and Learning,* 134, 65–74.
Epstein, R. (2017). *Attending: Medicine, Mindfulness, and Humanity.* Scribner.
Gannon, K. M. (2020). *Radical Hope: A Teaching Manifesto.* West Virginia University Press.
Kaufman, P., & Schipper, J. (2018). *Teaching with Compassion: An Educator's Oath to Teach from the Heart.* Rowman & Littlefield Publishers.
Ladinsky, D. (2003). *The Subject Tonight Is Love: 60 Wild and Sweet Poems of Hafiz.* Penguin Publishing.

Lazarsfeld, S. (1966). The Courage for Imperfection. *American Journal of Individual Psychology*, 22(2), 163–165.
Lee, F. I. (2018). *Joyful: The Surprising Power of Ordinary Things to Create Extraordinary Happiness*. Little, Brown Spark.
Levy, D. M. (2016). *Mindful Tech: How to Bring Balance to Our Digital Lives*. Yale University Press.
Lorde, A. (2007). *Sister Outsider*. Crossing Press.
Magee, R. V. (2017). One Field, Different Doors In: Contemplative Higher Education, Transformative Education, and Education for Social Justice. *ICEA Journal*, 1(1), 119–127.
Magee, R. V. (2019). *The Inner Work of Racial Justice: Healing Ourselves and Transforming Our Communities through Mindfulness*. Tarcher Perigee.
Murphy-Shigematsu, S. (2018). *From Mindfulness to Heartfulness: Transforming Self and Society with Compassion*. Berrett-Koehler Publishers.
Nepo, M. (2020). *The Book of Awakening: Having the Life You Want by Being Present to the Life You Have*. Red Wheel Weiser.
Palmer, P. J. (2007). *The Courage to Teach: Exploring the Inner Landscape of a Teacher's Life*. Jossey-Bass.
Petty, S. (2017). Waking Up to All of Ourselves: Inner Work, Social Justice, & Systems Change. *ICEA Journal*, 1(1), 1–14.
Pryor, A. A. (2000). *Psychology in Sufism*. International Association of Sufism.
Rendón, L. (2009). *Sentipensante Pedagogy*. Stylus.
Rendón, L. (2017). Embracing Contemplative Pedagogy in a Culturally Diverse Classroom. *ICEA Journal*, 1(1), 15–26.
Sherrell, C., & Simmer-Brown, J. (2017). Spiritual Bypassing in the Contemporary Mindfulness Movement. *ICEA Journal*, 1(1), 75–94.
Trail, J. (2019, April 24). *Faith in a Seed: Strategies for Nurturing and Embedding Contemplative Approaches on Our Campuses*. Webinar for Association for Contemplative Mind in Higher Education (ACMHE).
Zajonc, A. (2009). *Meditation as Contemplative Inquiry When Knowing Becomes Love*. Lindisfarne Books.

EDITOR BIOS

Bengü Ergüner-Tekinalp is Professor of Counseling at Drake University. Her research interests in positive psychology, multicultural counseling, and Adlerian and humanistic schools of thought have produced many journal articles and book chapters, along with four books written in her native language, Turkish. She is the current President of the North American Society of Adlerian Psychology (2022–2024).

Greta Gaard is Professor of English and Women/Gender/Sexuality Studies at the University of Wisconsin–River Falls. Her most recent volumes include her co-edited *International Perspectives in Feminist Ecocriticism* (2013) and her monograph, *Critical Ecofeminism* (2017). In 2018, the Mind and Life Institute awarded her a Think Tank grant for "Mindfulness Practices as Anti-Oppression Pedagogy," inspiring several participants to become contributing authors in this volume.

CONTRIBUTOR BIOS

Janelle Adsit is Associate Professor of English at Humboldt State University. She has written, co-written, and edited three books on creative writing pedagogy and, most recently, the book *Epistemic Justice, Mindfulness, and the Environmental Humanities: Reflections on Teaching* (Routledge, 2021).

Danaé Jones Aicher is an experienced equity and inclusion facilitator. Her career trajectory includes political journalism, political operations, and social/racial justice education. Taking time off to raise her young family—a revolutionary act for Black mothers—Aicher chartered a local chapter of Mocha Moms, Inc., and now serves on its national Board of Directors.

Jennifer Atkinson, PhD, is Associate Professor of Environmental Humanities at the University of Washington, Bothell. She is the author of *Gardenland* (2018) and creator of *Facing It*, a podcast exploring eco-grief and climate anxiety. Atkinson's upcoming book, *An Existential Toolkit for the Climate Crisis*, offers strategies to help young people navigate the emotional toll of climate breakdown.

Teysha L. Bowser is Assistant Professor in the Professional Counseling Department at the University of Wisconsin–Oshkosh. A central focus of her work is wellness and healing in minoritized communities. She serves as the Chair of the Association for Counselor Education and Supervision (ACES) Diversity & Inclusion Interest Network and is a member of the Diversity Committee of Sandplay Therapists of America (STA).

Franklin M. Chen received his PhD in chemistry from Princeton University, then worked for 25 years at Colgate-Palmolive, Johnson and Johnson, and Kimberly-Clark. After retirement, Chen joined the Chemistry faculty at University of Wisconsin–Green Bay, and was promoted to Associate Professor in 2008. Chen's scholarship emphasizes applied research and computations, producing over 20 publications in peer-reviewed journals, and over 50 U.S. patents.

Sam Cocks received his PhD in 19th/20th-century continental philosophy, and is currently Associate Professor of Philosophy at the University of Wisconsin–La Crosse. He has practiced Chan/Zen-based mindfulness for 31 years and teaches courses in Asian Philosophy and Zen Buddhism.

Jennifer Daubenmier, PhD, is Associate Professor in Holistic Health Studies at San Francisco State University. She conducts NIH-funded research on meditation and its impact on psychological well-being and stress-related health conditions and currently applies a social justice lens to the study of contemplative practices. She has been on the Buddhist path for 25 years and teaches courses on meditation.

Michele J. Eliason, PhD, is Professor of Public Health and Assistant Dean for Faculty Scholarship in the College of Health and Social Sciences at San Francisco State University. Her research and teaching have involved issues related to health of LGBTQ+ populations and other social justice issues, including implementation of social justice pedagogy.

Jan Estep is Emeritus Professor of Art, University of Minnesota–Twin Cities. In addition to her degrees in biology/art (BA), studio art (MFA), and philosophy (MA, PhD), she is trained in Mindfulness-Based Stress Reduction (MBSR) from UMass Medical School, Kundalini Yoga as taught by Yogi Bhajan (Levels 1 and 2: 460hr TT), Art and Yoga with Hari Kirin Kaur Khalsa, Emotional Liberation with Guru Meher Khalsa, and Prana Vinyasa Flow with Shiva Rea (200hr TT).

Maiya Evans, MPH, is a health educator, entrepreneur, and consultant. She is a lecture faculty member in the Holistic Health Studies and Public Health programs at San Francisco State University. In addition, she is a diversity consultant with the nonprofit The Mosaic Project. Her classes incorporate stress reduction techniques, mindfulness, and breathing exercises to provide a stress-free space that allows students to relax, practice self-care, and celebrate themselves.

David Forbes is Emeritus in the Urban Education Doctoral Program at the CUNY Graduate Center. He taught school counseling at Brooklyn College/CUNY for 19 years and consults with New York City schools on developing social mindfulness programs. Forbes co-edited the *Handbook of Mindfulness:*

Culture, Context, and Social Engagement (Springer, 2016). His latest book is *Mindfulness and Its Discontents: Education, Self, and Social Transformation* (2019).

Amney J. Harper is Professor of Professional Counseling at the University of Wisconsin–Oshkosh, where she focuses on social justice and multicultural counseling with a specific emphasis on the LGBTQ+ community. Harper has integrated mindfulness, experiential, and reflective activities and assignments in her classes over the past 11 years, and recently co-taught "Wellness, Mindfulness and Spirituality in Counseling."

Christopher J. Koenig, PhD, is Associate Professor of Communication Studies at San Francisco State University. His research focuses on the multiple relationships between communication and the social dimensions of health and illness. He maintains a 20-year yoga practice and adopts a contemplative approach to research methods and language use in everyday life.

Lisa Moore, DrPH, teaches in the Department of Public Health at San Francisco State University. Her work and interests have focused on the social production of infectious disease, especially HIV and with the intersections of the drug war and racial/class justice. She is a member and teacher with the sangha at the East Bay Meditation Center in Oakland, California.

Renee Owen is Assistant Professor of Education at Southern Oregon University in Ashland, Oregon. A scholar-practitioner in the fields of adult and K-12 education, Owen is founder and director of Rainbow Institute, which provides training and consulting to adults in schools and businesses in equity and holistic learning. Her ongoing research explores the potential for contemplative practices to promote transformative learning for teachers and adults in the workplace.

Darin Pradittatsanee is Associate Professor of English at Chulalongkorn University, Thailand. Her publications include *In Search of Liberation: Buddhism and the Beat Writers* (2007) and *Reflecting Upon Environmental Problems Through Contemporary American Literature* (written in Thai) in 2016.

Anne Raine is Associate Professor of English at the University of Ottawa. She has published articles on modernist literature, environmental writing, and earth art, including a chapter on "Ecocriticism and Modernism" in the *Oxford Handbook of Ecocriticism*. Her current book project is titled *Feminist Modernism and the Ends of Nature: Science, Nature Work, and Ecological Aesthetics*.

Renae Swanson is Associate Professor, Department Chair, and Graduate Program Coordinator in the Department of Professional Counseling at the University of Wisconsin–Oshkosh. She is also Clinical Director and practicing counselor at

Integrity Counseling, LLC, integrating mindfulness practices in all of her classes, her counseling, and supervision.

David J. Voelker is Professor of Humanities and History at the University of Wisconsin–Green Bay. He teaches courses on early U.S. history, environmental history, and environmental humanities. Voelker's publications include *The Powhatans and the English in the Seventeenth-Century Chesapeake* (Oxford University Press, 2020) and a co-edited volume, *Big Picture Pedagogy: Finding Interdisciplinary Solutions to Common Learning Problems* (Jossey Bass, 2017).

INDEX

Note: Page numbers in **bold** indicate tables.

4Rs (Relationship, Respect, Reciprocity, and Responsibility) 121, 123, **124** (Table 7.2)

accountabilibuddy groups 190
activism 60, 72, 76–77, 87, 103
Adsit, Janelle xiii, 17–31, 246
affect theory 72, 76; *see also* eco-affects
Agamben, Giorgio 84
Animal Dreams (Kingsolver, B.) 54, 57, 60
animality 56
animals 41, 56, 57, 59, 60, 61, 63, 68, 79, 91, 93, 96, 104, 105, 109, 111, 112, 123, 149, 158, 220
Animal's People (Sinha, I.) 54, 57, 60–61
anthropocentrism 56, 57, 83, 92
anti-oppressive pedagogy v, ix, x, xi, xii, xiii, 3, 6, 7, 8, 9, 10, 12, 14, 15, 18, 30, 41, 42, 109, 112, 149, 166, 178, 180, 187, 194, 235
art-making xi, 6, 11, 37, 45–46, 133, 134–136, 141–143, 145; sculpture 45–47
assessments of contemplative pedagogies: Fidelity of Implementation 91, 111; Five-Facet Mindfulness Questionnaire 13, 64, 85, 167, 177; informed consent 91, 111; Perceived Stress Scale 13, 98, 101, 111; pre- and post- tests 13, 64, 65, 91, 101, 102; qualitative self-reporting 13, 91; self-assessment learning reports 139, 143, 179; Toronto Empathy Questionnaire 13, 98, 101, 102, 112
Association for the Study of Literature and Environment (ASLE) xiii, 4, 69
Atkinson, Jennifer 10, 35–51, 246

Barbezat, Daniel P., and Bush, MIrabai 5, 7, 45, 52, 54, 92, 111, 225, 229, 230, 236
Batacharya, Sheila, and Wong, Y.-L. R. 8, 18, 22, 72, 138, 171
Berila, Beth xiii, 3, 5, 6, 7, 18, 19, 20, 71, 72, 75, 85, 92, 115, 172, 173, 199, 200, 202, 223
Black Lives Matter 77, 136, 197, 198
Bladow, Kyle 72, 75, 76, 88
body, importance of 171, 173; body-based therapies 186
Bowser, Teysha 11, 183–194, 246
Brach, Tara 87n2, 142
Brown, Molly 116–117, **119** (Table 7.1) **120** (Table 7.1), 124
Buddhism 8, 9, 14, 15, 16, 21, 53, 54,

70, 76, 88, 146, 192, 207; dependent origination 10, 53; eightfold path 8; Four Noble Truths 53; happiness 91; non-self 10, 53; socially-engaged 90; three characteristics of existence 53; three kinds of wisdom 53; three poisons 11; *tonglen* 53; *see also* dharma practice
Butler, Octavia 80–82, 88

Carson, Rachel 153–154
Cayoun, Bruno 87, 88
Center for the Contemplative Mind in Higher Education (CMind) xiii; *see also* Tree of Contemplative Practices
Chen, Franklin M. vi, 11, 147–165, 246
Chödrön, Pema 61, 74, 75, 82, 83, 88, 108, 124, 226
Cli-fi (climate change science fiction) 72
climate change x, 10, 11, 37, 38, 41, 45, 58, 62, 7, 73, 74, 76, 77, 78, 87, 103, 105, 106, 107, 109, 150; climate change denial 36, 42, 45, 72, 73, 76, 78, 85, 86
climate injustice 39, 41; climate justice x, 10, 36, 39, 41, 45, 47, 49, 51, 71–89, 90, 125
Cocks, Sam vi, 11, 129, 166–182, 247
consumerism 20, 82, 84, 87
contemplative campus 11, 233, 234; acting mindfully 241–242; beginning classes or meetings 240–241; centering teaching values 238–240; contemplative administration 234; contemplative communities of practice 11, 13; contemplative fellows 234–235; contemplative teaching 236–237; emptying the mind 242; mindful meetings 235–236
contemplative pedagogies: and anti-oppressive practices 9–14; campus-wide workshop series 197–214; measurement tools 13–14; strategies for integrating into courses 12
contemplative practices 147–163; *see also* mindfulness pedagogy; mindfulness practices
Cottrell, Stella 74–75, 88
Council of All Beings 117
creative writing 134, 140, 190
credibility, deficits and excess 186

cultural appropriation 8, 23, 133, 136, 137, 138, 185, 186, 187
Cunsolo, Ashlee 73, 75, 88

Dalai Lama 103, 199, 226
Daubenmier, Jennifer, et al. 13, 197–214, 247
DEAL Model for Critical Reflection 189
decolonizing 30, 31, 84, 89, 135; decolonization 73, 77, 83–84; yoga 136, 145, 146
D'Errico, Katja Hahn 3
dharma practice 8, 15, 31, 90, 103, 108, 149, 160; *see also* Buddhism
DiAngelo, Robin 19, 29, 215, 216, 222, 227
difficult [negative] emotions 168, 171

eco-affects: climate anxiety xi, 10, 35–37, 38, 43, 49n2, 73, 74, 76, 78–79, 80–81, 86, 10; climate depression 38–39; eco-anxiety and eco-grief xi, 10, 35–51, 246
ecocriticism 7, 53, 72, 74, 88, 245, 248
ecofeminism 10, 90, 245
ecological footprint 124–125
ecopoetry 73, 78–79, 82
Eliason, Michele J. 197–214, 247
embodiment (embodied) 7, 11, 17, 75, 90–92, 100, 133, 172, 203
empathy i, 7, 10, 13, 35, 36, 40, 68, 80, 91, 92, 94, 95, 96, 97, 98, 101, 102, 109, 112, 130, 132, 144, 145, 166, 183, 215, 222, 227
"Entanglement" (Singh, V.) 54, 58, 62
environmental health 92, 164
environmental justice i, xii, 5, 7, 10, 11, 33, 35, 36, 37, 38, 39, 41, 42, 47, 48, 51, 57, 61, 73, 76, 77, 118, 121, 125
epiphenomenalism 172
epistemic justice 10, 18, 21, 25, 29, 118, 186, 246
Ergüner-Tekinalp, Bengü i, ix, 3–16, 103, 129, 229–244, 245
Estep, Jan xiii, 11, 131–146, 247
Evans, Maiya 197–214, 247
experiential 53, 68, 71, 74, 76, 77, 85, 86, 133, 184, 186, 188, 191, 192, 197
externalism 174

First Nations 121, 123; *see also* Indigenous
Fiskio, Janet 72, 73, 88
Floyd, George 197
Forbes, David viii–x, xiii, 5, 7, 8, 9, 11, 14, 171, 247
Freire, Paolo 5, 15

Gaard, Greta i, ix, xiii, 3–16, 69, 90–112, 129, 150, 245
Genesis (Nuridsany, C. and Pérennou, M.) 56, 57
Germer, Chris 8, 15, 99, 111, 169, 170, 181
Ghosh, Amitav 75, 76, 78, 83, 88
Granados, Maria 73, 88
gratitude 8, 11, 40, 44, 69, 82, 98, 99, 101, 103, 104, 105, 107, 108, 112, 116, 117, 119, 125, 148, 149, 159, 160–163, 164, 165, 200, 222, 234, 235
grief 27, 40, 41, 48, 49, 116–117, 120, 143, 150; *see also* mindfulness pedagogy, mourning rituals
Grossman, Paul 76, 86, 88

habitual bias 11, 169, 175, 178
Hafiz 237
Hahn, Thich Nhat 8, 10, 53, 60, 77, 103, 149, 151, 153, 158, 160, 161, 202, 213, 226
Haraway, Donna J. 73, 84, 88
Harper, Amney J. 11, 183–194, 248
Hatch, Chris 73, 88
Haudenosaunee 119
heartfulness 118, 128
Hern, Matt 82–84, 88
heterosexism 9; homophobia 210
higher education 17, 20, 24, 117, 118, 148, 197–199; anti-oppression work 115; contemplative approaches to sustainability 7; contemplative pedagogies 5–7; mindfulness 13, 92, 229–239; student profiles of stress 4–5
history, United States 121, 122
hooks, bell 10, 23, 28, 30, 135, 145
Hopkins, Hop 75, 76, 84, 88
Hughes, Langston 122

humanities i, xiii, 36, 46, 48, 52, 72, 117, 120, 123–125; environmental 4, 7, 37, 41, 44, 53, 69
Huson, Freda 73

identity (personal) 174, 176
impermanence 81, 82, 176
Implicit Association Test (IAT) 221
Implicit bias 215–219; *see also* unconscious bias1
Indigenous 20, 22, 23, 39, 41, 42, 60, 73, 76, 83, 124; Indigenous ontologies 84; indigenous climate impacts 39, 41
inhabitation 10, 57, 59
inner tracking 115, 116, **119–120** (Table 7.1), 122; student responses 125–127
Institutional Review Board (IRB) 13, 91, 129, 204
intention 109, 126, 127, 148, 240–241
interactionist dualism 171
interbeing xi, 8–11, 13, 31, 52–54, 63–66, 76–77, 89, 97, 103, 108–109, 226
internalism 174
intersectionality and climate justice 75–77, 81–82, 84

Johal, Am 82–84, 88
justice 224; environmental, economic, multispecies, and climate as linked xi; gender 5; racial 18, 121, 126, 197; social viii, x, xi, xii, 4, 5, 11, 13, 25, 41, 116, 118, 121, 126, 127, 137, 145, 184, 185, 186, 187, 190, 192, 197–210, 211, 213, 231, 232; structural 7

Kabat-Zinn, Jon 8, 52, 70, 115, 129, 185, 200, 202, 213, 214, 223, 227
Kaza, Stephanie 74, 74–84, 87, 88
Keating, Annalouise 24, 25, 118, 127–128
Kendi, Ibram X. 118
King, Ruth 5, 18
Kingsolver, Barbara 78, 79, 84
Klein, Naomi 82, 87, 88
Koenig, Christopher J. 197–214, 248

Kolbert, Elizabeth 78, 82, 87, 88
Kornfield, Jack 87n2, 160

Ladino, Jennifer 72, 75, 76, 88
learning community 13, **119** (Table 7.1), 123, 229, 230, 232, 240
LeMenager, Stephanie 72, 88
LGBT 4, 41, 183, 192, 193, 247, 248; *see also* queer sexualities
literary studies 71, 109
Loy, David 72, 76, 89
Lustgarten, Abrahm 80, 88
Lyubomirsky, Sonja 11, 15, 103, 104, 106, 112

Macy, Joanna 116, **119** (Table 7.1), **124** (Table 7.2)
Magee, Rhonda 18, 19, 30, 137, 146, 183, 193, 197, 202, 213, 216, 224, 225, 226, 227, 231, 232, 237, 238, 244
McIntosh, Peggy 12, 17
McMindfulness 8, 15, 20, 72, 76
meditation *see* mindfulness pedagogy; mindfulness practices
Menakem, Resmaa 18, 30, 172, 173, 181
mental health 4, 5, 14, 15, 21, 37–39, 49, 50, 72, 150, 155, 157, 164, 165, 193, 204, 205, 231
Merola, Nicole 87n1
Mezirow, Jack 216, 217, 222, 225, 226, 227, 228
Mind and Life Institute xiii, 3, 213, 245
mindful meetings 235–236
mindfulness as anti-oppression pedagogy 6, 12, 115; benefits 6; environmental literature 10
mindfulness-based therapies: acceptance and commitment therapy 8; cognitive therapy 8; dialectical behavioral therapy 8; self-compassion 8; stress reduction 8, 184
mindfulness competencies 185
mindfulness in education 8; Mindful Schools 8; MindUP program 8
mindfulness pedagogy 3, 10, 12, 13, 72, 73, 74, 85, 86, 91, 183; body scan 57, 58, 75, 79, 82–84, 98, 168, 171, 185, 231; breath mindfulness xi, 6, 14, 17, 26, 37, 53, 56–61, 63, 69n2, 75, 77, 79, 82–84, 87, 92–94, 98–99, 119, 133–134, 137–138, 141, 143, 151, 156, 162, 164, 168, 198, 200, 202–204, 219, 223–224, 233, 235, 240–242, 247; eating 93–94, 149, 204; guiding principles 200–201; listening 11, 75, 93, 98–100, 149, 152, 200, 202–203, 205; loving-kindness (*metta*) 53, 57, 58, 61, 78, 79, 80, 82, 84, 87, 93, 169, 225, 226; mindful self-compassion (MSC) xi, 6, 8, 64, 70, 85, 91, 97–98, 112, 148, 169, 176, 181, 200, 205, 223–226; mourning rituals 36, 37, 40–44, 49; one-minute mindfulness 148, 150–151; poetry-reading 160–161; *tonglen* 53, 58, 61, 68 (ecological 78–79); walking 11, 53, 57, 60, 68, 98, 157–159; writing xi, 6, 11, 13, 53, 90, 95–98, 102, 134, 138 (as activism 87; creative 190; environmental 22, 27; self-reflective 14, 36, 37, 44–47, 133, 139–144, 190); *see also* contemplative campus; contemplative pedagogies; mindfulness practices
mindfulness practices: mindful walking xi, 6, 11, 53, 57, 60, 68, 98, 100, 149, 157, 158, 159, 203, 233; music 11, 42, **105** (Table 6.3) 155–157, 160, 235; observing thoughts 6, 18, 27, 92, 119, 134, 142, 224
mindful self-compassion *see* mindfulness pedagogy
Moore, Lisa 197–214, 248
multicultural learning 184
Murphy-Shigematsu, Steven 3, 118, 129, 149, 165, 243, 244

Neff, Kristin 8, 15, 70, 99, 109, 101, 112, 169, 170, 181, 224, 228
negative self-talk 168, 171
neuroscience of bias 222–223
nonhuman agency 76, 78, 79
Norgaard, Kari 71, 75, 76, 88

Oliver, Mary 54, 56, 70, 161
oppression i, vi, ix–xi, 6, 9, 12–14, 19, 20, 23, 29, 92, 109, 115, 133, 149,

166, 167, 173–174, 176, 179, 180, 181, 183–184, 189, 190, 205–206, 224, 245; dismantling 7; economic 170; institutional 172; interlocking 17, 27; internalized 118, 200, 202; structural 170, 172; systemic 80, 187, 197–200, 208; unlearning 3; *see also* racism; sexism; speciesism
O'Sullivan, Edmund 118
overwork 7, 100, 133, 231, 232, 234
Owen, Renee, and Aicher, Danae Jones vii, 13, 215–228, 248

pedagogy of love 237
phenomenology 173
Pihkala, Panu 43
Ponyo on the Cliff by the Sea (Miyazaki, H.) 54, 58, 62–63
Pradittatsanee, Darin 10, 52–70, 249
presence (self) 11, 20, 128, 134, 137, 138, 141, 142, 144, 148, 150, 163, 175, 203, 235, 236, 237
privilege 61–62, 82, 90, 92, 118, 122, 152, 173; able body 173; mindfulness and privilege 173–174; owning 41–42, 190, 207; position of 207–208; social construct 7, 41–42, 92, 136, 138, 174, 184, 187, 189, 200, 203, 206, 208; unearned 90; *see also* white privilege
Purser, Ronald 72, 76, 89

queer sexualities 4, 41, 90, 184, 193; *see also* LGBT

racism x, 5, 9, 17, 18, 24, 28, 39, 41, 75, 116, 118, 122, 126, 184, 187, 197, 210, 215, 216; dismantling 22, 29; disrupting 17; environmental 17, 36, 38, 76; interrupting 223; structural 224; systemic 116
Raine, Anne vi, 10, 71–89, 248
Ray, Sarah Jaquette 37, 38, 43, 49, 51, 72, 75, 76, 79, 89, 97, 116, 129
reflective pedagogy 123, 125, 189; practice 188; teams 190; writing 44–45, 189
Ricard, Mathieu 11, 15
Rich, Nathaniel 80–81, 89
Rowe, James K. 72, 73, 75, 76, 89

Sacco, Joe 84
Salzburg, Sharon 80, 89
secular/spiritual 7–9
self-awareness 119, 133, 139, 144–145, 155, 183, 188, 199, 200, 207, 230, 232, 238
self-care 72, 101, 134, 137–138, 141, 176, 185, 200, 204
self-compassion xi, 6, 8, 85, 91, 97–98, 169–170, 176, 200, 205, 223, 224–225, 226; scale 64
service learning 151–153
sexism x, 9, 41
Simpson, Leanne Betasamosake 41, 51, 73, 84, 89, 124
Slow Professor 145, 229, 232, 243
slow scholarship 131
"Smog Society" (Qiufan, C.) 54, 58, 62
Solnit, Rebecca 73, 83, 89
Somé, Sobonfu 122, **124** (Table 7.2)
Spahr, Juliana 78–79, 89
speciesism 38, 41, 109
spiritual bypassing 136–137,146, 244
Squarzoni, Philippe 77–78, 89
Sufi 9, 242
Swamp, Jake 116
Swanson, Renae vi, 11, 183–194, 249
"Systems Game" 117

"Tamarisk Hunter" (Bacigalupi, P.) 54, 58, 62
transformative learning xi, 7, 118, 128, 215, 216, 217, 218, 219, 222, 225, 226
trauma i, 5, 7, 38–39, 60, 80, 83, 92, 170, 187, 198, 200, 208; trauma-informed 85, 185, 186; Trauma Resiliency Model 186; traumatic stress 38, 75, 187
Tree of Contemplative Practices xiii, 6, 13, 148, 150, 202, 238–239
Treleaven, David 75, 89, 92, 112, 186, 187, 194

Van Dam, Nicholas T. 76, 86, 88
VanderMeer, Jeff 82–83, 89
Voelker, David J. 11, 115–130, 249

white privilege 12, 43, 60, 136, 197, 205, 206, 213, 223; white supremacy 17–18, 20, 26, 30, 38, 42–43, 76, 92, 118, 122

Wong, Yuk-Lin Renita 72, 76, 89
Work That Reconnects (WTR) 116, 117

yoga xi, xiii, 6, 11, 21, 37, 93, 111, 131–138, 140–141, 143–146, 148, 150, 168, 171, 185, 207, 210, 247–248; kriyas 133; mantra 133, 137, 139; mudra 133; pranayamas 133, 137

Young, Jon 116

Zajonc, Arthur 3, 52, 70, 92, 112, 147, 165, 197, 214, 236, 244

Printed in the United States
by Baker & Taylor Publisher Services